D1559881

with a

SWORD

in one hand &

JOMINI

in the other

with a

SWORD

in one hand &

JOMINI

in the other

The **Problem** of **Military Thought** in the **Civil War North**

Carol Reardon

UNIVERSITY OF NORTH CAROLINA PRESS *Chapel Hill*

THE STEVEN & JANICE BROSE LECTURES IN THE CIVIL WAR ERA
WILLIAM A. BLAIR, EDITOR

Designed by Kimberley Bryant and set in Miller by Tseng Information Systems, Inc.
Manufactured in the United States of America

The paper in this book meets the guidelines for permanence and
durability of the Committee on Production Guidelines for Book Longevity of the
Council on Library Resources. The University of North Carolina Press has been a
member of the Green Press Initiative since 2003.

Library of Congress Cataloging-in-Publication Data
Reardon, Carol.
With a sword in one hand and Jomini in the other : the problem
of military thought in the Civil War north / Carol Reardon.
p. cm. — (The Steven and Janice Brose lectures in the Civil War era)
Includes bibliographical references and index.
ISBN 978-0-8078-3560-9 (cloth : alk. paper)
1. United States—History—Civil War, 1861–1865—Campaigns.
2. Jomini, Antoine Henri, baron de, 1779–1869—Influence.
3. Military art and science—United States—History—19th century. I. Title.
E470.R285 2012
973.7′3—dc23
2011044954

16 15 14 13 12   5 4 3 2 1

For Steven & Janice Brose,

with sincere thanks for their unfailing and generous support

of the scholarly endeavors of the

George and Ann Richards Civil War Era Center

at Penn State University

CONTENTS

with a

SWORD

in one hand &

JOMINI

in the other

INTRODUCTION

"It has been said with good reason that many a Civil War general went into battle with a sword in one hand and Jomini's *Summary of the Art of War* in the other," wrote Marine Corps Brigadier General J. D. Hittle in 1947.[1] The subject of his observation, Swiss-born soldier and writer Antoine-Henri Jomini, enjoyed a lengthy literary career that spanned the first two-thirds of the nineteenth century. During that time, he became one of the most prolific and insightful chroniclers and analysts of the great campaigns of Frederick the Great, Napoleon Bonaparte, and other major military figures of the previous two centuries. He remains far more famous, however, for his efforts to formulate a "scientific" approach to the art of war through the deduction and application of immutable principles that guide an army's conduct on campaign and in battle. Jomini's substantial literary outpouring fully established him in European military circles as one of his generation's foremost authorities on war. His legacy in the United States, however, rests more specifically on the linkage of his ideas to the military conduct of the great sectional conflict of 1861–65.

Antoine-Henri Jomini's rise to prominence had not come easily.[2] Born on 5 March 1779 in the French-speaking Swiss canton of Vaud, he exhibited very early in life a passion for military affairs. His middle-class parents disapproved of his intention to make the army his career, so, after he briefly served in the Swiss armed forces, they sent him to Paris, where he obtained positions in banking and brokerage establishments. Attracted by Napoleon's battlefield successes, however, Jomini sought a military position and accepted the only one that he—as a foreigner—could find: a logistics assignment. The routine of his duties did not fully occupy his time, his mind, or his dreams of glory, so Jomini immersed himself in the study of great campaigns and the most influential works of military literature produced over the previous two centuries. Inspired by the power of the ideas with which he engaged—and confident enough to believe that he could improve upon them—he soon took up his own pen. *A Treatise on Grand Operations*, published in 1804 with the benefit of the patronage of Marshal Michel Ney, centered on Frederick the Great's campaigns in the Seven Years' War. Highly impressed, Ney soon found a place for

Jomini at his headquarters, until Napoleon Bonaparte himself promoted the young Swiss officer to the rank of colonel and attached him to his own staff. Jomini served closely with Napoleon during the Jena and Eylau campaigns of 1805. Soon enough, however, Jomini's military career became quite complicated. Chafing at his continued inability to escape staff duties for a troop command, he considered the offer of a commission in the Russian service and, in time, accepted a generalship in the tsar's army. (Since Jomini was a Swiss citizen, this course of action remained an acceptable option for him, although many of his French comrades-in-arms resented it.) When he tired of active service, he retired to Belgium and then to France to continue his writing. Until his death on 24 March 1869, Jomini continued to publish prolifically on the art of war, drawing upon Napoleonic campaigns as well as the broader sweep of seventeenth- and eighteenth-century European military history for inspiration and examples.

Jomini's literary roots ran deep into the intellectual movement that historian John A. Lynn has termed the period of the Military Enlightenment.[3] Between the seventeenth and mid-nineteenth centuries, each major European nation developed its own military institutions and professional military culture. As part of that evolution, a significant number of learned soldiers—and some civilians, as well—created substantial bodies of military literature that viewed war as a complex social institution, one best understood and perhaps even controlled through the agency of reason. During this period of great intellectual and literary vibrancy, writers attempted to create rigid "systems" of rules that comprised the foundation of a "science" of war. Others described immutable guiding principles, the situationally derived application of which became the "art" of war. Military writers of the era used the terms "science" and "art" interchangeably at times, borrowed freely (and often silently) from those with whom they agreed, critiqued their greatest rivals savagely, and revised and reissued their own works to refute the criticisms of others. No individual writer remained the unchallenged intellectual authority on war for very long.

The dynamic nature of these exchanges—which regularly crossed national and imperial boundaries—accurately describes the established intellectual milieu into which Jomini entered. He participated fully in the dialogue. Early on, he found himself drawn to the work of French military writer Jacques Antoine Hippolyte Comte de Guibert (1743–90), whose *Essai général de tactique* offered what historian Azar Gat has described as an early effort to describe a "definitive system of tactics, finally creating a science of war." While Guibert never completed the system he hoped to construct, he considered mobility, celerity, and boldness in active maneuver to be essential elements of an effective theoretical concept.[4] Jomini became intrigued by Guibert's unsuccessful quest, but he concluded that the Frenchman had overreached. As Jomini wrote in his first major work, *A Treatise on Grand Military Operations*, in 1804, "a simple theory . . . without giving absolute systems" will supply all the guidance an able commander requires to formulate the combinations that win victories.[5] He determined to identify the immutable principles that comprised that theory.

Jomini also found inspiration in the important work of Welshman Henry Humphrey Evans Lloyd (1718–83), a veteran of the Austrian army who authored a remarkable study on Frederick the Great's campaigns during the Seven Years' War. Lloyd, who trained as an engineer, viewed the army "as a great machine," and he heavily endowed his work with a mechanistic approach to war. Indeed, Lloyd believed that an army must operate on a similar principle as a machine, concentrating its energy and force toward the completion of its specific task. As he wrote: "That general, who, by the facility of his motions, or by artifice, can bring most men into action at the same time, and at the same point, must, if the troops are equally good, necessarily prevail."[6] Jomini—and many other military writers of his era—also embraced Lloyd's concept of "lines of operation" that linked an army in the field with its bases in a secure rear area. This specific notion took on even greater importance in Jomini's writing after he familiarized himself with the works of Prussian Adam Heinrich Dietrich von Bülow (1757–1807), whose geometrical diagrams explaining the relationship between bases and lines of operation exceeded in complexity even those of Lloyd.[7]

Lloyd and Bülow had differed from their peers in one particularly important way that greatly appealed to Jomini: both had shown a strong preference for studying the conduct of active military campaigns rather than adhere to the traditional emphasis of earlier writers on army organization and the design of battle formations. Jomini readily adopted their endorsement of skillful maneuver to concentrate combat power against important enemy positions—usually geographical points—while protecting the security of one's own bases and lines of supply and communication. The logical extension of their arguments—the selection of an appropriate objective, detailed planning, and striking hard only after maneuver had set up the conditions for decisive victories without unduly high losses—

also sat well with Jomini, who admitted on many occasions during his career that he cringed at the cost of even Napoleon's greatest victories. Although Jomini openly criticized some elements of Bülow's and Lloyd's works, the themes they advanced informed the entire body of his professional writings. At least partly for this reason, his modern critics recently have tended to view Jomini less as the herald of a new Napoleonic way of war and more as an intellectual reactionary who "set military thought back into the eighteenth century," where he felt "comfortable and safe."[8]

Jomini surely would have resented any such suggestion. Throughout his long literary career, he gave way to no critic, responding to the most serious challenges to his ideas with revised and updated editions of previous works in which he attacked his rival directly and, at the same time, incorporated without attribution any new ideas that appealed to him. When Austrian Archduke Charles published his *Grundsätze der Strategie* in 1814—after which some Europeans began to tout him as equal to, or even superior to, Jomini—the Swiss officer published a third edition of his *Treatise on the Art of War*, in which he greatly expanded and sharpened his discussion about the identification of enemy key points, their designation as military objectives, and the concentration of force against them—his new emphasis echoing major points the archduke had stressed.[9]

In like manner, Jomini's most famous work, his *Summary of the Art of War* (1838), stemmed in part from his desire to respond to the criticisms of both Archduke Charles and an influential Prussian rival, Carl von Clausewitz, whose own major study, *On War*, Jomini dismissed as simply a "declamation against all theory of war."[10] The *Summary of the Art of War*, the work that General Hittle had praised so highly, derived much of its enduring importance from Jomini's commitment both to define and refine the principles influencing the era's newest and most intellectually challenging concept: strategy. While nearly every major nation—including the United States—prepared a wide variety of drill manuals to instruct soldiers in the use of their weapons and tactics manuals to train them to deploy and fight as companies and regiments on the field of battle, comparatively few military thinkers addressed the planning and conduct of a comprehensive military effort in support of national policy goals.

Jomini, however, had tackled the issue with enthusiasm. As he considered it, strategy remained almost exclusively in the realm of military affairs, and he most succinctly defined it as "the art of making war upon the map." By its very nature—at least as Jomini observed Napoleon's execution of the concept—the strongest form of military strategy exploited the power of the offensive to defeat its rival. A strategic plan embraced the selection of a theater of war; it determined the decisive points within that theater; it selected from among those points the objectives most useful to achieving the army's—and its political leadership's—goals; it determined the location of bases and lines of operation and retreat to support army movements; it made plans for marches and maneuvers to reach and reduce decisive points; and it addressed a variety of other important matters, including the establishment of a reserve, decisions about diversions, and other activities exclusive of battle itself.[11]

While Jomini explained what a general needed to ponder and decide before launching major military campaigns, he did not explain in detail how to do any of them. He always believed that the unique circumstances of a situation and the commanding general's genius and skill would determine the most appropriate response. He noted only that whatever decisions the general made, he had to respect a "small number of fundamental principles . . . which could not be deviated from without danger." Jomini offered only four such principles. First, maneuver the mass of one's own army against decisive points in the theater of war, especially by threatening the enemy's line of communication while protecting one's own. To this end, he expanded upon Lloyd's and Bülow's concepts of lines of operation to describe "interior" and "exterior" lines of operation, establishing "interior" lines as the preferred choice. Second, when closing on the enemy, maneuver in such a way that one pits the mass of one's force against fractions of the enemy army. Third, on the battlefield, focus one's primary effort on the most critical point of the enemy line. Finally, when all was in readiness, "engage at the proper times and with energy."[12] The complex set of ideas articulated here, more than anything else, has secured Jomini's prominence in the development of the first generation of strategic thought. These ideas also provided the foundation for General Hittle's claim for Jomini's influence during the American Civil War.

Unquestionably, Hittle merits credit for the boldness of his assertion, but the claim presents Civil War historians with an evidentiary problem. During the eight decades between the start of the war and Hittle's observation, Jomini's name—let alone any detailed analyses of the principles he espoused—rarely appeared in any genre of Civil War literature. Indeed, Jomini accounts for only three citations in the index to the original 128-volume *War of the Rebellion: A Compilation of the Official Records of the Union and Confederate Armies.* In the profusion of postwar veterans' literature, Jomini's name appears only two times in the index to the fifty-two-volume *Southern Historical Society Papers*, not at all in the indexes to the full run of *Confederate Veteran* or the *Battles and Leaders of the Civil War* series, and only twice in the sixty-volume run of the Military Order of the Loyal Legion (MOLLUS) Papers. In most of these cases, eulogists used the Swiss writer's name chiefly as a bit of literary shorthand to confirm a deceased soldier's reputation for an above-average knowledge of military affairs. Jomini plays no major role in the military memoirs of Ulysses S. Grant, George McClellan, and most other Civil War generals.

Perhaps this helps to explain why, even after General Hittle's assertion, Jomini still remained outside mainstream Civil War scholarship until the mid-1950s. Then, within five years, he and his work became the starting point for two scholars who reached very different conclusions. First, historian David Herbert Donald drew upon Jomini and his ideas as a way to "rescue Civil War history from personal partisanship" and provide common ground on which the profession's Lincoln, Grant, and McClellan factions could discuss the Union war effort. To "understand why the commanders behaved as they did" and "to relate the military events of the conflict to broader economic and social patterns in American life," Donald determined to look at the war as an expression of specific social and cultural imperatives. That required, he argued, an exploration of "the theory of warfare behind the fighting." In the end, his findings presented him with an interesting conundrum. First, he determined that Jomini's writings about the art of war genuinely did present a number of quite useful concepts to explain military operations during the Civil War, and he cited as evidence the seeming influence of Jomini's works in the West Point curriculum. However, while factoring in important elements of the broader cultural landscape of antebellum America—the nation's strong antimilitary and antielitist sentiments as well as the restricted opportunities for many occupations to secure intellectual authority for their field of expertise—Donald ultimately concluded that Jomini's actual influence may well have been quite limited, suggesting that "it could be contended [that] most Union and Confederate army officers had no theoretical ideas about warfare at all."[13]

A second perspective on Jomini, first advanced by historian T. Harry Williams, harbored no such doubts. Williams argued in his influential 1960 essay "The Military Leadership of North and South" that the influence of Jomini on the Civil War was, in a word, "profound." Every graduate of West Point had been "exposed to Jomini's ideas, either directly, by reading Jomini's writings or abridgments or expositions of them; or indirectly, by hearing them in the classroom or perusing the works of Jomini's American disciples." This latter group included Dennis Hart Mahan, who from 1831 until his death in 1871 served as professor of military and civil engineering at West Point, and captain-turned-military-author Henry Wager Halleck.[14] For at least a generation, the Williams thesis held sway. Jomini's interpretation of Napoleon, wrote Russell F. Weigley in 1977, "became the foundation of the teaching of strategy at West Point."[15] In a similar vein, historian Joseph Harsh asserted in a 1974 essay that "West Point indoctrinated its students in Jominian ideas for many years."[16] Indeed, Civil War military historians seem to have granted Jomini a status he sought but never achieved in his lifetime: acceptance as the undisputed intellectual master of early nineteenth-century military thought.

Over the years, the initial conclusions reached by Donald and especially Williams unfortunately have become justifications to oversimplify quite complex intellectual processes. As it happened, neither Donald nor Williams considered Jomini against the broader context of the European military and intellectual history of his era. Indeed, few American military historians have given more than a nod to Jomini's intellectual debts and interactions with his own contemporaries; Archer Jones, John I. Alger, and John F. Marszalek rank high among the most prominent exceptions.[17] Thus, his role as an inheritor, refiner, and critic of ideas advanced by earlier generations of military thinkers has been obscured in favor of an image that touts an originality and a uniqueness that he never quite possessed. Most of the notions that Civil War historians have denoted as "Jominian"—such as concentration, a preference for maneuver over battle, and other concepts—existed in some form and appeared in European military literature well before Jomini began to write. Similarly, the adjective "Jominian" has become an all-encompassing term applied somewhat casually to the common language shared by all military professionals of that era. Therefore, a reevaluation of Jomini and his impact on the Civil War requires restoring him to his proper place, one in which he represents a single—though admittedly strong—voice among a mass of military authors whose ideas became available to the Civil War generation. This contextualized approach largely precludes the use of the sharp Jomini-Clausewitz dichotomy that has colored some recent Civil War scholarship, since Clausewitz's work had not yet been translated into English for popular distribution in the United States.[18] Similarly, it displaces twentieth-century military theorists popular with American historians in the post–World War II era, including British writers J. F. C. Fuller and

Sir B. H. Liddell Hart, both of whom Donald and Williams, among others, drew upon to make a case for recognizing the Civil War as the first "modern" or "total" war.[19] Jomini deserves to be considered the way he always functioned: as a part of, and not apart from, the vibrant and crowded intellectual environment that produced him.

This volume expands upon presentations delivered at Penn State University in March 2009 for the Steven and Janice Brose Lectures on the Era of the Civil War and explores several important questions relating to the influence of military theory during the conflict of 1861–65. It builds upon a growing body of scholarship that already has begun to loosen Jomini's powerful grip on the subject, and it establishes the existence of a previously unexamined public and professional dialogue among soldiers and civilians about major issues relating to the conduct of the war. To emphasize the dimensions of this intellectual exchange, this work will focus exclusively on the Northern war effort.

Simply put, the Jomini whom Donald and Williams placed on a pedestal has not survived scholarly scrutiny unscathed. As James L. Morrison's detailed analysis of West Point's antebellum curriculum has shown, for instance, cadets studied military strategy for only eight class periods during the spring semester of first-class (senior) year, and, until at least 1854, they read only extracts of Jomini's work.[20] No cadet had the opportunity, as Donald once suggested, to make "Jomini's works his Bible."[21] Moreover, the effectiveness of influential West Point professor Dennis Hart Mahan to inculcate a lasting appreciation of "Jominian" ideas into the minds of his cadets or the junior officers in his Napoleon Club has not been conclusively established.[22]

The evidence does not end there. By the late 1850s, the perceived staleness and potential inapplicability of the traditional "grand principles of war" after a period of rapid technological change raised concerns among thoughtful soldiers throughout the American officer corps. In 1859 Captain James St. Clair Morton, an engineer officer, urged his superiors to await the development of new principles from "some modern Vauban, Bülow, or Jomini" before adopting new tactical systems based on dated European notions. Admitting that "the stamp of European authority is pretty good evidence of the sterling value of a military dogma," he still believed it to be unwise to continue to "follow the old ones, which will . . . lead us astray."[23] Even more telling, when Senator Jefferson Davis and his congressional committee came to West Point during the summer of 1860 to evaluate the new five-year curriculum, they learned that the quality of instruction in military strategy recently had declined sharply. This was due in large part to the instructors' and cadets' open dislike of the text, the newly revised 1854 English-language edition of Jomini's *Summary of the Art of War*.[24] The army's chief quartermaster, Brigadier General Joseph E. Johnston, even suggested it be replaced by Prussian General Carl von Decker's *Tactics of the Three Arms*, finding that work "far more instructive to *young* students than Jomini's *Art of War*."[25] Historians Herman Hattaway and Archer Jones may have been correct to suggest, in terms reminiscent of Donald's own doubts, that Jomini "may well have made no impression" on the minds of the army's future leaders in antebellum West Point classrooms.[26] When the war broke out, however, soldiers and civilians alike embraced him as a familiar name, but they remained entirely open to the insights of others who were touted to be—or touted themselves as—established authorities on military matters.

The first chapter of this work, then, examines the unappreciated richness, complexity, and influence of the substantial body of military literature that became available to the wartime generation and their responses to it. Jomini's works remain part of this discussion, of course, but he represented only one voice in an increasingly expansive chorus. Many interesting approaches to the science and art of war appeared during the war years themselves, issuing from the pens of previously unheralded or underappreciated native-born writers—both military and civilian—or written by a wide array of previously unfamiliar European military thinkers representing a range of different military cultures and ideas. Taken together, their literary outpourings filled an important cultural need. The North's open society and free press made it impossible for the Lincoln administration to craft policy or the Union army's senior generals to plan strategy without public and professional critique, and both soldiers and citizens found in this burgeoning body of military literature the intellectual authority, conceptual frameworks, and specialized language for their debates, disagreements, and suggestions. Indeed, the cacophony of voices contributing to Northern public and professional discourse on military affairs during the Civil War foreshadows in some ways the modern-day media effort to consider in open forum a variety of strategic options shaping today's dangerous world.

Donald's suggestion that Jomini's theoretical foundations may not have influenced American soldiers very much—or even at all—merits closer consideration in one other way, as well. From the start, Northerners witnessed two kinds of public debates on the war effort: those that pitted one set of military ideas against another and those between individuals who engaged intellectually with military theory and others who rejected its usefulness entirely, deeming it too impractical, too pedantic, or simply incompatible with the common sense that lay at the base of Americans' national character.[27]

The second chapter in this volume builds on one of the most controversial themes to emerge from Civil War–era military literature: the qualifications for the generals that the Lincoln administration chose to entrust with translating abstract theory into positive action. Jomini and his contemporaries regularly attributed to the previous two centuries' most iconic generals a rare and innate quality designated as military "genius." Such men possessed a highly developed coup d'oeil—an intuitive understanding of the field of battle, or even of the entire theater of war—that let them quickly identify key points, decide upon a course of action, make a plan, and then act on it with boldness. Military "geniuses," proponents claimed, possessed the trait from birth, requiring only the opportunity to express it. If these men also understood the principles of war—whether from schooling, intuition, or self-directed study—so much the better, but how they acquired this knowledge mattered little. Most military writers of the era asserted that, in the end, true genius revealed itself not through strict adherence to any specific set of principles but through imaginative, creative plans—called "combinations"—that displayed an unpredictability and aggressiveness that inevitably crumbled enemy resistance.

The concept of "genius" fit comfortably into the culture of the antebellum United States. At a time when the spirit of Jacksonian Democracy blazed brightest, the belief that formal schooling actually frustrated the emergence of genius still flourished. Moreover, the course of national history, buttressed with long-standing fears of professional armies, seemed to validate the existence of military genius. Americans could point to the victories of George Washington and Andrew Jackson, neither of whom ever attended a military school, to argue against the need for professional military education of any sort, including the course of study at West Point.

The fault lines of this controversy did not split along the soldier-civilian divide. As William B. Skelton has noted, many antebellum American officers showed little genuine commitment to the study of their profession. A few, including General Winfield Scott, maintained a personal military library and developed a reputation for quizzing subordinates on their professional knowledge. But these men took few substantive steps to push for the establishment of an education system designed to promote the intellectual development of the officer corps. While they readily embraced opportunities to visit European armies, observe their field exercises, adopt useful elements of their tactical schemes and drill methods, attend their military schools, and witness their growing interest in the professional study of the higher arts of war, nearly every attempt to emulate Europeans' best practices in the U.S. Army foundered or failed, falling victim to institutional indifference as much as limited congressional funding and popular hostility. During the antebellum years, a few schools of application for company-grade officers several years out of West Point opened and quickly closed; early efforts to establish professional journals foundered for lack of authors and subscribers.[28] As active-duty officers fresh from service on the frontier gladly told the Davis Commission on the eve of the Civil War, few western forts possessed libraries, and even when one did exist, carrying heavy tomes into the field in their saddle bags slowed the officers down when in pursuit of marauding tribesmen.[29] With few exceptions, the small shelf of professional military literature authored by American officers contained mostly drill and small-unit tactics manuals, the only works considered important enough to warrant the calling of a War Department review board.[30] No professional advantage came to either of the two antebellum authors most recognized for their important works on military science. Both Captain Halleck's *Elements of Military Art and Science*—a 459-page tome appearing in 1846 and described by his biographer as the only "major American publication on military theory" before the Civil War—and Professor Mahan's useful *Elementary Treatise on Advanced-Guard, Out-Posts, and Detachment Service of Troops* that followed in 1847 were published without institutional support or encouragement and at the authors' own expense.[31] In the main, faith in the genius of generals remained strong.

Some antebellum Americans, however—both soldier and civilian—had begun to lose confidence in the concept. As industrialization, urbanization, and specialization of all sorts began to define a more complex society, relying upon the emergence of a single military genius at the right place and at the right time to guarantee the continuity of the republic presented terrifying risks. Thus, reformers rejected the popular faith in the genius of a single leader in favor of a new leadership concept based on cultivating the intellect of all officers in the U.S. Army. To that end, they defended West Point against its many critics and argued for the establishment of advanced schools to prepare company-grade and field-grade officers for the more complex duties that accompanied higher rank. Halleck had advocated such reforms in his book. So did all three members of the Delafield Commission—Major Richard Delafield, Major Alfred Mordecai, and Captain George McClellan—who served as the U.S. Army's military observers during the Crimean War in the mid-1850s. As Delafield admitted, "few new principles have been introduced with much success in the late contest," but he nonetheless noted that the most effective execution of operations in the Crimea largely had resulted from the success of "SPECIAL SCHOOLS of instruction, both theoretical and practical" for officers. The United States, he noted, possessed "a nucleus of military knowledge . . . barely sufficient for the wants of our army in time of peace," and he urged a substantial increase in efforts to promote "the diffusion of military information"—including instruction in military theory and war beyond the battlefield—through an American military education system for officers of all ranks and specialties.[32]

Interestingly enough, Jomini and other military writers of his era contributed to both sides of the leadership debate. The Swiss writer and most of his contemporaries acknowledged the existence of genius, but they generally endowed only the singular figure of the army's commanding general with that quality. Still, most of these writers represented military cultures that already had established military academies and advanced schools for subordinate officers, a system of professional education they also heartily endorsed. Thus, during the war years, both those Northerners who accepted uncritically the concept of military genius and those who advocated for the power of intellect could—and did—quote selectively from the very same authorities to support their own chosen position. The three-year quest to find the general who could lead the Union armies to victory opened frequent opportunities to revisit this debate, and Northerners did so with enthusiasm and not a little vitriol.

The third chapter in this volume examines one of the inherent limitations of Civil War–era military theory. Simply put, despite the expanse of the military literature available to the wartime generation, it could not answer every important question. Jomini's work and the growing library of tomes devoted to the art of war could not teach a lawyer-turned-general or a Regular Army lieutenant promoted to colonel of a regiment of volunteers everything he needed to know. The most sought-after military classics generally adopted a commander's-eye perspective in their discourses on the organization and operations of large military units. As a consequence, they tended to slight other essential elements of command that officers of all ranks simply could not afford to ignore. The fate of the Army of the Potomac from the start of the Overland Campaign in May 1864 through the opening week at Petersburg in mid-June 1864 illustrates one such matter largely left unexamined by Jomini and other major military writers of the period: the importance of human factors—or moral factors—in war and their ability to influence, for good or for ill, an army's operations.

The mechanistic approach that Jomini and other writers of his time had inherited from the Military Enlightenment had given their writings a highly institutional and impersonal tone. Even in the nineteenth century, Jomini's critics considered one of his greatest flaws to be his tendency to treat military units of equal size as equal in every other way.[33] If he recognized that tired, hungry, sick, wet, or traumatized soldiers did not fight as well as did the same number of rested, fed, healthy, and high-spirited men, he did not stress that lesson to his readers. Indeed, if the former could not match the latter in battle, most military classics of the era would describe this simply as a failure on the part of the commander to impose his will on his men and elicit their enthusiastic obedience. Morale flowed downward from the one to the many in most military works of the era, and strict discipline provided the single most important means of instilling it. Jomini touted the importance of an effective logistical apparatus to feed, clothe, equip, train, pay, heal, and provide spiritual comfort to preserve the combat power of the army, but he had little to say about how an army's failure to deliver these services impacted individual soldiers, especially in active campaigning. Antebellum military theory described an army as a series of well-meshed gears, but it apparently did not recognize the danger inherent in the breaking of individual cogs. A rival intellectual spirit defined as Military Romanticism had adopted a far greater emphasis on the importance of human factors in war, but few works of this nature—one being French marshal Auguste Frédéric Louis Viesse de Marmont's *Spirit of Military Institutions*—reached American readers during the war years.[34] Marmont considered soldier morale as the essence of an army's military spirit. To cultivate it, he gave each individual soldier a stake—and, by extension, a share of responsibility—in the army's success. Even if few Americans had heard of Marmont, they would have embraced his sentiments as entirely appropriate to a state that relied upon volunteers from the people for its defense.

Marmont also warned about the consequences of faltering soldier morale. During the Overland Campaign, the soldiers of the Army of the Potomac endured the most severe trials of the war to date. For an unrelenting six weeks—an unprecedented expanse of time for these soldiers—they marched, entrenched, or fought almost daily. They endured searing heat and knee-deep mud. Faithful comrades and long-trusted officers in great numbers died on the field of battle, suffered debilitating wounds, wasted away from chronic diseases and infections that they did not know how to prevent, became prisoners of war, or left for home when their term of service ended or sometimes just disappeared. Those who remained in ranks endured physical, mental, and emotional exhaustion of all kinds, suffering through weeks with irregular food supplies and little opportunity even to remove their shoes and attend to their hygiene. Many gave in to a wide range of behaviors that gave clear evidence of a sharp decline in both discipline and confidence. By the campaign's end, the names of over 54,000 Union soldiers were entered onto casualty lists. The army as an organization had suffered severely, but the individual soldier paid a far greater cost. Mahan often had expressed his disapproval of what he considered to be Napoleon's most serious flaw: "[H]e has shown a culpable disregard of the soldier's blood, and has often pushed to excess his attacks by masses."[35] Union survivors had every reason to wonder if Grant possessed the same weakness as the vaunted French Emperor.

Perceptive senior officers learned from their Overland Campaign experience, however. During the summer of 1864, as the rival armies faced each other in the trenches at Petersburg, observant brigade, division, and corps commanders finally had time to write their official reports covering the fighting and maneuvering that took their commands from their Culpeper encampment through the Wilderness, Spotsylvania, the North Anna, and Cold Harbor. Their writings revealed their growing awareness of a correlation between their recent operational reverses in the opening phases of the Petersburg campaign and the significant decline in the physical vitality and enthusiasm of their soldiers. They came to realize that success on the battlefield did not always go to the "strongest battalions" in a strict numerical sense. The Army of the Potomac continued to outnumber the soldiers that Lee deployed against them. But the physical, emotional, and mental state of many of the Union survivors, exacerbated by cracks in army infrastructure and gaps and lapses on all levels of army leadership, had made it increasingly difficult for them to sustain an effective effort against their enemies. The Army of the Potomac learned these painful lessons not because their leaders failed to heed the warnings of the masters of the art of war; the military literature of the era actually offered very few such warnings at all. Instead, the Army of the Potomac learned them at high cost from practical experience.

Military theory is an intellectually sophisticated and complex form of cultural expression. At the start of the Civil War, the U.S. Army and the people it defended barely had begun to demonstrate an interest in developing a capacity to think about war as an element of national life. They had done little to institutionalize such study. As a consequence, when the Civil War broke out, Northerners had few resources to turn to for insights on an American way of war, and they had no choice but to look to the military classics from across a cultural divide for the intellectual authority they sought. The works of Jomini—and many other figures who will be introduced in these pages—rewarded the patience and effort of objective and thoughtful readers who worked their way through dense prose; obscure references to unfamiliar battles and generals; complicated diagrams; and, often enough, tortured logic, contradictions, and ambiguities. But the classic works of Europe did not always impart the lessons their authors intended or the wisdom that American readers needed most to understand. It proved to be a simple matter to misinterpret or misapply their great military lessons, twisting their meanings or applying the fine art of selective quotation to secure evidence in support of a predetermined conclusion. A few American interpreters rejected outright the utility of all theory; for them, victory required only grit and the application of common sense. Just as the U.S. Army entered 1861 lacking the manpower, organization, and logistical infrastructure to engage in a conflict of the scale and scope of the Civil War, the absence of a strong and shared intellectual foundation to give direction and substance to its plans and its conduct also contributed to the struggle's duration and cost. For this reason, we must advance beyond Jomini to grasp the larger dimensions of this unappreciated element of the wartime experience. This book explores three important consequences of that lack of intellectual preparedness for war for which the army and the loyal North it defended paid a high price in lives and treasure.

1

EXORCISING THE GHOST OF JOMINI

Debating Strategy in the Civil War North

In September 1863 editor William Conant Church of the new *Army and Navy Journal* observed that, when the Civil War began, "American strategy, so much grander and more extensive than that of Europe, was a sealed book. And when that book was to be suddenly opened," the complexities of designing a plan to preserve the Union by force of arms entirely overwhelmed the North's senior military and political leaders. The search for authoritative direction had reminded Church of "calling for sailors among Mongol Tartars who had never seen the sea."[1] As a consequence, the Union's effort to forge a victorious military strategy followed no single path and endured many false starts. Early attempts drew heavily upon the principles contained in the greatest military classics of Europe, but when the lessons of the masters did not appear to apply to the American situation, Northerners did not hesitate to consider interesting schemes posited by unheralded and often self-taught students of military affairs. Others simply viewed the struggle for the Union as a national crusade that relied most of all on the spirit of the people and rejected the utility of all military theory in favor of the exercise of an acknowledged strength of nineteenth-century American character: common sense. Never restricted to generals and political leaders alone, dialogue about the design and execution of Northern military strategy drew in soldiers, politicians, and interested observers from across the loyal states and abroad. The dynamic nature of these exchanges illuminates an unappreciated element of this "people's war."

Although talk of war pervaded the nation well before Fort Sumter, it fell first to General Winfield Scott to open Church's imaginary book on American strategy. He had dreaded the time he might be called upon to do this, expressing in the fall of 1860 his concern that growing sectional tensions might lead to the "laceration and despotism of the sword." In March 1861, as Abraham Lincoln took his oath of office as president of the United States, Scott considered four likely courses of action open to the new commander in chief. Only one required offensive military action in the form of an incursion into the seceded states, a measure that might take "two or three years by a young and able general—a Wolfe, a Desaix, a Hoche—with three hundred thousand disciplined men." Scott clearly viewed this as the least desirable path. He feared that "the destruction of life and property on the other side would be frightful, however perfect the moral discipline of the invaders."[2] The first Confederate shell arching high over Fort Sumter in the predawn hours of 12 April 1861, however, shattered most hopes for peaceful resolution. While some voices in both the North and the South still cautioned restraint, the *New York Herald* announced: "The Civil War has now begun."[3]

Scholars have conjectured about Scott's age, health, Virginia birth, and personal political views as possible explanations for his apparent hesitation to take immediate decisive action against the seceded states in those highly charged April days. But other reasons compelled him to wait, as well. During the Mexican-American War, Scott had observed that President James K. Polk—and not the generals—had made the most important strategic decisions. Thus, immersed in a professional culture committed to the tenet of civilian control over the military, Scott needed to know both his new commander in chief's goals and the role Lincoln expected him and the army to play in achieving them. Although Civil War historians have shown a marked tendency to cite Clausewitz to stress the linkage of political aims and the use of armed force, Scott—who, like the great majority of the wartime generation, did not read the Prussian's work—could find similar notions about the connections between national policy and war in the military classics readily available on his bookshelf. Indeed, as Jomini himself had written, at the start of a conflict, a general in chief must make it his "first care . . . to agree with the head of the state upon the character of the war."[4] The concept of contingency planning in advance of potential threats and in the absence of specific political guidance did not exist as an element of American war planning, and Scott did not initiate such a practice.

Scott may have hoped for quick answers from the president, but Lincoln had much to think about. Lincoln readily had identified his fundamental goal: the Union must be preserved. But actions of any sort taken to secure it required him to consider a tangled web of domestic political imperatives and fine points in international law. Lincoln's decision to view the unrest officially, as legal historian Stephen C. Neff has argued, as "a law-enforcement enterprise (albeit one on a large material scale), rather than as a war," solved some of the president's problems, but it certainly compounded Scott's difficulties.[5] Nearly every major work on military theory available to the general began with definitions of different kinds of war, and not one of them offered a perfect fit with Lincoln's decision. Many military authors, including future Union Major General Henry W. Halleck and the Austrian Archduke Charles, simply acknowledged two forms of war: offensive and defensive. But others viewed it as a far more complex institution; Jomini himself analyzed at least ten different kinds of war in his *Summary of the Art of War*. Applying those definitions alone, Scott could identify elements of an offensive war "to reclaim rights"; a defensive war from the political point of view (to preserve the integrity of the Union) but offensive in its military operations; a war of "opinion" that pitted one ideology against another and enlisted the people's "worst passions"; a "national" war, since the new Confederacy had begun to build military and governmental institutions to help to establish its identity as an independent political entity; or a civil war that resulted from political sectarianism—a kind of conflict that Scott found especially troublesome since, as Jomini had noted, "to give maxims in such wars would be absurd." The Swiss writer wrote nothing about the conduct of domestic "law-enforcement operations," of course, asserting only that "governments may in good faith intervene to prevent the spreading of a political disease whose principles threaten social order."[6] Scott needed a clear answer to this important question, since the nature of the war would suggest the most effective applications of military force to end it.

Even if Scott had been able to discern a clear answer, however, he knew it only led to more vexing problems. Scott confronted a challenge of unprecedented scale and scope with little institutional flexibility or readiness to respond to it. At the three-story house that served as army headquarters, he had a small personal staff, but, unlike the major European armies, he had no general staff to design, as Jomini had described it, a "system of operations in reference to a prescribed aim."[7] The U.S. Army had no officially adopted doctrine on strategy or the higher arts of war to consult during the Civil War; the definition of "strategy" most readily available to Scott and his staff appeared in Colonel Henry L. Scott's *Military Dictionary* published the previous year. Colonel Scott had defined the concept as "the art of concerting a plan of campaign, combining a system of military operations determined by the end to be attained, the character of the enemy, the nature and resources of the country, and the means of attack and defense."[8] The entire entry consisted of fewer than eleven lines of text. It contained the same three elements—ends, ways, and means— that modern military professionals apply to discussions about strategic options, but it centered solely on military factors and offered no useful insights on how to translate theory to action.[9]

Beyond securing Washington from attack, Scott hardly knew where to start, even after the president made preservation of the Union his clear and unequivocal policy goal. Prodding from an ambitious subordinate forced him to clarify his thinking quickly, however. On 27 April the new commanding general of the Ohio Volunteers, Major General George B. McClellan, sent Scott a plan of operations "to relieve the pressure on Washington, & . . . to bring the war to a speedy close." McClellan offered two possible scenarios. First, with a force of 80,000 volunteers, he planned to cross the Ohio River and march up the Kanawha River valley of western Virginia to advance upon Richmond, the Confederacy's new capital. Alternatively, he might cross an army of the same size at Cincinnati or Louisville, march directly on Nashville, and "thence act according to circumstances." McClellan made clear his lack of experience in thinking on the grand scale. Scott's own notes criticized his plan to "subdue the seceded states by piecemeal, instead of enveloping them all (nearly) at once."[10] McClellan's plan also lacked specificity about ends, ways, and means, and Lincoln's secretaries John Nicolay and John Hay—never well-disposed toward "Little Mac"—remembered it later for its "astonishing crudeness."[11]

Scott's reply to McClellan on 3 May preserves useful insight into his thinking. He made three points. First, since the Lincoln administration already had planned to call for 25,000 additional Regular troops and 60,000 three-year volunteers, he deemed it inexpedient to rely on a force of three-month volunteers for either of the ambitious options McClellan proposed. Second, he spelled out a plan to combine the naval blockade of southern ports that Lincoln already had instituted with "a powerful movement down the Mississippi to the ocean," establishing a cordon of posts at appropriate points to "envelope the insurgent States, and bring them to terms with less blood-shed than by any other plan," which was in concert with the president's desire at the time to limit loss of life and property. Raising the troops and building the gunboat flotilla to transport men and supplies would take time, so Scott's third point centered on patience. He considered "the greatest obstacle in the way of this plan" to be "the impatience of our patriotic and loyal Union friends."[12]

Scott's initial thoughts reveal the difficulties he faced in attempting to draw a blueprint for army operations. Scott read widely in both military history and military theory—not merely Jomini, Mahan, and Halleck but also M. A. Thiers's *History of the French Revolution* (1842), French General Paul Thiébault's *Manual* of staff practices (1813), and many more works— and he previously had applied their lessons to solve practical problems. As historian John F. Marszalek has asserted: "Scott was a product of these ideas. Scott's books told him that war should be reasonable, that it should be waged according to civilized rules, and that it should be conducted only by meticulously trained army units."[13] Still, his comments of 3 May indicate that he could not apply his knowledge to craft a war plan on the scale now needed. He merely had built on Lincoln's blockade by adding a very general proposal for a single line of operation down the Mississippi valley. He badly underestimated the size of the force required to execute even that limited offensive, ignored the threat of newly organized enemy armies, and underestimated the new political realities that accompanied the formation of the Confederate States of America. He proved to be entirely correct only in his assessment of the temper of the Northern people.

By contrast, few Northerners outside official Washington worried over details, definitions, or theories. Moreover, they harbored no qualms about calling the conflict a "war" or demanding that the rebels be quickly crushed. Public interest in military affairs filled lecture halls, increased the sale of newspapers, and inspired hundreds of armchair generals to circulate their plans in the open forum of editorial pages, public rallies, and even the pulpit. Demand for books on military theory and military history spiked, and booksellers could not keep them on their shelves. Publishers rushed to market hastily prepared reprints of military classics; just after Fort Sumter, a New York printer reissued a translation of *Napoleon's Maxims* "as a publication timely for the occasion," its brief foreword purporting to be approved by "Winfield Scott" himself.[14] "Americans are the best observers in the world," a naval officer later noted, and the outbreak of the war encouraged "the utmost freedom of discussion by the people of every feature of it."[15]

Scott learned the accuracy of that observation as soon as his first fragmentary ideas for military action became known to the public. Unimpressed Northerners countered with their own ambitious ideas, some sending lengthy screeds directly to the commander in chief himself. Long-retired Brevet Brigadier General Joseph Gardner Swift, one of the very first graduates of the U.S. Military Academy, ignored ends and means entirely in suggesting "a simultaneous movement of two forces," one from the region around Mobile and Pensacola and a second from Memphis, against some unnamed "point or position between the Mississippi & Georgia & South Carolina." These maneuvers were to be made before Jefferson Davis could "propose armistice or any other delay."[16] A Philadelphia journalist designated the capture of Abingdon, Virginia, to be key to a Union victory. "Richmond, Fredericksburg, Winchester, Lynchburg, and above all, Abingdon, in the extreme southwest corner of Virginia, should be occupied, and connected together by impregnable posts," he wrote, asserting—without explanation or justification—that this "latter point may be looked upon as the great strategetical point which overlooks Tennessee and North Carolina, and holds them in check."[17]

Scott's concerns about popular impatience proved even more well founded when public opinion quickly solidified around a military operation that the general opposed. Deeming Scott's ideas for a naval blockade and advance down the Mississippi valley too indecisive and too slow to crush the South, the editor of the *New York Tribune*—quickly joined by other voices in the press, on the stump, and in Congress—demanded: "Forward to Richmond at once!" After Governor Henry A. Wise of Virginia voiced his resolve to stand with the new Confederacy, even though his state's proximity to the Union's growing military power in the environs of Washington might make the Old Dominion "the victim of an anaconda," Northerners quickly transformed his colorful reference into a criticism of Scott's notions to increase the pressure on the South slowly and purposefully until it submitted.[18] They did not approve of the "Anaconda Plan." They far preferred a viper's deadly bite, citing the authority of any military classic that touted the importance of taking possession of the enemy's capital. After all, as Jomini himself had stated, "All capitals are strategic points, for the double reason that they are not only centers of communications, but also the seats of power and government."[19] John Nicolay and John Hay, Lincoln's secretaries, considered the so-called Anaconda Plan to be "premature and therefore necessarily incomplete," a series of unrelated notions that "remained in the shape of a purpose, rather than a defined project."[20] That did not matter to the Northern public. In the end, the general's name became attached to the intended insult, and "Scott's Anaconda Plan" became synonymous with ineffective early-war strategic planning. At the time of the Civil War Centennial, military historian Theodore Ropp, who viewed the Anaconda Plan as little more than a "vague strategic notion," challenged scholars to reconsider their use of the term, but clearly it still endures.[21]

By mid-May, for the first time and certainly not the last, inaction by Union arms quickly raised an army of critics throughout the North. Their impatience, as Scott predicted, drove some—including professional soldiers—to demand that Scott reject the conservatism of European military theory for the practicality, energy, and righteousness of the loyal men of the North eager to take the fight to the Confederates. As Colonel Samuel B. Holabird demanded, even as he completed his translation of Jomini's 1804 *Treatise on Grand Military Operations*, "If we must borrow let us only accept that portion applicable to our circumstances, the necessities of our warfare and the genius of our people." In just the few weeks after Fort Sumter, he complained, he had begun to sense that "nothing is gold with us until it has been coined in Europe" and pondered whether or not the army would ever make a move unless "some Frenchman suggests it."[22] Other Northerners rejected not merely the ideas contained in the European military classics but all military theory, regardless of its origin, suggesting that recent technological change rendered the thinking of the past obsolete. "Take our word for it," a Pennsylvanian asserted, a Northern man would soon "produce some patented Secession-Excavator, some Rebel-Thresher, some Traitor-Annihilator[,] some Confederate State Milling-Machine, which will grind through, shell out, or slice up this war."[23]

It grew difficult for Scott to ignore the cacophony, but he tried his best. After all, as Napoleon had counseled, a general in chief had to "remain firm and constant in his purpose; he must not allow himself to be elated by prosperity, nor to be depressed by adversity."[24] Besides, his call for patience won popular support, too. "The more cautious and reflecting are contented to say, 'Forward to Richmond as soon as possible, consistent with safety and absolute success,'" a midwestern editor wrote. "There are thousands of facts connected with such a forward movement—a movement on so grand a scale—of which no one save Gen. Scott himself, can form any adequate conception," he added, damning as "the height of human folly" any censure of the general for perceived dawdling.[25] A Maine man also counseled patience, averring that he was "yet to be convinced that editors of newspapers know more about the necessities of the time, or the principles of the art of war, than Lieut. Gen. Scott and the officers on whose skills he relies."[26]

The gentleman from Maine had made an important point. The public's increasing calls for action also made it increasingly clear just how little most Northerners understood the language and concepts that governed the art of war. As shown by the frequency with which "strategy" appears in daily and weekly papers, political speeches, and private communications, Northerners quickly attached great importance to the term. It is equally apparent, however, that many did not grasp its full meaning. For every Northerner who captured at least some of its essence—such as the Massachusetts editor who wrote that strategy "consists in always being stronger than your enemy at the point of attack"—one could find the victor of a small skirmish accorded such praise as: "His plan is full of strategy!"[27] They even struggled to adopt a uniformly accepted adjectival form of the word. While most adopted "strategic," others opted for "strategical," and a few even added an extra syllable, describing the results of even the smallest actions as "strategetical."[28]

Under great public pressure, Scott soon became overwhelmed. As he and Secretary of War Simon Cameron fought with state governors who tried to control the recruiting process, Lincoln's desire to keep the border states of Missouri, Maryland, and Kentucky in the Union required premature deployments of raw troops in and around those regions, unavoidably establishing a pattern of scattering small Union armies around the Confederacy's periphery rather than concentrating them for Scott's proposed thrust down the Mississippi valley or any other large-scale offensive. Few Northerners appreciated Lincoln's political needs, however; they demanded quick and decisive military results.

On 16 July Scott finally ordered Brigadier General Irvin McDowell's 35,000-man force to advance from Washington toward Manassas Junction on the road to Richmond. Even though Scott did not participate actively in the campaign, he nonetheless became the target of angry Northerners who demanded an explanation for the army's failures at Blackburn's Ford and especially the rout at Bull Run on 21 July. Apparently forgetting Scott's deep opposition to the move on Richmond, some Northerners now blamed him for the defeat, as if the advance had been part of his grand vision from the start. "Why is it that this Anaconda that was to crush the enemy in its folds," an angry but uninformed New Yorker demanded to know, "has been compelled to drag its wounded length back to Washington, staining its track with blood, and palpitating in agony?"[29] German immigrant Carl Schurz—an early leader of the Republican Party—joined in the growing number of civilians who tried to use the language of professional soldiers to critique recent military affairs, indicting Scott for his violations of basic principles of war. Schurz found it hard to accept that such a respected general could disperse his troops and make himself "strongest everywhere except upon the decisive point; the enemy were weak everywhere, and Gen. Scott permitted them to become strongest on the point where the battle was to be fought."[30]

Although Scott did not retire officially until 1 November 1861, his effectiveness as the U.S. Army's general in chief and primary strategic thinker waned quickly after Bull Run. On 22 July Lincoln ordered General McClellan to take command of the Division of the Potomac, the troops defending Washington. McClellan's quick promotion relied only in part on his recent success in western Virginia. He also brought with him a reputation for understanding the higher arts of war, which he demonstrated in his formal report as a member of the Delafield Commission during the Crimean War. Congress already had ordered the printing of the commission's report as a matter of procedure, but not long after the general's rise to national prominence, the Philadelphia publishing house of J. B. Lippincott reprinted the report for public sale. While McClellan had devoted much of his attention in the Crimea to cavalry operations, his thoughts about the art of war penned as a captain provided significant clues about how he would approach his duties as a general. In his introductory chapter, entitled simply "The Crimean War," he cited no specific military theorist by name but revealed a deep familiarity with the intellectual foundation of his profession. Not content merely to narrate the major events of the Russian army's major operations, he applied generally accepted principles of war to the various options open to its commanders, condemned political interference in military matters, and stressed the need for a commander to possess complete and timely intelligence about enemy strength and intentions. Those who read his study at length may have found it unsettling that, before McClellan himself held high command, he criticized the allied generals for losing sight of their objective and failing to "press rapidly and unceasingly towards it." Even more troubling, perhaps, was the fact that he considered the "finest operation of the war" to be the conduct of the final Russian retreat.[31]

As early as 2 August 1861, in response to a presidential request, McClellan described the current conflict as he saw it. Nations usually fight wars "to conquer a peace and make a treaty on advantageous terms," he wrote, but the restoration of the Union required both the defeat of enemy armies in the field and the display of such "overwhelming strength, as will convince all our antagonists, especially those of the governing aristocratic class, of the utter impossibility of resistance." The slow pressure and limited offensive operations of Scott's Anaconda could not accomplish these things. Only "taking their strong places" with "overwhelming physical force" combined with a pursuit of "a rigidly protective policy as to private property and unarmed persons" would produce the desired results. Then McClellan laid out his plan and manpower requirements. He called for a main "Army of Operation" comprised of 273,000 troops of all arms "to restore peace to its citizens, in the shortest possible time." Leading this army in person, he planned an ambitious operation designed first to take Richmond and then proceed to Charleston, Savannah, Montgomery, Pensacola, Mobile, and New Orleans to "crush out this rebellion at its very heart." While he, too, called for a strong movement on the Mississippi—leaving the size of that army to be determined by local commanders and Lincoln—he did not lay out a similar series of cities to take; he merely acknowledged that this secondary force's advance, along with the progress of his own massive army, would "materially assist each other by diminishing the resistance to be encountered by each." He also identified a number of geographical points along the Union's southern borders that required protective detachments, including Cairo, Illinois; Baltimore; Fort Monroe; and Washington, and he placed great emphasis on building, reopening, and protecting railroads.[32] He emphasized maneuver and position, not combat. In short, he envisioned a very traditional "war of posts," one very much shaped by prevailing nineteenth-century military theory that emphasized the capture of enemy strong points, the security of one's own important bases of supply and communication, and minimal interference in the lives and affairs of noncombatants. The plan did not promote a concentration of effort or resources, but it set forth a goal, offered an action plan, and presented a rough idea of the means required to execute it. It also fit Lincoln's political goals as they existed in the fall of 1861. But McClellan's ideas did not include a timetable for execution. Moreover, as long as Scott filled the position of general in chief, McClellan did not yet possess the command authority to turn thought into action.

On 1 November 1861, however, General Scott finally retired, and McClellan succeeded him, as he never doubted he would. On the day before he took command, McClellan submitted to Secretary of War Cameron some thoughts that suggested his strategic vision had widened to embrace a responsibility to design a unified plan for coordinated action by all of the nation's military resources to achieve Lincoln's policy goals. To guarantee soundness in the direction of all Union military affairs, he asserted, "the entire military field should be grasped as a whole not in detached parts; one plan should be agreed upon & pursued; a single will should direct & carry out these plans." He fully intended that the "single will" be his own, without outside interference from politicians or the public. But he could not do any of these things, he reminded Cameron, until he obtained the necessary resources even to initiate operations against his first target: the Confederate army at Manassas. Reports of massive enemy troop concentrations limited his immediate options. He could either go into winter quarters, continue to build his army, and begin active operations in the spring of 1862, or he could go on the offensive immediately with a smaller force than he deemed "desirable & necessary." He bemoaned the political circumstances in Missouri, Kentucky, and elsewhere that hampered the War Department's ability "to concentrate the resources of the nation in this vicinity," especially since, he claimed, "the nation feels, & I share that feeling, that the Army of the Potomac holds the fate of the country in its hands."[33] Thus, even as he staked his claim as the U.S. Army's strategic leader, McClellan revealed increasingly dangerous blind spots for Lincoln's political needs and for the fortunes of Union armies outside his immediate direction.

Northerners had welcomed the arrival of McClellan during the summer, but they also expected him to back up his bold talk with action. The constant delays both east and west through the fall of 1861, the disaster at Ball's Bluff in October, and then McClellan's decision to go into winter quarters and again delay his advance into Virginia turned hope into frustration. In early 1862, the editor of the *New York Times* mused, "It would be amusing to look back to the Northern journals, and see how much of the pompous programme of 'our Fall campaign' has been fulfilled." After listing a number of the cities that McClellan planned to take but had not yet done so, the editor expressed great dismay that, at the end of 1861, "the good public is presented [only] with a strip of sand at Hatteras, and an inlet at Port Royal."[34] Many still ardently believed that the 1862 spring campaign, whenever it finally started, would "vindicate General McClellan's high reputation for military strategy," but others were not so sanguine.[35] In Washington, the newly organized Joint Committee on the Conduct of the War demanded immediate action. A correspondent from Massachusetts visiting Washington in January 1862 reported back to his hometown a widely circulating "hotel-joke" describing McClellan's newest strategic plan. It called for Little Mac to wait "for the Chinese population of California to increase to such a vast number that they will be able to cross the Rocky Mountains and bring up his right wing, by which time the Russian Possessions and Greenland will have a redundant population, which can be drafted down to the support of the grand left wing of the Union army—and that when these great events take place, the war will commence in earnest."[36]

McClellan's continued delays into the new year deeply concerned Lincoln, who, as James M. McPherson has argued, began to truly embrace his role as commander in chief. Candidate Lincoln had enjoyed telling stories of his military prowess in the Black Hawk War, but he had no additional military education or experience. Thus, President Lincoln, during the first year in office, became a voracious reader of military works. But the extent of his study—and the authors he read—remains unclear. Library of Congress records show that Lincoln checked out Halleck's *Elements of Military Art and Science* on 8 January 1862 and returned it on 24 March 1864, but no other military classics, including Jomini, appear on the list.[37] Nonetheless, by early 1862, Lincoln's correspondence reveals an increasing facility with the language and theoretical concepts of the professional soldier, and he applied his newfound knowledge to make clear to his generals both what he wanted to accomplish and how he expected it to be done. On 13 January 1862, he explained his thoughts quite clearly in a letter to Brigadier General Don Carlos Buell:

> I state my general idea of this war to be that we have the *greater* numbers, and the enemy has the *greater* facility of concentrating forces upon points of collision; that we must fail, unless we can find someway of making *our* advantage an over-match for *his*; and that this can only be done by menacing him with superior forces at *different* points, at the *same* time; so that we can safely attack, one, or both, if he makes no change; and if he *weakens* one to *strengthen* the other, forbear to attack the strengthened one, but seize, and hold the weakened one, gaining so much.[38]

Lincoln had indentified the key problem. His plan could not work without a general in chief capable of developing a unified plan for coordinated action and then executing it. The aftereffects of McClellan's bout with typhoid fever in December 1861 and his obsession with planning the Army of the Potomac's spring campaign—as well as his fighting with his superiors and senior subordinates who were opposed to his Urbanna plan— suggested that he might not be up to the challenge. Although he insisted that when he assumed command in November, he had embraced "the whole field of operations—regarding the Army of the Potomac as only *one*, while the most important, of the masses under my command," he had paid far less attention to western matters. Major General Henry W. Halleck, commander of the Department of the Missouri, advised him in late January 1862 to order an end to the "pepper-box strategy" of scattered troop deployments in the western theater. Halleck even offered his own plan to amass a force of 60,000 troops—a mere fragment of the force McClellan contemplated—and advance them up the Tennessee and Cumberland Rivers. Such a move would permit the concentration of force upon the scattered Confederate defensive scheme, and it would divert military efforts away from the Mississippi River itself, which, Halleck argued, did not meet accepted standards of "a proper line of operations."[39] While Halleck had offered a worthy plan, McClellan supplied little in the way of advice or support. Lincoln himself had cleared the way for Halleck's advance that led to Brigadier General Ulysses S. Grant's victories at Fort Henry and Fort Donelson in mid-February.

Even the success of his subordinates—and the public praised heaped on them—did not inspire McClellan to action. When the Army of the Potomac still did not move on 22 February, as the president himself had ordered, even the Richmond press began to poke fun at Little Mac, crowing: "So much for 'strategy'! So much for the comprehensive 'plans' of George B. McClellan! So much for the terrible 'anaconda' which was to crush rebellion in its fold!"[40] The Joint Committee demanded Lincoln relieve McClellan. When Lincoln asked Senator Benjamin Wade who might succeed him, the Ohio Senator barked: "Why, anybody." Lincoln is supposed to have replied: "*Anybody* will do for you, but not for me. I must have somebody."[41] On 13 March, for a host of reasons, Lincoln relieved McClellan from his position as general in chief. Interestingly, perhaps because he did not want to joust with Joint Committee members who favored McDowell or John C. Fremont, Lincoln did not name a successor. Between mid-March and July 1862, he and his closest advisers from his cabinet—especially new secretary of war Edwin M. Stanton—provided direction for the conduct of the war. As a strategic leader, McClellan had failed Lincoln. The president retained him in command of the Army of the Potomac, a move that presidential secretary John Hay deemed "a very great kindness" that might give Little Mac "an opportunity to retrieve his errors."[42] But, in time, that decision backfired, as well.

McClellan had arrived in Washington in July 1861 hailed as the next Napoleon. Thus, after his inaction as general in chief and his subsequent cautious advance up the Virginia peninsula bounded by the York and James Rivers toward Richmond during the spring of 1862, Northerners sought answers to explain why a general of such promise produced so few results. Some detractors pointed to the growing disconnect between McClellan's personal politics and those of the Lincoln administration. Others saw political conspiracies hatched by the Joint Committee or other anti-McClellan partisans in the cabinet or the Congress to undermine him. Still others sought their answers in military science, especially in the wake of the casualty lists of Fair Oaks and the Seven Days Battles that ended with the Confederate capital still in Southern hands and McClellan's army pulled back to a position of safety through what he and his partisans deemed a particularly skillful "change of base."

These last detractors, whether truly inspired to learn more about the art of war or simply desiring to criticize McClellan and other military leaders with at least a veneer of intellectual authority to support their charges, continued to apply the language of the military classics. Compared with the first months of the war, the selection of works now available to them had expanded dramatically. Two publishing houses—D. Van Nostrand in New York City and J. B. Lippincott in Philadelphia—took the lead, each offering a rapidly lengthening list of tactical manuals, fortification and engineering treatises, and comprehensive works on the art of war. These last volumes supplied much of the grist for public discourse on strategy. Not only did the publishers enjoy brisk sales, but the popularity of such works with the general public earned them detailed reviews in newspapers across the North and in such widely circulating periodicals as the *North American Review* and the *Atlantic Monthly*.

Among the most popular works, of course, was a new edition of Jomini's *Summary of the Art of War*. J. B. Lippincott now featured a revision so up-to-date that it included notice of the U.S. Navy's Port Royal campaign of November 1861. Captain George H. Mendell and Lieutenant William P. Craighill, two West Point instructors, translated the work not merely to meet the needs of newly commissioned army officers but also to benefit "those not thus accustomed heretofore" to reading military works "but who are becoming more interested in such subjects (and this class must include the great mass of the American public)." To help readers understand Jomini's preeminence, the editors explained that he "is admitted by all competent judges to be one of the ablest military critics and historians of this or any other age," but, interestingly, they did not dub him a "theorist." They did, however, suggest that readers begin their study with chapter 3, "Strategy." Then, if they read the entire work with a map at hand, they easily could master his most important concepts.[43] If a reader wanted to learn more about the highly contentious interaction of military and political affairs, then he might read Captain Stephen Vincent Benet's new translation of Jomini's *The Political and Military History of the Campaign of Waterloo*, a title previously unavailable to Americans who did not read French.[44]

The two leading publishing houses did not limit their offerings to the work of Jomini, however. Public interest in all kinds of military literature encouraged them to introduce newly translated works of less-familiar European writers to their customers. Nearly each new selection bore the imprimatur of a U.S. Army officer to vouch for its intellectual value. For instance, Brigadier General George W. Cullum—a close associate of both Scott and Halleck who spent much of the war at West Point—introduced French engineer captain Édouard De La Barre Duparcq's *Elements of Military Art and History* as "the best book" he could find on the subject "among the many excellent productions of the French and Germans."[45] Duparcq's definition of strategy reflected the common understanding of the era: "Strategy, the science essential to the general-in-chief, is the art of properly directing masses upon the theatre of war, for the defence of our own, or the invasion of the enemy's country." But, unlike Jomini, Duparcq also wrote in flowing prose and offered novel insights into such topics as urban combat and irregular warfare, two elements of the current war most military writers, including Jomini, ignored.[46]

A bit more popular among Northerners—as evidenced by the increasing frequency with which newspaper editors and journalists cited the author in their own commentaries—was *The Spirit of Military Institutions*, written by Auguste Frédéric Louis Viesse de Marmont, one of Napoleon's marshals. Marmont urged readers to study only works written by successful battlefield commanders like himself "because little good is to be gained" from campaigns described by staff officers—a jab clearly aimed at Jomini. Such men, he claimed, produced works that were little more than "a tissue of errors and misrepresentations." Marmont asserted that "every art has its theory," but his definition of strategy reflected no profound and innovative insights beyond those common to his era, centering on concentration and security of one's own communications while threatening those of the enemy. Indeed, he disliked detailed discourses on military theory, preferring instead to philosophize about the importance of morale and other human factors and use military history to showcase "the talent of employing it with advantage"—a personality-centered approach that appealed to American readers.[47] Marmont's work caught the eye of Henry Coppee, a retired West Point instructor who was serving as a professor of English literature at the University of Pennsylvania. A strong supporter of the Union cause, Coppee believed this work, more than others, would provide the loyal citizens of the North with "some exact elucidation of military questions now arising, explanations of our military successes, and reasons for the reverses we have sustained."[48] Though little appreciated by modern Civil War historians, Marmont's work found an enthusiastic wartime audience. Massachusetts soldier John Chipman Gray, for one, found himself "very much pleased with it," especially when he noted "how strikingly applicable to General McClellan are many passages in it. It seems as if there must have been some McClellan of those times whom he had in his eye in writing."[49]

Certainly, the McClellan of 1862 inspired what became perhaps the most widely discussed book on military strategy to appear in print that year. Although it bore a familiar title, *The Art of War* that appeared in the J. B. Lippincott catalog in the late spring of 1862 came from the pen of Emil Schalk, a newcomer to the field of military writing. A mysterious figure who apparently arrived in the United States from Germany just at the start of the war, Schalk seldom revealed much about himself except for his deep familiarity with the military literature of the eighteenth and nineteenth centuries and his ardent support for the Union. Appalled by McClellan's performance, he dedicated his short treatise to the Northern volunteer soldier.

As Schalk explained, he decided to write because "war is a science, and a difficult one." For the Union to reverse its early losses, he argued, "every officer should know the great principles of war." Although inspired by the complex theories of Jomini and other European writers, Schalk purposely chose to write in a manner easily understood even by "the civilian who has never before been connected with military occupations."[50] Schalk grounded his concept of strategy on three great principles. The first paralleled a notion found in nearly every contemporary book on the art of war: "Concentrate your force, and act with the whole of it on one part only of the enemy's force." Schalk differed from the principles advanced by Jomini, Halleck, and others, however, when he challenged their injunction to mass one's forces against the enemy's strongest point. He wrote instead: "Act against the weakest part of your enemy." Finally, reflecting his own frustration at Union delays, Schalk asserted that once a commander had settled on a plan, "act with the utmost speed, so that you may obtain your object before the enemy suspects what you are about." This dictum likewise challenged Jomini, McClellan, and others who argued that deliberation, based on a full knowledge of enemy capabilities, paid far greater dividends than speed. It also greatly appealed to Northerners outraged by McClellan's inactivity on the peninsula and Halleck's slow advance on Corinth after Shiloh.[51]

Schalk then attempted what neither Scott nor McClellan had yet tried: he applied his strategic principles to pit "imaginary armies, . . . equally brave and equally well organized," against each other over an expansive theater of war that included all of the states in rebellion. He subdivided the Confederacy into three "zones," but, interestingly, all of his maps reversed the traditional scheme of orientation; he positioned the South at the top of the map and the North at the bottom. Thus, Virginia and the Carolinas became his "Left Zone"; the traditional western theater of Tennessee, Mississippi, Alabama, Georgia, and environs became the "Centre Zone"; and the "Right Zone" equated to the trans-Mississippi theater. He then divided the entire Union army into eight smaller forces and posted them in the approximate locations of then-current deployments, stretching from the approaches to Richmond westward to Missouri, with each facing a smaller Confederate force. He then presented the frightening consequences that inevitably would follow if the commander of each of the eight Union armies "trace[d] his own plans" and forgot that, as "only part of *one* great plan," he was obliged to "co-operate as much as possible with the armies nearest to him." Under those conditions, the smaller Southern armies could utilize their interior lines of communication and transportation to mass first against one Union army, defeat it, and then turn to crush others sequentially, thereby winning the war.[52]

In June 1862, with his ambition fully primed, Schalk presented a copy of his book to President Lincoln. In a lengthy letter, he outlined his zones and principles and then presented two options for the Lincoln's consideration. First, invading armies could strike at all accessible points on the enemy's periphery. Second, the invading army could "act with the *entire force* against a part only of the enemies [*sic*] country," subdue it completely, and move on to the next key point. Schalk reminded Lincoln that, during 1861 and early 1862, the Union armies had followed the first course, with the results being a dilution of effort that was already "obvious." He now called for an immediate coordinated offensive of the several Union armies already concentrated in the Left Zone (Virginia), the theater he deemed the most decisive. If those Union armies each marched seventeen miles a day, followed the lines of operation he laid out for them, and lived off the land, only two possible fates awaited the Confederate army: a fight to its inevitable destruction with its back to the ocean or a surrender. Then the victorious combined Union forces could let circumstances dictate where to go next. In any case, Schalk explained, he expected the whole campaign to be "finished in less than four months."[53]

Lincoln could only dream of such a quick end to the war. The active campaign season in the spring of 1862 had permitted his "War Board" few opportunities to develop strategic plans. Worse, the momentum gained by initial Union successes in the west at the river forts and at Shiloh, Island No. 10, New Orleans, and Corinth from February through May had drained away by June and July. Political vulnerabilities at a crucial time in a midterm election year also commanded Lincoln's attention. In mid-July 1862, with Stanton now taking much of the public criticism for the war effort's lack of progress and for McClellan's defeat on the peninsula, and while the Joint Committee openly questioned McClellan's loyalty, Lincoln finally named General Halleck—generally conceded to be the foremost American student of the art of war—to the position of general in chief.[54]

Halleck's appointment coincided with important political developments that portended a fundamental change in war aims. Hints throughout the summer that Lincoln might push for an end to slavery, culminating in the issuance of the Emancipation Proclamation in September, ended any lingering hopes of political conciliation and paved the way for a new "hard war" policy. Both the Confederate army and the South's entire socioeconomic infrastructure that supplied its many needs—including the slaves in those areas of the Confederacy not yet under Federal control—could now be considered legitimate military targets. With a call for 300,000 new three-year volunteers already issued—to much popular grumbling—and indications that Congress would approve both conscription and the recruiting of black soldiers, Halleck could count on a substantial increase in manpower for his armies to execute a coordinated operation to crush Confederate resistance.

Most Northerners knew little about Halleck apart from the press coverage of his early-war western operations. Partially to fill that void—and also to take advantage of an opportunity to showcase a rare native-born military writer—J. B. Lippincott quickly reprinted Halleck's *Elements of Military Art and Science*. But those who anticipated quick and decisive action soon saw their hopes dashed. From the start, Halleck quickly made it clear that he viewed his position primarily as an administrative and advisory one. He freely offered advice to the president and to Secretary of War Stanton, but he admitted to his wife that "they seem willing to give me more power than I desire on some points."[55] He willingly advised the commanders of the various widely scattered Union armies, but he left to them the responsibilities of designing their own campaigns. Moreover, as biographer John F. Marszalek has explained in detail, Halleck exhibited strange physical ailments, suffered a debilitating mental breakdown during the fall of 1862, and proved unable to forge effective working relationships either with his own staff or with senior members of the administration.[56] After the Second Bull Run campaign, a distressed Secretary of the Navy Gideon Welles confided to his diary that "Halleck, destitute of originality, bewildered by the conduct of McClellan and his generals, without military resources, could devise nothing and knew not what to advise or do after Pope's discomfiture."[57]

The public and the army saw none of Halleck's quirks that so concerned Washington insiders, of course. But they also saw no plan, no progress. By the late fall of 1862, Secretary of the Treasury Salmon P. Chase summarized the deepening frustration felt by the general in chief's critics: "Defeat before Washington poorly compensated by the expulsion of the rebels from Maryland; Ohio & Indiana menaced; military stagnation throughout the South, with danger of expulsion from the points gained on the Atlantic Coast; Tennessee nearly lost, & Kentucky nearly overrun. Was there ever anything like it?"[58] Equally disconcerted, Emil Schalk contacted Lincoln again, this time offering his services in uniform if the president would only offer him a commission at the rank of colonel.[59] Lincoln did not accept the offer. Two rare and costly winter battles—a bloody repulse of Major General Ambrose Burnside's Army of the Potomac at Fredericksburg and Major General William S. Rosecrans's tough fight at Stones River in Tennessee—underscored yet again what appeared to be the bankruptcy of Union military strategy.

Intellectually, Halleck knew what needed to be done. He clearly believed that coordinated efforts by the individual armies under his command was desirable, even required. He had come to accept Lincoln's hard-war philosophy. But he simply failed to produce a unified action plan to direct actions of his individual armies toward a common goal. Few Civil War historians have found much to praise in Halleck's performance as a strategic leader. Halleck biographer Marszalek and historians Herman Hattaway and Archer Jones represent important exceptions, but they base their positive assessments primarily upon Halleck's ability to call Lincoln's attention to one specific element of the entire area of operations: the importance of the western theater.[60] By early 1863, impatient Northerners demanded Halleck's relief.

Indeed, the general's seeming lack of initiative and vision made him the whipping boy of editors, politicians, soldiers, and the Northern public at large. Polish count Adam Gurowski felt no qualms in proclaiming that "Hell itself would be too good a place for Halleck; imbeciles are not admitted there!"[61] Upon Halleck fell the blame for all the Union army's ineffective military efforts, even those for which he had no responsibility. Northern editors now scathingly dubbed the independent and uncoordinated activities of the various Union armies as the "scattering plan" or "scatteration policy." As the *New York Evening Post*'s editor proclaimed, his newspaper never supported the so-called Anaconda Plan "devised by Gen. Scott, and followed by Gens. McClellan and Halleck," because it violated "one of the most fundamental and inflexible maxims of war": concentration. A capable general in chief would have designed a plan to "concentrate . . . disposable forces toward single decisive points, and not scatter them to every direction of the needle, to strike a dozen different blows, which, supposing them all successful, nevertheless determine little or nothing."[62] Similarly, a Boston editor who found inspiration in Schalk's imaginary campaign now rejected any "scheme of 'surrounding' the rebellion, of 'hemming it in with fire,'" including the anaconda concept. He marveled that reasonable men could continue to embrace any strategy of "excessive division of forces"; he was entirely convinced that "success in this war will depend upon concentration and the overwhelming of the enemy's armies, as a preliminary to any extensive occupation of posts or any general adoption of the scheme of combined advances from different points."[63] A Wisconsin editor, likewise viewing Schalk's work as an essential corrective for poor or absent planning in the past, urged that "if we are travelling on the highway to disaster, it would certainly be wise to stop and change our direction."[64]

Many of Halleck's critics attributed the general's numerous failures to his resistance to thinking beyond—or rejecting entirely—his faith in the correctness of the "scientific" principles of war. In his gentler tirades, Count Gurowski frequently referred to the general in chief as "Jomini-Halleck," intending it as a gross insult. (In time, Gurowski attached "Jomini" to the surname of nearly every West Point–educated general whom he disliked, and he compiled a very long list.)[65] Halleck's performance reinforced the doubts of those who, from the start of the war, questioned the applicability of theoretical principles deduced from past wars to the conduct of the current one. As John Chipman Gray now surmised, intractable cultural differences made it unlikely that even the most educated and active Northern general grounded in the works of European military theory could win a war in North America. As he wrote to his friend John Codman Ropes, "the character of our country" and advances in technology "have entirely changed the nature of strategy" and "have worked the greatest change the world has ever seen in the principles which must govern it." Gray expressed little surprise at Halleck's failure to produce a grand plan for victory. As he noted, "All theories seem to be upset and our generals groping in the dark, and so they will have to grope until some master mind can discover the principles which should regulate warfare under our new circumstances."[66] No one had defined those principles yet, but some Northerners felt confident that they would come in time. "[T]his war will give birth to new treatises on the art of war," one midwesterner declared, noting that these works will "bear the character, if not the title, of the 'Art of War in North America.'" After all, he continued, "we have already learned that it differs radically from the practice of war in Europe. Extent of territory and comparatively boundless frontiers of mountains and forests make a fundamental difference at the outset. 'Bagging' great armies may be accomplished in Europe [but] "genius has not devised methods by which it may be done here."[67]

In the early spring of 1863, Emil Schalk returned to the public eye—and to much greater controversy—with the publication of a new book, *Campaigns of 1862 and 1863, Illustrating the Principles of Strategy*. Schalk reviewed the military events of the past year and, once again, had little positive to note. "In passing in review the campaign of 1862," he wrote, "we have seen how a wrong general plan, a division of force, a choice of indecisive lines of operation, led to insignificant results, and even reverses."[68] He had nothing good to say about McClellan's Peninsula and Maryland Campaigns. He devoted most of his work, however, to his own suggested plan of operations for 1863, essentially the unified action plan he outlined to President Lincoln in June 1862. Among other points, Schalk insisted that the Confederacy had succeeded so far largely because its commanders had adhered more closely to the principles of war than had the Union's senior commanders. While he condemned the Union response to Stonewall Jackson's Shenandoah Valley campaign in the spring of 1862, he praised the Confederate operation as "one of the most apropos movements executed during the war" in preventing a juncture between McDowell's Union forces at Fredericksburg and McClellan's army outside Richmond—a particularly successful exercise of "war upon the map." His Northern reviewers did not challenge him on that point.[69]

Schalk's second book, far more than the first, drew both ardent supporters and vehement critics, military and civilian alike. His partisans described him as "a cultivated military student," and one Philadelphian expressed admiration for the clarity with which Schalk explained "how, where, and when, our armies, violating the great principles of the art of war, failed in securing the successes which their valor might have expected to achieve."[70] Another Pennsylvanian drew attention to a specific statement in Schalk's work that struck him "as important and worthy of the consideration of our Government. It is in brief, that instead of undertaking to capture *places, forts, towns, &c.*, we should ignore and pass by these and beat the *Rebel armies* wherever we can find them."[71] Civil War historians frequently praise Abraham Lincoln's foresight for urging Major General Joseph Hooker to make Lee's army—and not Richmond—the objective of his Spring 1863 offensive, but clearly that idea already had entered the public domain.

Reviewers convinced of the correctness of Schalk's ideas demanded that the Union army immediately take the all-important next step: apply those principles to its contemplated operations. Indeed, after reading Schalk's new work and believing him to be "no conjurer," the editor of the *New York Evening Post* wondered if it were "not too late . . . to suggest to our military authorities a careful revision of the plans of campaign which they are now trying or are about to execute."[72] A Philadelphia editor actively endorsed Schalk's call for concentration and cooperation since it represented a position for "which we have constantly advocated." Even if he did not feel quite prepared to advocate the specific lines of operation that Schalk recommended, the editor still viewed the writer's suggestions as worthy of the consideration of the army's senior generals.[73] A month before his death in battle at Fort Wagner, Colonel Robert Gould Shaw of the 54th Massachusetts—who had found Schalk's first book "quite interesting"—wrote to his family that he recently had perused the most recent volume; while he considered it a "good thing to read," he also admitted he did not "know how much humbug or how much solid stuff it contains."[74] Count Gurowski even sent an autographed copy of Schalk's book to General Hooker at the headquarters of the Army of the Potomac.[75]

In mid-May, Lee defeated Hooker at Chancellorsville and Salem Church, and Northern editors clamored for Schalk's analysis of the Union army's performance. He did not disappoint. In a detailed commentary reprinted widely in newspapers throughout the North, he placed the blame for the defeat almost entirely on Hooker. While he completely approved of the general's intention to rely upon maneuver and speed to turn Lee's left flank, Schalk deplored Hooker's decision to utilize only four of his seven corps in the movement. If he had concentrated all of his combat power on his enemy's weak point, Schalk argued, Hooker could have set up the "great decisive battle of the war." Instead, he yielded the interior lines of operation to Lee, who took full advantage of them and fully proved himself to be "one of the ablest generals of the present age."

But Schalk did not intend this commentary solely as a campaign analysis. Indeed, he viewed Chancellorsville as additional evidence of the continuing poverty of Union military strategy. After criticizing Hooker's failure to make the best use of all the forces available to him, he turned his wrath toward Halleck for the same fault on an even grander scale. Only Halleck possessed the authority to stop detaching troops to coastal operations to serve "as sentries to prevent blockade runners from coming into Southern ports." Only he could "mass all these troops" so that they might "crush with this superiority the enemy's main armies." But Schalk simply had given up on expecting any such action from "a general-in-chief who advanced against Corinth with a snail-like pace" and committed so many other errors. Schalk's frustration was palpable. "Have there not been useless butcheries and failures of operation enough to warrant finally the adoption of sound military plans?" he asked. "Till this is done, we can only hope that fortune will once more smile upon the country of freedom."[76]

Even if they shared his lack of confidence in the Union high command, not all of Schalk's readers embraced his proposed solutions. Indeed, they saw plenty of "humbug" in his writings. Some genuinely felt that, no matter what schemes Schalk might suggest, the North had no choice now but to continue the scattering policy already charted. Others rejected the validity of Schalk's—and Lincoln's—insistence that Confederate armies, and not Southern cities, comprised the most important targets. "The principle contended for by Jomini, and exaggerated by Schalk, that modern warfare is no longer a war for positions, is altogether a mistake," a traditionalist noted, adding that any person who rejected the importance of capturing the South's major cities to turn "exclusively to the massing of our armies and the fighting of desperate battles" misunderstood the art of war.[77] The editor of the *New York Times* printed a letter from "A Yankee Observer" who simply dismissed the importance of all of Schalk's commentaries with this pithy remark: "Strategy and novel writing afford the most unlimited play to the imagination. Both deal in imaginary scenes. One peoples the world with imaginary people, who act just as the author chooses, and the other takes up the map of a country and marches armies over it, and fights battles to suit his own fancy."[78] Likewise, Lieutenant Colonel John Pilsen, who had served as John C. Fremont's chief of artillery in the 1862 Shenandoah Valley campaign, published a public letter in which he rejected Schalk's analysis as so entirely lacking "any foundation in fact" that he could not concoct "a sufficient measure of [Schalk's] culpability."[79]

Schalk's evident notoriety and his stridency even made him the subject of an unflattering poem. "What do our successes balk!" it began.

> Want of simple rules, says Schalk.
> Daily I am shocked to see
> Utter lack of Strategy.

After scathing commentary on Schalk's complex, contradictory, and sometimes confusing prose, the poem ended with a tongue-in-cheek warning:

> So if you'd your battle win
> And would properly begin
> Choose your scientific man,
> Fight the European plan,
> And to stop all further talk
> Win them by the longest Schalk![80]

Unaccountably, after his brief but notable literary prominence, Schalk disappeared entirely from the public press just before the Gettysburg campaign.

Schalk's success, however, helped to sustain public interest in military affairs. Commentaries and critiques by professional soldiers evaluating the war's early campaigns entered the market with frequency in 1863, some of the most intriguing of these representing the perspectives of military cultures generally unfamiliar to an American audience used to French works. Interestingly, while insights on tactics and battles might have differed, their conclusions about Union military strategy raised the same familiar concerns. Charles Cornwallis Chesney, an instructor at Sandhurst, studied all the campaigns from the peninsula through Chancellorsville, thought well of Confederate chances for victory, and blamed the failure of Union arms to date on "a divided command opposed to unity of action" and "a contempt for the principles of war."[81] Major Ferdinand Lecomte, a staff officer in the Swiss army and editor of its professional journal, served briefly on McClellan's staff in the spring of 1862 before returning to Europe to report his observations. Despite his connection to Little Mac, he still argued that the U.S. Army, as a whole, lacked "unity of command and"—noting its lack of a general staff—"strength of government." Additionally, he acknowledged "a super-abundance of criticism, and of political wheel-work, which complicates the progress of military affairs."[82] Hungarian-born Emeric Szabad, who cited Prussian General Karl von Decker as his greatest inspiration, asserted in his *Modern War: Its Theory and Practice* that the massive size of the theater of war should no longer be accepted as an excuse for the Union high command's inability to orchestrate coordinated efforts, noting that "the mere extent of a theater of war, it must be remembered, affects little the principles of the plan of war, especially with the present means of communication."[83]

The bloody year of 1863 also spawned new—though not always feasible—ideas for shaping a successful strategy, and one theme that gained particularly strong popular interest set itself apart from earlier efforts in its emphasis on achieving victory without excessive loss of life. The editor of the influential *New York Herald* sounded a familiar note in arguing that Union armies needed to apply the principle of concentration against the decisive point, but he sounded a new note by emphasizing that if these efforts truly conformed to the principles of war, they would eliminate all "necessity for an attack on Vicksburg, Port Hudson, Charleston or Richmond" because of its high associated cost.[84] Schalk's plans, his critics noted, invariably ended in crushing battles, thus rendering them unacceptable to those Northerners upon whom the war's great loss of life and treasure weighed heavily. High casualty rates had concerned Winfield Scott from the first, and a number of antebellum military writers, including Dennis Hart Mahan, had considered victory with small loss to be the clearest mark of great generalship. Jomini himself had written that "battles have been stated by some writers [he meant Clausewitz] to be the chief and deciding features of war." But, he contended, this "is not strictly true, as armies have been destroyed by strategic operations without the occurrence of pitched battles."[85]

During this period, John Watts de Peyster, a brigadier general in the New York militia, became the most articulate advocate of low-cost, maneuver-based strategy as the surest route to victory. De Peyster did not set out to be a military writer. When the war broke out, he attempted to enter Federal service at his militia rank; when that effort failed, he turned his prodigious energies to writing a series of pamphlets and articles to promote his own unique notions about military science. In a brief 1862 work entitled *Winter Campaigns*, he drew upon the history of seventeenth- and eighteenth-century European offensives launched during the year's coldest months that defeated enemy forces and demoralized their leaders through shock and surprise, shortening wars and cutting down on waste of all kinds.[86] The results of the winter Civil War battles at Stones River and Fredericksburg soon after the pamphlet's publication briefly undermined de Peyster's credibility, but his ascendency into the public eye relied far more on his 1863 pamphlet entitled *Practical Strategy*.

De Peyster offered yet another rejection of the Union's poorly conceived, overly costly, and indecisive strategy of the war's first two years. Citing the dubious authority of such notables as Washington Irving and William Shakespeare, as well as a long list of European military authors, he argued that superior military strategy ended in victory with full ranks. De Peyster openly wondered if the war's long casualty lists were "absolutely necessary" and whether or not they were "chargeable to ignorance or incomprehension of the plainest rules of true generalship." These two concerns shaped his search for what he dubbed "practical strategy." The best strategy, de Peyster concluded, avoids unnecessary battles. "To fight requires mere courage," he wrote, and "to coerce without fighting, science." Maneuver, stratagem, an emphasis on secrecy in operations, and a calm that forbade impetuosity lay at the heart of his concept.

Practical strategy, de Peyster noted, "preserves life." He believed that few Union generals truly understood that axiom, so he introduced his best example from history: Otto Ferdinand, Count von Abensperg und Traun, an Austrian field marshal who served in the War of the Polish Succession (1733–38) and the War of the Austrian Succession (1740–48). Appreciating that very few Americans likely recognized Traun's name, de Peyster explained in detail the field marshal's use of maneuver rather than battle to achieve imperial goals. Indeed, de Peyster considered it to be "undeniable" that Traun represented the "greatest practical strategist . . . of the middle half of the XVIII Century." To de Peyster's way of thinking, only Major General William Rosecrans in Tennessee and Brigadier General Quincy Gillmore at Charleston showed any evidence of an ability to apply the principles of war as well as Traun had done.[87]

Indeed, as Northerners reviewed the progress of the Union's Tullahoma campaign in central Tennessee during the summer of 1863, Rosecrans's popularity briefly spiked, based on his successful effort to push General Braxton Bragg's Confederates south into northern Georgia with very few losses. Praise for this kind of bloodless progress also filtered into press coverage of military affairs in the eastern theater; while most observers decried the Army of the Potomac's lassitude after Gettysburg, a few described General George Meade's maneuvers in Virginia during the fall of 1863 as an outstanding illustration of "the scientific character of pure strategy," far superior to "any former campaign in that state during the war"—even though they accomplished little.[88]

Because he was well established in New York military and political circles, de Peyster's work commanded attention. Unfortunately, the intemperate nature of his personal attacks on a number of serving Union generals—those he deemed careless of their soldiers' lives—very quickly transformed him from sage to target. While he proved himself to be quite well-read in the military classics, his writing showed amazingly little integration of the ideas of others or his own original thought. His pamphlets, wrote one reviewer, comprised little more than "a jumble of quotations," and his translations were merely "perversions of a foreign tongue." Worse, he probably contributed more to the confusion surrounding the term "strategy" than he enlightened readers about its complex nature. It seemed impossible to tell from de Peyster's essay, one critic noted, "whether *strategy* means strategy, as the word is received among military writers, or stratagem, or tactics," or something else entirely. Indeed, understanding the concept of practical strategy as written, the critic claimed, would "test the genius of the world's future Alexanders, Hannibals, Caesars, Napoleons, and Watts de Peysters!"[89] The New Yorker's time in the spotlight peaked in late 1863, but he continued to contribute to public discussions of the Union army's strategic options, often under a pseudonym.

This blossoming of military writing represented by Schalk, de Peyster, and many more new voices in the spring and summer of 1863 repeatedly reminded Northerners that, despite victories at Gettysburg and Vicksburg in July, the war seemed no closer to its end than it had the previous year. Legitimate challenges to the Anaconda policy all but destroyed what had served as the only strategic framework Northerners possessed, and while a number of new ideas provided the grist for discussion, no one with actual military or political authority stepped forward to offer a workable plan. Frustration and impatience held sway. To reenergize public interest in the larger art of war, however, two new publications appeared in 1863 that offered open forums for soldiers and knowledgeable civilians to exchange ideas, critique current practice, and consider future options. Providing an environment free from command influence and overt political partisanship, William Conant Church's *Army and Navy Journal* and Henry Coppee's *United States Service Magazine* contributed greatly to moving forward a substantive discussion about Union military strategy.

Church, a young man still in his twenties, came from a family of journalists. When the war broke out, he served as a staff officer through most of the Army of the Potomac's 1862 campaigns. He left active duty in 1863, however, determined to start a weekly newspaper devoted entirely to news of the war and discussion of military affairs. He hoped to draw readers who would embrace his new project and support it not only with subscriptions but also with submissions of articles, letters to the editor, and other worthy items. After William R. Dyer and Sitwell Harris of Philadelphia launched the *Army and Navy Gazette* in May 1863 but could not make a go of it, Church took it over and renamed it the *Army and Navy Journal*. He began publication in August 1863.[90]

From the start, the *Army and Navy Journal* became an important forum for informed discussion of the need for—and the content of—a truly unified military strategy for the Union armies. Contributors quickly showed themselves eager to apply concepts from the military classics, especially Jomini's model of interior and exterior lines. An author calling himself "Anti-Jomini," for instance, reviewed Union reverses in the late summer and early fall of 1863 to explain why the momentum of July's victories at Gettysburg and Vicksburg had evaporated so quickly. Rather than blame army commanders Rosecrans and Meade, he aimed his greatest criticisms at Halleck. "I must be wrong in supposing that the loyal gentleman who commands our armies, and who once wrote a work on military science, can have made any errors in his military combinations," he wrote, blaming Halleck for preventing Lee from using his interior lines to send two divisions of General James Longstreet's corps to Georgia to help Bragg win at Chickamauga. Then he blasted the general in chief for failing to reinforce Meade for an advance on the remainder of Lee's army during Longstreet's absence.[91] Similarly, another correspondent to the *Army and Navy Journal* complained that Rosecrans fought unsupported at Chickamauga while the Army of the Potomac remained "inactive on the banks of the Rapidan, like a horse fighting flies in Summer time."[92] Not understanding the degree to which President Lincoln still participated in these decisions, the public blamed the general in chief for the failures.[93] In the public mind, only Halleck possessed the authority to shake off such lethargy, and readers did not restrain their language in condemning him. It was during this period that Secretary of the Navy Welles confided to his diary one of his most pithy assessments of the general in chief: he "originates nothing, anticipates nothing, to assist others; takes no responsibility, plans nothing, suggests nothing, is good for nothing. His being at Headquarters is a national misfortune."[94]

The defeat of General Rosecrans's army at Chickamauga in September 1863 set in motion a broader discussion of Union strategy. As one writer noted, Chickamauga represented not only a tactical defeat but also "a fresh illustration of that principle of which the whole course of the war is a series of illustrations; namely, that all the success achieved by both the Union and [Confederate] arms are the result of correct military action, and the defeats that have befallen both us and the enemy the result of incorrect military action." For Rosecrans to have advanced while no other major Union army moved in concert "is simply to invite the enemy to a concentration against that particular portion for its annihilation." News that reinforcements reached Rosecrans only after the battle ended angered the critics even more.[95]

It did not take long for the editor and contributors to the *Army and Navy Journal* to switch from campaign critiques to an assertive literary offensive against the current conduct of the entire war. In addition to complaining about the slowness of the Union army's operations, they also decried what they deemed to be the operations' essentially defensive and nonaggressive nature. "The theory of war is offensive," Church himself wrote, adding that Union military strategy "should be made to conform." He found it "mortifying to be lost in this bewildering coil, waiting to see what the rebels will do, instead of, as masters of the situation compelling them to following OUR lead."[96] Union generals should not parry Southern thrusts like so many fencers, another contributor argued. Rather, the Northern armies should start "attacking him stroke after stroke, wrenching the rapier from his hands, and exposing him helpless to the mercy of the sharpened steel. Nothing short of this can be called success."[97]

By the fall of 1863, numerous contributors to the *Army and Navy Journal* openly called for a new plan based on concentrated, coordinated, successive, and rapid blows. "Concentration" became the watchword of the day. Writers now called the Anaconda policy a "a false theory." The whole early-war plan to squeeze the life out of the Confederacy now struck Church as a "preposterous notion—so thoroughly characteristic of a people utterly inexperienced in war." He regretted that the plan had early on become "fixed and formulated by a phrase (the authorship of which tradition assigns to General Scott)" and had "seized hold of the popular fancy" as "the certain and sovereign prescription for the cure of the rebellion." Instead, its use of exterior and indecisive lines of operation defied "the most fundamental principles of war."[98] Contributors seemed to agree that, of all the Union army commanders then in the field, only Major General Ulysses S. Grant—then taking up his new assignment at Chattanooga—understood what needed to happen. "The concentration of all the Western forces under General Grant has given the campaign in the central zone properties which can only be fitly designated by the word *colossal*," Church wrote, noting as well that the general did not go to Chattanooga "for the purpose of being *safe*, but for the purpose of routing and destroying the armed forces of the rebellion."[99]

At the end of 1863, Halleck submitted his annual report, and contributors to the *Army and Navy Journal* used it as a tutorial to identify the most important military questions still facing the Union. Few acknowledged Halleck's solid service as an administrator and adviser. The very first question raised an important issue: "*With whom rests the ultimate responsibility for the direction of our military affairs?*" Church himself quickly restated it: "*Who has been exercising the supreme direction of military affairs?*" Halleck's report, at least to Church's way of thinking, provided the worst possible answer: "Sometimes the supreme guidance of military operations has been exercised by the President, sometimes by General Halleck, sometimes by Secretary Stanton, and sometimes by the general in the field."[100] He pushed yet again for Halleck's relief.

Church soon found support for his cause—and help in his efforts to improve the quality of public and professional discourse on military matters—with the publication of the first issue of the *United States Service Magazine* in January 1864. Henry Coppee, the University of Pennsylvania professor and former army officer who already had contributed translations of European military writings to the North's growing body of military literature, now became editor of this new monthly journal "devoted to the interests, descriptive of the progress, and illustrative of the honorable services, of the United States Army and Navy, Regular and Volunteer."[101]

Both Church and Coppee—and the majority of their contributors—greeted with enthusiasm the March 1864 promotion of Grant to command of the entire Union army. They cheered as well the reassignment of Halleck to the newly created position of chief of staff, the administrative office for which he was far better suited. Church noted that the *Army and Navy Journal* already had substantiated "how lamentably incoherent had been the exercise of the central military power" under Halleck, but Grant, he asserted confidently, "shall really *command* the 'armies of the United States.'"[102] He, like other perceptive Northerners—including the newspaper editor who denounced the operations of "General Scatteration"—had expressed frustration with January and February's uncoordinated independent actions at such distant locations as Olustee, Fort Pillow, Pleasant Hill, and Meridian. But now, with Grant's promotion, they could be deemed simply as *"legacies from the times preceding* the creation of the Lieutenant-Generalship."[103] Coppee now encouraged both Grant and Lincoln, then entering into the discussions for the spring campaign, to concentrate the Union forces to "pour large masses upon the enemy at one point,—let it be Richmond or Atlanta." Or both. As he noted, the old scatteration policy needed to be discarded, as evidence by the dismal reality that Union armies had enjoyed "few victories with decisive immediate results."[104]

Upon first meeting Grant, Lincoln had told him that all he had ever wanted was a general who would take responsibility and act, and he applauded the general's plans for a coordinated offensive in the spring of 1864. As Grant explained to Major General William T. Sherman, he planned to "work all parts of the army together, and somewhat towards a common centre." Grant himself would accompany Meade's Army of the Potomac on its advance against Lee's Army of Northern Virginia, while smaller Union armies in the Shenandoah Valley and on the same peninsula that McClellan had made famous would launch cooperative efforts simultaneously with Meade. At the same time, Sherman would lead the combined Armies of the Cumberland, the Tennessee, and the Ohio into Georgia against General Joseph E. Johnston's Army of Tennessee to "break it up and get into the interior of the enemy's country as far as you can, inflicting all the damage you can against their war resources." Other Union forces would be charged with pinning down Confederate units in their fronts to prevent them from reinforcing the Confederacy's two largest armies. Grant did not draw upon any specific discernable body of military theory to design this plan. He frequently admitted that while he enjoyed reading history and novels, he had not studied the great classics on the art of war beyond the effort demanded of him at West Point. But he understood clearly, as he admitted in his memoirs, that during the first three years of the war, individual Union armies "acted independently, and without concert, like a balky team, no two ever pulling together."[105] James

McPherson has called the design of the spring campaign of 1864 a "concentration in time," but editor Church dubbed it a concentration in the "*direction of power*, of whatever military character upon a point or series of points: not always uniting men, but combining movements."[106] Grant's unified action plan fully satisfied Lincoln, who remembered when he had urged "Buell & Halleck et al" in 1862 to move quickly to "bring into action our great superiority in numbers."[107]

As the spring campaign opened in early May, Northern journalists— and their readers, too—overwhelmingly welcomed the new concentration policy. Ohioans read with interest an expansive editorial clipped from the *New York Tribune* expressing joy that "concentration, resolution, and vigor" now replaced "dispersion, indecision, and heartless purposeless strategy." The editor of the *New York Herald* likewise asserted that "in 1861, 1862, and 1863, the fatal policy of our military operations . . . was to scatter our armies about as much as possible"; but "under the opposite system of concentration," he could foresee Grant pressing on "with the perfect assurance of success." Philadelphians knew that "concentration is now the order of the day" and "the true principle of determined vigorous warfare." At a Republican rally in New York City's Union Square, a senator was met with loud cheers when he announced his support for the new concentration strategy over "the previous system of isolation and disintegration."[108] Only the soldiers in the ranks adopted a wait-and-see attitude as they wondered about the price they and their comrades would pay for the new strategy's success.

The eager anticipation of March and April, however, quickly changed to May and June's numbed horror at the concentration strategy's bloody toll. Like other advocates of the new plan, Church counseled patience as long casualty lists from Grant's "hammering" operations at the Wilderness, Spotsylvania, North Anna, and Cold Harbor and Sherman's efforts in north Georgia arrived with alarming frequency. He realized that "our sacrifices will be immense" with no "immediate adequate results," but past experience clearly showed the emptiness of early-war dreams of ending the war in a single decisive battle. The new experience of continuous operations not only added to the casualty lists; it also made it nearly impossible for serving officers to contribute to the journals as the editors had hoped. Nonetheless, Church and Coppee remained committed to providing the kind of sound campaign analysis that quickly made their publications favorites in army camps. In letters to his wife, General Meade commented positively on the overall accuracy of their reporting and the astuteness of their analyses; Sherman actually took time during the fighting at Kennesaw Mountain to jot notes to Coppee for an article on Grant.[109]

Still, war-weary Northerners bristled at the cost of the spring and early summer operations. When Lincoln issued his July 1864 call for 500,000 more recruits to refill the ranks, one Northerner loudly denounced the president's demand for his "semi-annual fresh installments of fresh victims to his incapacity."[110] That summer's selection of newly translated European military works included *Strategy and Tactics*, authored by General G. H. Dufour, a former chief of staff of the Swiss army who had commanded his nation's forces against an insurrection in 1847. As a reviewer for the *Atlantic Monthly* noted, Dufour not only had applied correct military principles to concentrate his forces but also had crushed the rebellion in only six days with little loss of life.[111] Especially after the bloodletting at the Crater on 30 July, Church acknowledged the "conspicuous failure, gloom spread everywhere." Some Northerners groused loudly, and the editor admitted that "while that temper was not praiseworthy, it was not wholly unpardonable."[112] Still, while Northerners continued to decry the lengthening casualty lists wrought by the campaign's tactics, there was no great public outcry openly condemning Grant's strategy. In the end, patience and commitment won out. Indeed, as the stalemate of summer gave way to the U.S. Navy's victory at Mobile Bay, Sherman's capture of Atlanta, and Major General Philip H. Sheridan's early success in the Shenandoah Valley, a new spirit of hope surged in the North. The reason behind these triumphs of autumn seemed clear enough. After one of Sheridan's successes in September 1864, a war correspondent attributed recent Union progress to the replacement of a "hydra-headed system of control . . . to an active Army under one head."[113]

The unfolding of Grant's strategy, of course, occurred simultaneously with public interest in the 1864 presidential election that pitted Lincoln against former general in chief McClellan. In print and on the stump, Lincoln's supporters adopted the particularly confrontational tactic of revisiting the strategic situation of 1862 to offer starkly negative assessments of McClellan's performance that compared poorly with the progress of the Lincoln-Grant team. McClellan's friends had no choice but to respond.

Supporters of both candidates drew their battle lines, and partisan charges and countercharges flew. A Republican speaker at a rally at the Union League in Philadelphia recalled how "the country waited, waited, and waited, many a patient week and month for the army to move," and when asked to explain his delay, McClellan's "universal reply was in two words *strategy* and *anaconda*." Thus, he left the nation "in a state of suspense for many months, between strategy and anaconda, and by way of variety between anaconda and strategy."[114] The *New York Times* added McClellan's name to a list of generals known both for their intellectual mastery of the principles of war and their failure on the battlefield, equating him with two other "very conspicuous and striking additions" to that roster: Confederate General Joseph E. Johnston—and Jomini himself.[115] McClellan's Democratic supporters, of course, defended him against all partisan attacks upon his strategic vision. Especially after the fight at Cold Harbor in June, Little Mac's supporters pointed out that several of his successors—including the current incumbent—had failed to take Richmond with plans of their own design, and now Grant's choice to fight on the same ground where McClellan fought Lee during the Seven Days Battles two years previously invalidated all criticism of Little Mac's selection of strategic bases and lines of operation and proved his "superiority as a military man, over all the popinjays who have sought to traduce him."[116]

Lincoln's reelection in November paved the way for a final push for military victory based on concentration of effort. Northerners continued to praise Grant's strategic vision for demolishing what one New Yorker described as the "old exploded anaconda plan of fighting around the circle" with exterior lines of operation. More and more, they approved of his new actions that encouraged "cutting and cutting through the vitals of the enemy's country."[117] However, in late November, Confederate General John Bell Hood quite suddenly marched north into central and western Tennessee, hoping to lure Sherman north from Georgia. The move unnerved Northern civilians once more. "West of the Alleghenies, the field of war presents the singular spectacle of two great antagonistic chieftains, *both* at once acting on the offensive!" editor Church marveled.[118] Bloody repulses by Union troops under Major General John Schofield at Franklin in November and especially by Major General George Thomas's command at Nashville in December, however, destroyed the bulk of Hood's force. Hood's destruction restored Northern confidence.

The successful conclusion of Sherman's march to the sea in December 1864 gave Northerners further reason to appreciate the effectiveness of Grant's unified strategy. While Grant's key subordinate conducted his operation through the heart of Georgia out of the public eye, European soldiers marveled at the novelty of the effort, and the Northern public had held its breath in anticipation until its success was assured. "When the movement of Sherman is developed in its full character," Church assured his readers in November, "a new turn will be manifest in the kaleidoscope of the war."[119] By early December, he could boast of the "novelty and daring which mark the conception of Sherman's latest and most brilliant campaign," even as he relied mostly on snippets of information from Southern newspapers to chart the Union army's course.[120] The operation's true worth, wrote editor Church, stemmed not merely from the bisection of the Confederacy and the severing of communication between east and west, but, even more important, from the "destruction of his military supplies and storehouses all along the protracted route" and the "staggering blow . . . against the enemy's self-confidence." In short, Church concluded, Sherman's campaign "teaches a lesson in strategy. It shows us that we may accomplish as much by going where the enemy does not want us to go, as by taking the route he prescribes for us."[121]

After praising Sherman's victory all the more for its success at a cost of "no more than 1,000 or 1,500 men—the price we often pay for a reconnaissance" in Virginia, he predicted more grand-scale success as the general transformed his army into "a disturbing influence in the campaign of Lee."[122] As Sherman marched north through the Carolinas, Northerners relished the elimination of Fort Fisher and every perceived option remaining open to the vaunted Confederate chieftain. By late March 1865, during the war's last days, "concentration" became "once more, and more palpably than ever, the watchword of the hour."[123]

With the end of military operations in April 1865, Northerners reveled in their grand victory. But when they began to identify the conflict's great lessons to be preserved for future generations, the processes of collective memory quickly began to filter the events of the previous four years through the minds of millions of Northerners, each of whom tended to focus on specific aspects of the war and remember them only in the way he preferred. Seldom intending to pervert the truth, they nonetheless ignited literary wars of all sorts. On the conduct of the war on its highest levels, few disagreed that the Grant-Sherman team had led the way to victory. But all efforts to forge a consensus on such matters as the relative importance of the eastern and western theaters—a topic that was somewhat muted during the last year of the war, as Northerners understood that victory depended on the collaborative effort of *all* the Union armies—entirely collapsed, with each side turning to the theories of the most useful military authority, however credentialed, to make their cases. One writer who praised Grant's crushing of Confederate resistance at Petersburg and his pursuit of Lee to Appomattox called upon the "ingenious" Emil Schalk, who had recognized as early as 1862 that "the destruction of the power of the confederacy east of the Alleghanies would inevitably result in the restoration of the authority of the United States over the whole valley of the Mississippi."[124] Meanwhile, another observer drew upon the same source to reach an entirely different conclusion. In an intriguing 1865 piece entitled "Emil Schalk—Is Gen. Sherman His Pupil?," the author called upon Schalk's strategic plans of 1863 to argue that "the South could not be vanquished through Richmond." Georgia had to be invaded and Augusta captured to ensure the Confederacy's fall. In short, "Virginia must be conquered in Georgia." He concluded that Sherman had "followed the charts laid down by Schalk" to carry out that plan.[125] The veterans of the two theaters and their supporters reached no agreement during that era, of course, and historians have argued the importance of the individual areas of operation ever since.

As the civilians and volunteers who loyally followed the Union cause resumed their peacetime pursuits, many professional army officers gratefully returned to the more tranquil life of the peacetime army. The most astute among them understood that the postwar U.S. Army simply had to adopt a more intellectually sophisticated approach to the study of war. As General Sherman noted in a public speech at St. Louis in July 1865: "War means success by any and every means; it is not fighting alone. Bulls do that, and bears, and all beasts, but men attain objects by intellect, and the introduction of physical power, moved upon strategic points."[126] Nonetheless, after four long years of war, the army still lacked an "immutable clear and thorough explanation, accepted by all, of the technical terms" of the higher arts of war. During the war years, American soldiers had been exposed to a far wider variety of military writers and their ideas than ever before, and they felt overwhelmed by it all. "Open Rocquescourt, Dufour, Jomini, Bismar[c]k, DelDurro, Vial, Duparcq, &c, &c, French, Spanish, German, Swiss and Belgian, all differ," one officer complained, and readers will find that "all mingle strategy more or less with tactics, and make maneuvering not a link of union, but of confusion."[127]

The verdict on Jomini himself—the erstwhile father of strategic thought—remained unsettled, as well. One contributor to Church's journal continued to insist that the Swiss officer's "labors have been as useful, or, perhaps, more useful than those of any other one man," ranking Jomini as "amongst the first, if not the very first, who has pretended to 'raise the curtain which shrouded in mystery and darkness the science of war.'"[128] But Colonel L. P. DiCesnola, a veteran cavalry officer, saw only Jomini's limitations, considering his works—"which I have seen carefully read by our Volunteer officers"—to be "laboriously written," lacking any "power of genius," and inferior to the writings of Archduke Charles.[129]

The U.S. Army saw the merits of moving into the future on a stronger intellectual foundation. But many veterans of the Civil War voiced a very specific stipulation about the body of military theory they studied: they required one of American design. "We had much to learn, and began late to study," one man commented, "but we made no mean progress when we did set about it. We began aright by trying the efficiency of adhering to military science" of the past, but, in so doing, "we have been obliged to mark out our own paths." In time, the senior leadership of the U.S. Army itself would come to believe in the necessity for an intellectual framework for the study of war that combined a respect for the ideas of past masters with new additions supplied "by American ingenuity." Such a change loosened—but did not release—the grip of Jomini and his generation, but it made "the campaigns of Grant, Sherman, Sheridan and Rosecrans . . . the studies of military schools for years to come."[130] It would take almost two decades, however, for the U.S. Army to start down that path.

2

WHO SHALL COMMAND?

The Cult of Genius versus the Primacy of the Professional

In late 1863 an exasperated Northerner remembered that, in the exciting first days of the Civil War, "it was the fashion to sneer at those who had made the profession of arms their study, and an experience in Congress was apparently regarded as a more essential qualification to command than a course of study at West Point." Indeed, he recalled with dismay a time when a "conscientious regard for the essential principles of military science" might be deemed a hindrance.[1] The commentator clearly regretted those sentiments, but he barely hinted at the heated disagreements that inspired them. Just as Northerners had argued over the planning of Union military strategy, they also disagreed sharply about who should be entrusted with its execution.

The dual nature of the nineteenth-century American military tradition lay at the base of the controversy. From the early days of the Republic, the United States maintained a small standing army in peacetime but expanded it exponentially with citizen-soldier volunteers in times of national crisis. Each wartime mobilization revealed inherent tensions between the "professionals" and the "amateurs," and the process for commissioning general officers during the Civil War provided an especially contentious illustration of that phenomenon. Over time, additional dichotomies suggested themselves. Historian Thomas J. Goss, for instance, has explored the Lincoln administration's selection of "professional" and "political" generals for the necessary skills each group could bring to the conduct of a "people's war." The modern American military profession uses Civil War generals as examples to make distinctions between "leaders" and "managers."[2] But all of these dichotomies serve as specific illustrations of a far broader nineteenth-century cultural framework that shaped the North's public, political, and professional discourse on the selection, promotion, and assignment of generals to command the Union armies. This framework pitted faith in the inspiration of "genius" against the authority of "intellect."[3]

To antebellum Americans, the concept of "genius" represented a specific innate quality present in an individual from birth. Formal education could not introduce genius into a mind not already possessed of it; indeed, it was generally believed that the formalism of the classroom might block its full development. Military writers of the seventeenth and eighteenth centuries regularly identified genius as the element that set the era's most successful generals apart from their peers. Well before Napoleon's rise to prominence, for instance, Welsh military theorist Henry Lloyd, a veteran of the Austrian army during the Seven Years' War, noted that the best generals followed no sets of formal rules for choosing key positions, claiming that "genius alone can do it, and precepts are in vain."[4] Most military writers recognized that any given age produced few men blessed with genius, and a nation could count itself fortunate if the commanding general of its armies was one of them. After all, as Napoleon himself famously proclaimed, in war, "men are nothing; it is the one man, the master mind, that sways the multitude." Most Europeans equated military genius with the possession of a finely honed coup d'oeil, essentially an inner eye that permitted a general to look at a map, grasp the situation at a glance, and intuitively know how to plan and secure victory, often employing bold and creative methods to achieve it.

A belief in military genius also thrived in antebellum American culture. After all, the history of the young nation certainly seemed to validate it. The rise of George Washington during the Revolutionary War, followed by the ascendency of Andrew Jackson during the War of 1812, fit the model of the untutored genius who rose from the people to lead American armies to victory. It also reflected the spirit of Jacksonian Democracy that touted advancement based upon individual merit rather than the benefits of privilege, fortune, or education.

The strength of this popular conviction revealed itself regularly during annual congressional hearings over the funding and future of the U.S. Military Academy at West Point. Controversial since its founding in 1802, the school regularly became a target of fiscal conservatives who complained of its expense, antimilitarists who opposed any institution that supported a standing army, and antielitists who feared the creation of a permanent American warrior class. But the most telling criticism simply asserted that a school for soldiers was irrelevant. As Senator Thomas Hart Benton, an ardent critic of the school, frequently asserted, the Military Academy's strict discipline and rote pedagogy "blocks up the way against genius." He, and many others, did not doubt that, if war threatened, the nation could count on "barefooted genius—such as this country abounds in, and which the field alone can develop" for its protection.[5] The popular understanding of the concept of genius also rested on a belief that the quality lay dormant until a man possessing it found an opportunity to express it fully.

Noting the rising power, wealth, and ambition of the world's greatest nation-states, however, a small number of Americans interested in military affairs warned against a continued reliance upon the timely appearance of a Washington or a Jackson at the first hint of national crisis; they viewed it as a misplaced confidence that carried an unacceptably high degree of risk. Starting in the aftermath of the War of 1812, they began to consider options for improving the quality—but not the size or cost—of the Regular Army, and officer education, in particular, attracted their interest and advocacy.

From their readings in European history and military theory, these reform-minded individuals understood that the iconic geniuses Napoleon and Frederick the Great had not won wars single-handedly; they had required subordinate commanders and staff officers capable of translating inspiration into decisive action. By midcentury, every major European military power had developed at least the rudiments of an officer education system. Even Jomini had included the establishment of "an organization calculated to advance the theoretical and practical education of its officers" among his twelve conditions for a perfect army and frequently proclaimed a "well-instructed general staff" to be "one of the most useful of organizations."[6]

The military-education reform impulse produced no lasting positive results during the antebellum years, however. Congressional appropriations committees generally proved hostile, and even the army's senior leaders did not demand change. Education proponents damned the shortsightedness of their critics. As Captain Henry W. Halleck wrote in 1846: "If professional ignorance be a recommendation in our generals, why not also in our lawyers and surgeons? . . . Is it less important to have competent [officers] to command where the lives of thousands, the honor of our flag, the safety of the country depend upon their judgment and conduct, than it is to have competent surgeons to attend the sick and the wounded?"[7] But the U.S. Army did not follow the example of its major European counterparts.

The useful dichotomy of "genius" versus "intellect" could be entirely disrupted by a third element—indeed, a wild card—that, depending on individual circumstances, could supersede either of the others in importance: the influence of character. Jomini himself had explained its overarching importance by creating an imaginary situation in which he had to choose between two senior officers to fill a corps commander's billet. One candidate was an officer of long service with little formal military education but a solid record of boldness and success in leading troops—enough to suggest the possibility of genius—while the other was a very well-schooled senior staff officer with highly effective service in successful campaigns but without significant command experience. Jomini equivocated in the end, admitting that his selection had to be guided by each man's unique blending of military knowledge (however acquired) and his character.[8] As he wrote: "Two very different things must exist in a man to make him a general: *he must know how to arrange a good plan of operations, and how to carry it to a successful termination.*" The first might be the product of either genius or intellect, but the second depended almost entirely on individual character.[9] Indeed, Jomini argued that, for generals, sometimes "the character of the man is above all other requisites."

Specifically, Jomini wrote, a general must possess "*A high moral courage, capable of great resolution*; Secondly, *A physical courage which takes no account of danger.*"[10] As Jomini concluded: "He will be a good general in whom are found united the requisite personal characteristics and a thorough knowledge of the principles of the art of war," irrespective of the manner in which he acquired such knowledge.[11] European military writers considered a whole range of desirable character traits and personal attributes in an effort to define the ideal military character—from age, emotional stability under stress, and endurance to such affectations as maintaining a string of the finest horses to serve as an ornament of pride to his troops—but only two qualities stood unchallenged: physical and moral courage.

When Fort Sumter fell in April 1861, all three elements—genius, intellect, and character—factored into Northerners' discussions about who should lead their armies, but genius reigned supreme. Indeed, some believed that the North already possessed its genius: the seventy-five-year-old general in chief of the U.S. Army, Brevet Lieutenant General Winfield Scott.[12] In many ways, Scott neatly fit the accepted definition. A native

Virginian, Scott originally planned to practice law. Unimpressed by his prospects, however, and inspired by his brief stint with a Virginia militia after the *Chesapeake v. Leopard* incident in 1807, he leveraged his family's political connections the next year to obtain a direct commission into the U.S. Army as a captain. Thus, Scott began his distinguished career with no formal military education. His advancement did not suffer, however. His battlefield heroics during the War of 1812 at Chippewa and Lundy's Lane—where he fell badly wounded and secured his reputation for physical courage—made him a general and a national icon. According to a member of his staff, Scott "was profoundly learned in the campaigns of Turenne, Condé, Saxe, Frederick the Great, by Jomini, Napoleon and others." He maintained a traveling library of military tomes for quick reference. But, as one of Scott's modern biographers has argued, the general seldom showed evidence of deep reflection upon the material he read. While he frequently quizzed subordinates on their military knowledge, he did not make it a priority for himself or for the U.S. Army to cultivate the habit of professional study.[13] If his readings in military theory inspired his decisive, daring, and innovative Mexico City campaign of 1847—closely followed and much remarked upon by European military writers—he did not acknowledge it.[14] Thus, to most Americans, Scott represented the born soldier whose patriotism and personal energy had served him and his nation well. In the war's first days, the North briefly embraced him as its first hero-general, lavishing copious amounts of praise upon him, sometimes undeservedly and often entirely disproportionate to the results achieved. In late June, a Pennsylvanian gave Scott complete credit for the nearly bloodless capture of Harpers Ferry by a small Union force, proclaiming the win "as a greater triumph of military genius than though thousands had been slain in capturing the place." A Philadelphia account echoed those sentiments, according to Scott the laurels of "a victory of superior generalship. It is an achievement of pure military genius."[15]

Scott did not enjoy the national limelight for long. His age, among other factors, triggered doubts about his capacity. While a New York evangelist offered prayers that Scott might continue to "preside at the centre, with his clear eye looking out as on a map over the whole theatre of war," a New Hampshire editor struck a more common note when he opined that "too many grave misfortunes have occurred in our own and other nations' histories from the employment of generals in whom the fire and energy of youth had burned out." The North needed to avoid the error of Napoleon's enemies in throwing against him generals who were, "says Jomini, 'exhumed from the Seven Years' War, whose faculties were frozen by age.'"[16] Public reports of both lethargy and confusion emanating from Scott's headquarters disappointed those who hoped for rapid, decisive action. "There are a few plodding pedants, with maps, rulers, and compasses," one visitor reported, while "some ignorant, and not very active young men" in uniform loitered around aimlessly, the whole effect suggesting "no system, no order, no knowledge, no dash!"[17] Scott's loyalty also came came under public scrutiny after Virginia's secession triggered rumors of his resignation. Despite the general's repeated denials and his eagerness to take a public oath of allegiance—one commentator facetiously explained to readers that Scott willingly took it "after every meal, and the first thing when he gets up in the morning"—the general's character lost much of its former luster.[18]

If Scott were to give way to a younger general, as seemed increasingly likely, Northerners openly wondered who might fill his place as general in chief. Would he be a West Point graduate of long service, or might he be one of the newly commissioned generals who entered the army directly from civilian life with no military education or experience? The unpredictability of the operation of genius suggested that neither pool could claim any particular advantage over the other. Two Union reverses in Virginia in June 1861 at Big Bethel and Vienna, however, launched the war's first substantive public discussion about the responsibilities of high command.

On 10 June Benjamin F. Butler, an influential Massachusetts Democrat with militia experience whom Lincoln recently promoted to the rank of major general of U.S. Volunteers, ordered a force of 3,500 troops from Fortress Monroe to advance against Southern troops blocking the road to the Confederate capital at Richmond. After a sharp fight at Big Bethel, the Union forces withdrew from the field, losing seventy-nine men to only eight Southern casualties. The numbers shocked the sensibilities of Northerners still new to war's destructive power, and the deaths of two men—First Lieutenant John T. Grebel, the first Regular Army officer and West Point graduate to fall in battle, and Major Theodore Winthrop, a promising young author from a prominent Massachusetts family—led to public funerals, flowery eulogies, and a demand for answers. Northerners heaped most of the blame upon Butler's senior subordinate, Ebenezer W. Pierce, a brigadier general in the Massachusetts militia who had exercised actual field command that day. Few defended Pierce's performance, but Grebel's death particularly infuriated his fellow Regulars. A Philadelphia editor noted the drawing of battle lines over the qualifications for high command, noting that "subordinate officers and privates in the regular army" made it known that "they are unwilling to be butchered through the incompetence of civilians holding posts as field officers."[19]

A brief skirmish at Vienna, Virginia, on 17 June unleashed a torrent of similar complaints, this time targeting Brigadier General Robert C. Schenck, an Ohio politician and ardent Lincoln supporter who had helped to deliver his state's votes for the Republican ticket the previous year. Possessing neither military experience nor military education, Schenck commanded a brief reconnaissance outside the Washington defenses, falling back in disorder after Confederate soldiers ambushed his small force near Vienna. The Northern press made much of the "disaster." The *New York Herald* dubbed it another Big Bethel and attributed the defeat to the same cause: "another ambuscade of the enemy fallen into by the incompetence of militia generals." The editor warned that such disasters would "continue to befall our army to the end of the chapter if civilians are placed in high command," concluding: "You cannot improvise a general." While he admitted that a schooled soldier would not "always make a good officer, just as study and practice of law will not always make a good lawyer," he also believed that "without such study and experience the chances are one hundred to one against success. A genius may arise here and there who is a natural general, but such men are extremely rare, and even they would be vastly improved by education."[20] These two early Union defeats briefly undermined the popular faith in genius and triggered a popular demand for generals who had received an education in the art of war.

The public's new embrace of intellect took many forms. In a common reaction to recent events in Virginia, the Pennsylvania legislature in June 1861 passed a resolution urging all Northern governors to choose brigadier and major generals for state troops only from men who were "*competent persons of military education, experience and skill.*" Likewise, it encouraged the War Department in Washington to refuse to commission generals based on "private friendships or associations," along with "all political hacks, all contractors who have neither capital, character or credit, and all mere politicians." With little appreciation for Lincoln's need to build broad-based public support for the war effort even among Democratic Party loyalists, these Pennsylvanians argued that political affiliation had no place in the selection of generals. Instead, they urged every man seeking high rank to consider this question before further pursuing his quest: "Can I drill a company or a regiment, or carry a brigade successfully into action without first looking at Scott's Tactics?"[21] If recent events did not convince all Northerners of the wisdom of such a change, advocates of military education quickly pressed their case by compiling for their local newspapers long lists of distinguished generals who graduated from French military schools before they rose to prominence on Napoleon's victorious battlefields.[22]

The course of military events during the summer of 1861 seemed to augur well for a popular conversion from a trust in genius to the embrace of intellect. The loyal North welcomed good news from Missouri, where a mere colonel named Franz Sigel—a German immigrant, former soldier, and prominent leader of St. Louis's German-American community—effectively stopped the pro-Confederate Missouri Home Guard from taking control of the state and leading it out of the Union. An admiring observer attributed Sigel's "quickness of combination, which disclose the practiced eye and the fertile mind" to his education at "one of the best military schools of Europe."[23] Brigadier Generals Irvin McDowell and Nathaniel Lyon both had graduated from West Point, but neither the former's defeat at Bull Run on 21 July nor the latter's death in a losing effort at Wilson's Creek in southwest Missouri on 10 August triggered significant public outcry against Military Academy graduates. While a few Northerners condemned Regular Army officers who "talk[ed] learnedly of the art of war" but possessed too much "pride in uniform and gold lace" to "soil them in the smoke and gunpowder," others continued to voice their disapproval of entrusting positions of great military responsibility to those intellectually unprepared to accept it.[24] Indeed, after Bull Run, a Massachusetts editor demanded to know why so many Regular Army officers, including West Point graduates, served as subordinates to more senior political appointees "who really knew no more about the science and art of war than children."[25] Northern newspapers circulated lists of recent defeats suffered by generals selected directly from civilian life and victories achieved by West Pointers to demonstrate that "every step of the war which has been of important advantage to us has been accomplished by regularly educated military men," while "every *fiasco* . . . has resulted from the incapacity of civilian appointees."[26]

In the turmoil after the defeat at Bull Run, President Lincoln ordered Major General George B. McClellan to Washington.[27] No hint of future controversy greeted his arrival in the nation's capital. A Pennsylvanian and West Point graduate, McClellan had enjoyed a solid antebellum military career as an engineer and military observer before he resigned his commission in 1857 to enter the railroad business. He took command of Ohio's state troops soon after Fort Sumter and won a quick promotion to the rank of major general in the U.S. Regular Army the next month. In June, Union forces in western Virginia under his nominal command defeated a series of small Confederate armies, including one led by Robert E. Lee. Although McClellan's personal role in these fights remained murky, his reports of success had delivered good news when the North needed it. His performance in the western Virginia mountains had stamped him "as a commander of first class military genius." Interestingly, however, the journalist who reported the victory corrupted the usual definition of genius by attributing the general's capacity in part to his thorough education "in every department of military science."[28]

Now, with banner headlines blaring "McClellan Must Come Here," Little Mac answered the call. "We want such a leader as McClellan," a correspondent avowed, adding a plea that the general weed out the army's incompetents.[29] Editors, politicians, and the Northern public at large praised his military education, professional knowledge, commanding presence, youthful energy, and recent battlefield success as clear evidence of his readiness for his new posting. McClellan's flaws still remained largely hidden from public view. The praise bestowed upon him stoked his ambition and his confidence. He showed great impatience with those who did not share his breadth of vision, and he felt real frustration that he lacked the authority to shape the course of the war to his liking. He never doubted that he would succeed Scott as general in chief, but until his superior retired, Little Mac could do nothing but perfect the defenses of Washington and organize his Army of the Potomac.

With Scott still at the helm, however, an ugly Union defeat at Ball's Bluff near Leesburg, Virginia, in October 1861 ignited a series of events that had profound consequences for future discussions about the qualifications of generals. During that fight, Union soldiers had crossed the Potomac River and climbed a steep cliff on its south side. When the soldiers emerged in the open fields at the top, Confederate infantry advanced upon them and pushed them headlong off the crest in precipitous retreat. The specter of the bodies of dead Union soldiers floating down the river and the cries of wounded men drowning in its currents created a special horror, one compounded by the death of Brigadier General Edward D. Baker, a popular senator-turned-general and close friend of Lincoln. While Baker bore much of the blame for the circumstances leading to his demise, public opinion placed most of the responsibility on Baker's immediate superior, Brigadier General Charles P. Stone, a West Point graduate. An outraged Northern public quickly vented their anger upon Stone, as well as upon McClellan and other West Pointers who rose to his defense. Now damning professional soldiers, a number of editors reversed a tactic used successfully during the summer by advocates of military education, publishing lists revealing the backgrounds of some of Napoleon's other "most renowned captains and commanders," including a hairdresser and a drawing teacher, to demonstrate that soldierly proficiency did not require "any scientific military education" whatever.[30]

Congress, too, demanded answers, and after Ball's Bluff, the U.S. House of Representatives and Senate passed legislation creating the Joint Committee on the Conduct of the War. Under the leadership of its most vocal members—Radical Republican senators Benjamin Wade and Zachariah Chandler and Congressman George Julian—the Joint Committee quickly became a haven for the Congress's most strident enemies of professional soldiers. As historian Bruce Tap has asserted, most of the committee's members "were woefully ignorant of military matters and seemed particularly unqualified to pass judgment on military issues." From the start, they reduced the complexities of the military art and science to an oversimplified trust in offensive action, best led by generals animated by the Radicals' goals to preserve the Union and end slavery.[31] They did not understand the time, effort, specialized knowledge, or resources required to build, train, move, and command a people's army. Instead, they regularly attributed a general's delay, missteps, or defeats to a real or alleged political allegiance to the Democratic Party or, just as often, to the treasonous influence of West Point, an institution most of the committee members heartily opposed. They consistently took the side of the citizen-soldier, and they also searched for that general of genius who possessed not merely innate military talent but, it would seem, also strong Radical Republican political views. From the start, the Joint Committee threw its support behind generals such as Major General John C. Fremont, who supported emancipation, and launched vicious personal attacks on those such as McClellan and his senior subordinates, who did not.

The committee quickly made its authority felt. After General Scott retired on 1 November 1861, Lincoln and much of the Northern public hoped that McClellan's ascendance to general in chief would portend a swift advance and decisive victory. As civil engineer Charles Ellet wrote to Lincoln: "Mr. President, *winter is approaching*, and the delay still continues. These are truly precious moments, richer than the mines of California in golden opportunities."[32] But McClellan did not move, and as 1861 gave way to 1862, the public's frustrations aimed at professional soldiers after Ball's Bluff continued to grow. The Joint Committee, already critical of McClellan's defense of General Stone, openly chafed at his refusal to inform them of his plans or his timetable for action. As Joseph T. Glatthaar has argued, McClellan also demonstrated clear signs of paranoid personality disorder, becoming increasingly distrustful, secretive, and unresponsive to those with legitimate authority over his actions.[33] A bout of typhoid overwhelmed him in late December 1861. Congress did not care about McClellan's mental or physical well-being, however. In January 1862, on the floor of the House, Representative John A. Gurley of Ohio—not a member of the committee—aimed his ire directly at McClellan: "Our army has long been ready, and our soldiers were burning and panting for the battle-field. We had earnestly cast about for a bold and daring leader, ready for the great contest, and it was painful to confess at this late day, that the country had looked in vain for a Commander-in-chief exhibiting the will and the requisite enterprise and genius to lead our forces on to victory."[34] Even some of Little Mac's own troops—who truly admired their general for his concern for their welfare—openly wondered if he was the commander who would lead them to great victories. "Why has not a Napoleon appeared on this scene?" one soldier asked. "Why have not the great issues involved in this struggle created the military genius necessary to overwhelm this rebellion? Why has not this social earthquake thrown up the great men which revolutions always produce . . . the Cromwells, the Napoleons, the Washingtons of other revolutionary times?"[35]

The erosion of public confidence in Stone, Scott, and especially McClellan spawned a distrust of professional soldiers as a class and restored the popular faith in innate military genius. In January 1862 the congressional debate on annual legislation on the U.S. Military Academy's budget sent the school's most ardent critics to the floor to oppose all such measures. Late in the month, Congress voted down a bill to enlarge the corps of cadets. Senator Wade, who long believed the academy served as a haven for the Democratic Party, continued to demand the school's closure. Although his motives clearly served a political purpose, his public argument relied upon the strength of an enduring cultural belief: "There is no doubt, if the war continues, that you will have men of genius enough, educated in the field." Others continued to argue that the school's emphasis on mathematics and engineering habituated its graduates to systematic and deliberate thought processes, incapable of creativity and spontaneity. "Take off your engineering restraints," a frustrated Senator Lyman Trumbull demanded, and "dismiss from the army every man who knows how to build a fortification."[36] The acerbic Count Adam Gurowski, who closely followed the congressional hearings, added: "Engineers are the incarnation of defensive warfare" and belonged to a military specialty "which does not form captains and generals for the field."[37]

Ever-impatient Northerners far from the seat of power also continued to seek signs of genius anywhere they might appear. Some indulged in nostalgic glances back to the Republic's past, when untutored military geniuses rose from the masses to lead the nation's armies to victory. "Who led our army successfully through the Revolution? A Virginia planter, without a Regular military education," wrote a New Yorker. "Who were the ablest generals that served under Washington?" he asked. "Not [Charles] Lee and [Horatio] Gates, who were bred in the British army . . . but [Nathanael] Greene, the son of a Quaker anchor-smith . . . [Israel] Putnam, a Pomfret farmer," and a long list of other men of "strong faculties and native energy."[38] Other commentators cast their net wide and manufactured evidence of genius in Union generals who did not graduate from the Military Academy. Franz Sigel—his German military education now forgotten—surfaced once again, now impressing western observers with his possession of "something neither to be taught nor learned—a something seen you know not where, and you know not how—that high, incommunicable gift, prized, like the diamond, even more for its rarity than for its splendor, and which men call GENIUS."[39] Western generals with West Point educations experiencing genuine success—especially Brigadier General Ulysses S. Grant—enjoyed brief flurries of positive popular notice, but they did not reverse the damage to the public trust in the authority of the professional soldier caused by reports of McClellan's refusal to cooperate, communicate, or act.

In mid-March 1862, a frustrated President Lincoln relieved McClellan of his position as general in chief, limiting his authority to the command of the Army of the Potomac. Little Mac finally took the field, transporting his army by ship to Fortress Monroe, at the tip of the Virginia peninsula bounded by the York and James Rivers, from which he intended to advance and take Richmond. Once he began to move, his most ardent supporters—and he continued to inspire many, especially among Democratic Party loyalists—railed against those who had diminished their hero and expressed admiration for his stated intention to protect property rights of Southern civilians, his opposition to emancipation, and his commitment to protecting his soldiers' lives. They lauded his ability to mass his forces in front of Yorktown in such strength that the Confederates evacuated it without the need for a costly Union assault. In his apparent preference for maneuver over battle—to take Richmond with the smallest possible loss, in conformity with the military thought of the day—his partisans claimed that his "genius triumphed over gunpowder."[40]

But in July 1862, McClellan's campaign ended in defeat, and Northern anger erupted. Little Mac had promised a quick victory, but his cautious advance up the peninsula ended in a stunning reverse that pushed the Army of the Potomac from the gates of Richmond to a defensive position at Harrison's Landing. Worse, he showed no sign of renewing the offensive. McClellan had to be held accountable for the 5,000 Union casualties at Fair Oaks on 31 May and 1 June, the additional 16,000 casualties suffered during the Seven Days Battles from 26 June through 1 July, and the thousands of soldiers felled by disease in the fetid Chickahominy swamps—all sacrificed to no effect. During the summer and fall of 1862 and then again during his 1864 presidential run—and to a degree no other Union general ever experienced—McClellan, and his performance on the peninsula, became the focus of intense public scrutiny that eclipsed for a time the usual nature-versus-nurture dichotomy of "genius" versus "intellect." As Brigadier General John G. Barnard, McClellan's chief engineer during the Virginia campaign, concluded: "The question of Gen. McClellan's responsibility for our disasters ceased to be a mere abstract question about which men might differ without prejudice to the public interests; it became a national question, and one of vast import."[41]

Toward the end of 1862, William Henry Hurlbert divided the massive amount of public commentary about McClellan's performance on the peninsula into four general classes: comments on "the constitutional unfitness of General McClellan for the conduct of operations requiring boldness in the conception and decision in the execution"; criticisms relating to "the presumed bias of that commander's political opinions"; comments supportive of McClellan and centering on "the constant interference of an 'Aulic Council'"; and praise of the "superior military abilities of the Southern commanders."[42] Of the four, only the first category truly rested on the triad of genius, intellect, and character as described in the military classics.

Public consideration of McClellan's fitness for command demonstrated that he could still elicit support from a large army of ardent admirers, but his critics carried the day. Their most vehement condemnations began in one of two ways. Some used the results of the recent campaign to deny categorically that Little Mac possessed military genius. George Wilkes, editor of the popular tabloid *Wilkes' Spirit of the Times* and once an admirer of Little Mac, recalled the days when "nine-tenths of the hopes of the nation were centered on his genius." Now, however, he concluded that McClellan "is either a genius or he is nothing, for he follows none of the ordinary theories, and does everything by inversion. He does not believe at all in the policy of attack; he sees no moral loss or disadvantage in enduring siege from inferior numbers; and, with a principle of strategy, not very well established, prefers to fight against heavy odds, to having them."[43] Wilkes clearly concluded that McClellan was no genius. Others outlined the progress of his recent operations to demonstrate an absence of evidence of the general's vaunted intellect. Such accusations inspired West Point's opponents to demand once again that the institution be closed, since McClellan's rigidity, caution, and unimaginative approach to his campaign once again validated their most serious concerns about the school's curriculum. After reading about McClellan's command performance on the peninsula, a Union man in far-off Utah declared: "Nothing is more mathematically proven than the plans of attack taught to boys at West Point and other academies," as long as "armies can be reckoned into blocks of stone, which will stand still to be measured, weighted, calculated, and then one to be lifted over another as if by cranes and pulleys."[44] Whether critics attacked McClellan's genius or his intellect, they met on common ground to assault his character. Reports of his frequent absences from the front lines, leaving his soldiers "uncheered by the personal presence of the Commander-in-chief, where whizzing shot and screaming shell baptized them in the fires of battle," helped to label him a coward, and cartoons of the general observing his army's battles from the safety of a Union gunboat in the James River dogged him for years.[45] The antebellum years had supplied three main touchstones for evaluating fitness for generalship—genius, intellect, and character—and, as his many critics loudly proclaimed, McClellan failed on all counts.

Arguments that Hurlbert applied to his fourth category actually complemented those he placed in the first. Because Robert E. Lee had commanded the Army of Northern Virginia only since 1 June 1862, few Northerners made direct personal comparisons between his command ability and that of Little Mac. It seemed to be sufficient simply to assert that the Confederate army had been handled far more competently than had the Army of the Potomac. McClellan's scattered deployments during the Seven Days Battles had allowed the Confederates to demonstrate a superior use of the principle of concentration at Gaines Mill, Mechanicsville, and other fights, resulting in the smashing of isolated elements of the Army of the Potomac. Even the general's complaints about the superiority of Southern numbers never convinced these critics, who argued that "the country has no evidence that McClellan was outnumbered, but only that he was outgeneraled."[46]

Hurlbert's second and third categories, however, had no foundation in the European military classics or in the traditional way in which Americans previously considered fitness for high military command. McClellan's critics now accused him of permitting his personal political views to exert inappropriate influence on his professional military decisions. Rather than blame the defensive legacy of Dennis Hart Mahan or other military theorists whom McClellan might have studied, critics blamed his unwavering stance that Southern noncombatants and their property, including their slaves, should be protected—a stance directly opposed to the public and political demands of Northerners with strong Radical Republican leanings—for cultivating in him a caution that precluded boldness. His public disagreements with his commander in chief made him increasingly vulnerable to such charges. On 7 July, less than a week after he pulled back to Harrison's Landing, McClellan addressed a letter to the president to summarize his own views on the current state of the conflict, a missive that Lincoln read in the general's presence. McClellan now declared that the rebellion "has assumed the character of a War," and "it should be conducted upon the highest principles known to Christian Civilization." Thus, he opposed any "war upon population," advocating violence only "against armed forces and political organizations," and he opposed "confiscation of property, political executions of persons, territorial organization of states or forcible abolition of slavery." Furthermore, he added, "a declaration of radical views, especially upon slavery, will rapidly disintegrate our present Armies" and turn his soldiers into criminals.[47] McClellan's trespass into policy did not go unchallenged. "If this rebellion could possibly be put down by conciliatory means," wrote a Northern pamphleteer, "we believe General McClellan qualified to command our armies. . . . [But] we believe this rebellion will be put down by fighting, and kept down by a radical change in the feelings and aspirations of the ruling class of the South." If McClellan could not command his army on these terms, then he must be relieved.[48]

McClellan's friends found their voice in Hurlbert's third category, blaming the results of the recent campaign squarely on political interference from Washington. For months, they had targeted the members of the Joint Committee on the Conduct of the War for their uninformed military views. As McClellan had inched his way up the peninsula with politicians' criticisms dogging his every move, one of his advocates countered that if Little Mac had responded the way the committee demanded, "perhaps they would have over again the catastrophes which befell Burgoyne at Saratoga or Cornwallis at Yorktown."[49] On the very day McClellan delivered his views on the war to Lincoln, Senator Chandler unleashed a personal attack on the general on the floor of the Senate, condemning the general's open embrace of antiemancipation views and his opposition to the recently enacted Confiscation Act. In retaliation, McClellan's advocates condemned the Michigan senator and the entire Joint Committee for their partisan approach to military matters. As one stated bluntly: "These politicians were unacquainted with military tactics, and were not competent judges of the movements of a great army."[50] They also charged Secretary of War Stanton—and, by extension, the president himself—for conspiring to deny McClellan the resources his army needed, especially by refusing to send McDowell's corps from Fredericksburg to the peninsula, a reinforcement Little Mac repeatedly had requested. They made sure that the general's telegrams pleading for additional support became available to the public, along with his blunt accusations of Washington's perfidy. The *New York Herald*, always sympathetic to McClellan, painted Stanton especially as "the tool of the abolitionists, the organizer of disasters, the author of defeats," blaming the secretary's "reckless mismanagement and criminal intrigues" for McClellan's discomfiture and the needless loss of Northern lives.[51]

The public dissection of McClellan's recent operations came at a time when the way in which Lincoln selected his generals for promotion or assignment had begun to change. In 1861 Lincoln's attention had centered on the officer accession process, his choices shaped as much by his need to satisfy various political constituencies to build broad popular support for the war effort as by his need for proven soldiers. By the summer of 1862, he now had his choice of dozens of experienced army, corps, division, and brigade commanders and senior staff officers with a year or more of active service—some professionals and some not—to fill important posts. Even more important, the summer and early fall of 1862 witnessed a fundamental change in the Union war effort. The wishful thinking of 1861 that fed expectations for a short and comparatively bloodless war had evaporated, and the conciliatory approach of that first year had begun to give way to "hard war." During the summer of 1862, Congress had passed the Confiscation Act that prohibited the return of slaves to their Confederate masters. Lincoln circulated within his cabinet a draft of a preliminary emancipation proclamation. Reports of involuntary conscription and the possible raising of regiments of African American soldiers for the U.S. Army had begun to filter into Northern newspapers. In short, the Lincoln administration had raised the stakes, and, as Jomini had long ago suggested, it became imperative that Lincoln now find proven generals who supported his expanded war aims—or at least who would not permit their personal political views to color their professional duties. Members of the Joint Committee, however, continued their practice of pushing forward the careers of generals who shared their political views, even if a year or more in command had revealed them to be lackluster talents at best.[52] Since Congress retained approval authority over presidential nominations of general officers, politicians' interests could not be ignored.

During the politically charged atmosphere of mid-July 1862, Lincoln named General Halleck to fill the post of general in chief. In many ways, the president had made a logical selection. Halleck graduated from West Point ranked third in the class of 1839. While he had not seen combat in Mexico, he served in California and became known as one of the army's foremost experts, not only in military theory but also in international and mining law, harbor defenses, and other military subjects. He had resigned his commission in 1854 to enter business and start a law practice, and he parlayed his background and experience into a major general's commission soon after Fort Sumter. In the fall of 1861, as General Scott's retirement date approached, Halleck had emerged as the only significant challenger to McClellan for elevation to general in chief. Scott, in fact, stated a strong preference for Halleck, largely due to his reputation as a military intellectual and his experience in civil-military relations. When Little Mac received the nod, however, Halleck quickly received a plum assignment to command the western theater. In November 1861 the Northern public had welcomed the appointment. "As a statesman, as a lawyer, as a man, he has shown himself to be just the person for that Western Command," a Philadelphian asserted, confident that the general could restore order to the chaos reigning in fractious Missouri.[53] His soldierly qualities merited positive comment, as well. A New York reviewer of his *Elements of the Military Art and Science* touted the work as "esteemed in Europe as well as here [as] one of the great standard modern works on military polity and strategy."[54]

But Halleck's tenure in the west had not gone smoothly. He won a modicum of public praise as the architect, if not the executor, of the Union victories at Forts Henry and Donelson and at Shiloh, but he also bristled at the Northern press's fawning over his field commander, Brigadier General U. S. Grant. While a Northern editor dubbed Grant as "a Napoleon of military genius and daring," Halleck openly criticized his subordinate's military professionalism, citing his inattention to proper administrative procedures, his failure to report regularly, and his tendency to take action without obtaining his superior's expressed permission.[55] The slowness of Halleck's advance on Corinth and the lack of aggressiveness and imagination in his operations suggested that he, like McClellan, might suffer from both a bad case of "the slows" and the absence of even the most obvious signs of true genius. But others saw in his caution "a triumph undimmed by blood; and this is the highest glory of the soldier."[56] Halleck had not made a point of publicizing his political views—he proved far wiser than McClellan in that regard—but that left an open question that members of the Joint Committee on the Conduct of the War could not ignore. They pushed instead for the appointment of John C. Fremont, who clearly shared their commitment to emancipation. But Lincoln had prevailed.

Public reaction to the news of Halleck's selection showed neither great enthusiasm nor significant discontent. Northerners simply adopted a wait-and-see attitude about their new general in chief. As a Massachusetts man concluded, Scott and McClellan "have had to give way. Halleck is now tried. The third time never fails, they say; but if the third does fail, we still have John Charles Fremont, and with him, if not without him, will come liberty and victory." He ended his narrative pessimistically, however, concluding that it was probably good that candidates for the nation's most important military post were "not confined to the major generals."[57]

Lincoln hoped he had found a general in chief who could do two things for him: plan a unified "hard war" strategy consistent with the administration's new war aims and actively exert his authority over the commanders appointed to lead the various individual Union armies to advance the war effort. Unfortunately, Halleck excelled at neither of these things. Colorless and quirky, he showed far more willingness to advise than command, to act primarily as an intermediary to pass on presidential wishes to his field commanders, and to allow his subordinates to develop and execute campaigns of their own design without ordering that they conform to a single master plan. But he did embrace the "hard war" philosophy that McClellan had abhorred, and he made his subordinates aware of it. Soon after he acceded to command, Halleck had advised Grant to handle Confederate sympathizers in Mississippi and Tennessee "without gloves, and take their property for public use. . . . It is time they should begin to feel the presence of the war."[58] Halleck might not have possessed the fire that Lincoln sought, but he was thoughtful, thorough, and well-read in the military classics. He also proved to be a capable and useful administrator. Besides, Lincoln could identify no viable alternative.

Because Halleck preferred to "advise" rather than "command"—and because Lincoln had learned to deal directly with field commanders during the period between March and July 1862, when he left the general in chief slot unfilled—the president now took a deep interest in Halleck's senior subordinates: the generals who led his individual armies. Since this pool of men might, in time, produce a future general in chief, Lincoln took their measure. Nearly all of them had graduated from West Point, accumulated years of experience in field and staff assignments, and successfully commanded large units in battle. Even if the public still indulged in a search for military "genius," Lincoln had opted for men of military intellect.

Students of the Civil War are familiar with the long list of failed army commanders of 1862 and 1863. At Second Bull Run in late August 1862, a bloody defeat of Major General John Pope's Army of Virginia resulted in his quick relief. Even though the Joint Committee applauded his enthusiasm in carrying out a "hard war" policy in Virginia, Pope's battlefield performance did not match his aggressive rhetoric and led to his quick reassignment to Minnesota. With Lee already advancing into Maryland, Lincoln reluctantly authorized McClellan to take command of the combined Army of Virginia—Pope's old command—and the Army of the Potomac, drawing howls of protest from cabinet members and the Joint Committee alike. Lee's unchallenged return to Virginia after the war's bloodiest day at Antietam on 17 September—yet another failing that would be well documented in committee hearings later that fall—counted as only one reason for Little Mac's relief from command on 7 November, however; Lincoln had issued the Emancipation Proclamation after Antietam, and McClellan's open opposition to the changing political goals of the war made his removal necessary.

In the west, the bloodletting at Perryville in October ultimately led to the sacking of Major General Don Carlos Buell, whose lack of boldness and strong preference for maneuver over combat finally terminated his acceptability to the Lincoln administration. Major General Ambrose E.

Burnside's costly Union defeat at Fredericksburg, compounded by the poisoning of the senior command climate of his army—Stephen W. Sears labeled it "the revolt of the generals"—quickly terminated his army command.[59] Lincoln appointed the aggressive Major General Joseph Hooker to command the Army of the Potomac in January—despite his qualms about the general's outspokenness, his conniving ways, and his seeming inability to grasp the president's vision to target Lee's army and not Richmond. But Hooker, too, failed at Chancellorsville in May, and even his cultivation of the most influential members of the Joint Committee could not save him from his relief from army command in late June. Through it all, Halleck simply watched, without much sympathy for the plight of men he could have helped but failed to support. As he once observed: "The Government seems determined to apply a guillotine to all unsuccessful generals. It seems rather hard to do this where the general is not in fault, but perhaps with us now, as in the French Revolution, some harsh measures are required."[60]

The fates of two army commanders—Major General George G. Meade of the Army of the Potomac and Major General William S. Rosecrans of the Army of the Cumberland—deserve a closer look. A West Point graduate, a topographical engineer, and a successful brigade, division, and corps commander, Meade defeated the Army of Northern Virginia at Gettysburg after less than a week in command and then basked in celebratory praise that only a victory over Lee could inspire. But the accolades did not last. After Lee recrossed the Potomac unmolested to the security of Virginia, a critic used Meade's inaction to summarize Northern frustration over its inability to find an aggressive and decisive leader: "If any foolish one, unmindful of the sore lessons of two years' warfare, expected [in Meade] a wonderful military genius . . . a new Napoleon ready made for the crisis, he must be disappointed." Meade, like his recent predecessors, did not lack "in science or skill—all that the books can teach he has, and in addition, boundless bravery, fine judgement, and experience won on many a bloody field." But that had not been enough. The critic ended with the most generous assessment he could muster: "Meade is not a great General . . . [but] he is a good one now—a safe one, a brave one, and he will not disgrace his government by his conduct."[61]

While Meade won at Gettysburg, Rosecrans conducted his Tullahoma campaign, an operation marked by a series of rapid flanking marches, minimal fighting, and low casualties that resulted in pushing General Braxton Bragg's Confederate army out of Tennessee. Some Northern observers, noting the creativity of his plan, attributed Rosecrans's success to military genius. Others, more familiar with the military classics, saw in his actions the purest distillation of the teachings of Jomini and the other great European theorists of the era. Moreover, proponents of both genius and intellect found common ground in their shared approval of his comparatively bloodless road to victory. John Watts de Peyster, the New York military writer, singled him out for favorable comparison to major European generals of the previous two centuries who successfully had employed similar methods.[62] General John Wool identified "Rosecrans . . . perhaps, more than any other" as the Union general most capable of handling large bodies of troops without excessive loss of life.[63] When Rosecrans and large portions of his army crumbled under the ferocious attacks of Bragg's army at Chickamauga in September 1863, however, his star fell quickly.

Both Meade and Rosecrans enjoyed reputations as men of character and integrity. Meade had impressed no one with his genius, and he won no accolades for his intellectual accomplishments, but he won a major battle at Gettysburg. In Lincoln's mind, Meade's failure rested with his lack of aggressiveness during the pursuit. Rosecrans, on the other hand, had impressed great numbers of his countrymen with either his genius or his intellect, and he skillfully maneuvered an entire Confederate army out of Tennessee with little loss before losing at Chickamauga. Meade stayed in command; Rosecrans was relieved. Neither man had proved to be an abject failure as a soldier. Mostly, they seemed to lack a killer instinct. Lincoln had come to believe that the war would end only when the Confederates lost their main means of armed resistance. Both Meade and Rosecrans had opportunities to smash their opponents or at least display an aggressive spirit toward that end. But Meade's reluctance to attack Lee at Williamsport during the retreat from Pennsylvania and during much of the following autumn convinced Lincoln that the general once described as a "damned old goggle-eyed snapping turtle" was not his man. Likewise, Rosecrans's plaintive complaint to Secretary of War Stanton not to overlook the decisive result of his Tullahoma campaign "because it is not written in showers of blood" did nothing to help his standing with Lincoln, even before Chickamauga.[64]

As Rosecrans's and Meade's experiences demonstrated, the clash between genius and intellect that shaped the antebellum and early-war controversy about generalship proved less and less useful as the war continued. In those heady days in early July 1863, however, when news of victories at

Vicksburg and Gettysburg—both achieved by West Point graduates—sent the North into a grand euphoria, those who had embraced intellect over genius sensed an opportunity to revisit the original cause that the antebellum military reformers had espoused. During the first two years of the war, so much interest had swirled around the qualifications of the commander of the army that military reformers essentially forgot their commitment to the professional development of the entire officer corps. The time had come to reinvigorate their push for a military education system for the intellectual betterment of army officers of all ranks. The same two publications that revitalized the midwar consideration of Union military strategy now took up the cause of officer education.

When the *Army and Navy Gazette*—the predecessor to the more influential *Army and Navy Journal*—published its first number in May 1863, editors William R. Dyer and Sitwell Harris voiced the desperation of Northerners still seeking the nation's military genius. "A great general, like a great poet, is born, not made," one editor wrote, as he lamented the North's rapidly dimming prospects for finding one. After all, he surmised, only five men—Wellington, Nelson, Washington, Scott, and Decatur— "represent the military genius of the Anglo-Saxon race, during a period of a thousand years." While Hooker and other recent army commanders served as well as their skill allowed, "we have not yet had that man who could step forward, with a mind sufficiently comprehensive to grasp the contest in detail, and to lead a noble, intelligent, patriotic and enthusiastic army to complete and unconditional success."[65] The Union's generals were simply "men of fine talents" who could carry out "the mandate of some commanding genius," but they "cannot create." The only Union general in whom one author saw genius was politician-turned-general Benjamin Butler.[66]

When the *Army and Navy Gazette* quickly fell into dire financial straits and William Conant Church took over, however, the editorial position of the newly renamed *Army and Navy Journal* changed immediately.[67] From the start, Church declared himself to be exhausted by public complaints about the nation's failure to find in the army's ranks "an unmistakable master mind, capable of directing the strategetical movements of large bodies of troops." Moreover, he condemned Northerners—from partisan editors and journalists to political stump speakers and loyal but unreflective readers—for continuing to accept the validity of the concept. Church had become convinced that unless Northerners interested in military affairs developed a sound grasp of the requirements of generalship, they deserved to be dismissed as "would-be military critics without the ability to fill the most inferior military positions" who had no right to damn even one general for failing to "leap into the field as a full-fledged Napoleon."[68]

Church found a ready ally in the like-minded Henry Coppee, editor of the new *United States Service Magazine*. For the rest of the conflict, these two men welcomed the submissions of all interested parties—serving officers and civilians alike—who wished to discuss objectively, and without the intrusion of political agendas, the benefits and limitations of military education. Additionally, they provided an important service in regularly recommending recently published military literature from the United States and Europe that supported their position, and they utilized their reviews as an additional forum for proeducation commentary. While not particularly impressed by John Watts de Peyster's use of historical example, for instance, a reviewer expressed his entire concurrence with the New Yorker's assertion that, since very few generals could ever equal Napoleon, it was foolish for the Union army, the government, and the Northern people "to *sit waiting* for a Napoleon" to rise from the masses.[69] In 1864, amid his decidedly mixed feelings about the quality of General Halleck's translation of Jomini's *Life of Napoleon*, another reviewer took the opportunity to observe that, "in our days, we no longer believe in what Chatham called 'heaven-born generals.'" Indeed, he asserted, "It is the MIND, DISCIPLINED AND INSTRUCTED, which leads armies and builds up empires; mind, not stultified with pedantry, but the development of thought and inward will, conferring the power of discerning, analyzing and combining means essential to . . . [the] self-culture of the soldier."[70]

A War Department proposal in the fall of 1863 to replace the army's seniority-based officer promotion system with a new one based on merit quickly won the support of Church and his readers. Although suggested reforms only targeted officers below the rank of major, contributors openly wondered why merit-based standards could not be applied to officers of all ranks, even to the promotion and assignment of general officers. "Good corps commanders are invaluable men, and as rare as they are invaluable," an officer wrote, claiming that a significant number of the army's current major generals likely could not master "the educational discipline" to command so large a unit. The army's chances for success stood to improve greatly if the contemplated changes blocked the assignment of ill-prepared—but very senior—generals to corps or army commands. Although he did not choose a particularly apt example, he looked back upon General Meade's appointment to command the Army of the Potomac—a move that jumped him over Major Generals John F. Reynolds, John Sedgwick, and Henry W. Slocum, all his seniors in lineal rank—as evidence of the benefits of merit-based postings.[71] Since any objective standards might interfere with Congress's ability to influence senior appointments, however, the proposals failed.

The controversy, however, encouraged interested soldiers and civilians to give greater attention to measuring merit, and educational attainments offered one potentially useful standard. In the fall of 1863, Church began a year-long discussion—taken up by Coppée's journal after it began publication in January 1864—by requesting contributor input on one small piece of a very large issue: the need for educated staff officers. He had made an astute decision. Jomini, Halleck, and other influential military writers frequently addressed the qualifications for the specific position of "chief of staff," the officer appointed to serve as senior military adviser and head of the official family of an army commander. The chief of staff of a field army, Jomini believed, should be a general officer of "recognized ability" capable of working in "perfect harmony" with the commanding general to advise and update him on the condition of his army and to transform his vision—whether it be inspired by genius or the product of intensive study of the art of war—into practical orders to move and fight. The Civil War generation had begun to value the importance of the man assigned to that position. Indeed, that posting—and not the position of general in chief—demanded a knowledgeable senior officer possessing strong administrative skills. The chief of staff and not the commanding general, noted Lieutenant Colonel C. W. Tolles, "is really the head of the organization, the director of all the business of the command . . . [and] the official medium through which the commanding officer communicates and acts."[72] To strengthen their argument, soldiers and civilians alike cited the example of the French, who educated their staff officers both in the classroom and in two-year assignments with field units before joining a general's official family.

From discussion about the qualifications for a general's chief of staff came a wide-ranging exploration of the need to sharpen the expertise of all officers assigned to supply, transportation, ordnance, communication, intelligence, finance, and medical efforts and other logistical requirements. Some argued for the establishment of a specialized staff school; one reformer even drew upon the authority of Jomini himself to argue for a small and highly selective program to identify a small group of officers already "thoroughly trained in the three arms, acquainted with logistics

... versed in topographical engineering, and above all, gifted with the *coup d'oeil militaire*" and prepare them for immediate assignment as staff officers at the division, corps, and army levels.[73] If such a process existed, then citizens of privilege could no longer leverage their political clout to obtain comfortable and comparatively safe staff billets for their sons or "any boy fresh from college, whose idea of military duty is confined to wearing good clothes and riding a good horse."[74]

As readers and contributors warmed to the subject, they continued to expand their thoughts on military education far beyond the discussion's starting point. One of Coppee's active-duty contributors explained how he already had begun to incorporate military education as a key discriminator in evaluations of all his subordinates. He split his officers into three groups. "Regulars" possessed a West Point education and had put their knowledge into practice. "Irregulars" entered service directly from civilian life with little previous military education, but they committed themselves to learning necessary skills through experience and study. "Defectives" included those officers "without necessary brains" for their responsibilities and for whom schooling offered no cure. This contributor understood that the current crisis required an increase in the number of Irregular officers, but he lamented that so many Defective officers, too often "rich men's worthless sons, and the relatives of influential politicians," still remained in the army during the war's third year.[75]

The cause of military education benefited from a successful experiment in officer accession. The army's need to find capable company and regimental commanders for newly raised units of the U.S. Colored Troops (USCT) offered a chance to make specialized schooling a requirement for commissioning. Building on early-war review boards that had evaluated the performance of volunteer officers, Major General Silas Casey oversaw a Philadelphia-based school of instruction for officer candidates seeking commissions in USCT regiments. Classroom instruction centered on the administrative duties and tactical roles of company-grade and field-grade officers, and successful applicants had to complete all curricular requirements and pass a rigorous examination for commissioning. Importantly, the school report noted that "every candidate stands upon his merit," and the test score largely determined if a graduate would receive a second lieutenancy or be commissioned at a much more senior rank. After the first round of testing, 560 candidates passed, but 491 were rejected. As one of the school's instructors proclaimed, the nation had tired of political interference in military affairs and now "appreciates the worth of a system [designed] to end forever the emptying into our regimental and brigade commands the unsifted grist of [state governors' offices] that grind out commanders."[76] The school won the endorsement of all supporters of military education and even the Joint Committee on the Conduct of the War.

Unfortunately, the detailed, provocative, and constructive discussions about military education for commissioned officers that filled the pages of Church's paper and Coppee's journal seldom engaged a wider public audience. Indeed, during the war's final eighteen months, only three issues related to leadership—ongoing concerns about the mission and future of West Point, the campaigns of Ulysses S. Grant and William T. Sherman, and the presidential aspirations of George McClellan—captured the interest of both the regular readers of the military publications and the Northern public at large in sufficient measure for open exchanges of conflicting ideas.

Despite important victories won by Union armies commanded by West Point graduates at Gettysburg and Vicksburg, criticism of the Military Academy continued unabated. As late as June 1864, Senator Benjamin Wade still denied any need for the institution, noting that young men straight from home made the best fighters and "the old idea that a soldier must be in training for several years before he is fit for the field is not at all applicable to our soldiery."[77] During annual deliberations over appropriations, popular opposition to the expense, elitism, or militarism of the Military Academy continued to fill the public press. Now, however, Church reprinted the most outrageous charges leveled against the academy to encourage his readers to respond. In turn, the public press reprinted—and often condemned—the defenses of West Point offered by Church's readers.

Nonetheless, emboldened West Point graduates and their friends launched their most substantial counteroffensive of the war years. Captain Edward C. Boynton, adjutant of the Military Academy, adopted a positive tone in his popular new history of West Point, a volume that emphasized the school's military and engineering contributions to the building of the nation and not simply its service in national defense.[78] But most authors chose instead to confront specific criticisms. West Point graduates long had objected to accusations that the Military Academy taught treason. As one alumnus asserted, "the doctrine of our perpetual nationality was ever placed at the forefront of instruction and practice there."[79] Brigadier General Truman Seymour, an alumnus, wrote a widely publicized letter to proclaim that at West Point, "no peculiarity of sentiment as to political affairs has ever been inculcated. In my day politics were never even referred to."[80] In the *North American Review*, a friend of West Point took on another set of critics, the "ignorant men" who feared that the institution might become "a miniature praetorian guard" and still believed "the pruning-hook is in great danger from the sword; a uniform is the Devil's livery, and an army only a howl in Pandemonium."[81]

Friends of West Point tried especially hard—and not always successfully—to convince their countrymen to respect the Military Academy's primary mission: the education of American army officers to fight and win the nation's wars. They launched eloquent counterarguments against those critics who continued to blame the Military Academy for failing to produce a military genius to win the current conflict. One supporter turned the complaint back upon those who lodged it, asserting: "The question might be asked, does ever any school produce the genius?" He then rejected the validity of the critic's challenge, pointing out that "it is contrary to the definition of genius to be produced by such instrumentality."[82] Another friend of the Military Academy adopted the same line of argument, noting that, by definition, West Point could not provide genius to a single one of its students because that quality had to be considered "a gift of God to individuals; it is only soldiership that is an acquisition." That said, West Point's partisans then took great pains to emphasize that, even if they conceded that the Military Academy could not create genius, it remained true nonetheless that "no uneducated genius has been found to take the place of [those the school has] educated."[83] Several years of war had proven that West Point–educated officers, more than any others, best combined the two important virtues of loyalty and ability. "Grant, Meade, Rosecrans, Thomas, Gillmore, and a hundred others" had already earned far more respect from their soldiers for the competence they brought to their duties than the nation at large accorded them.[84]

At the time that this man wrote, however, not one of these vaunted figures yet had emerged as the general possessing a demonstrated capacity to win the war. In March 1864 the long-suffering Northern public had every reason for at least a measure of cynicism when President Lincoln announced U.S. Grant's selection for promotion to the rank of lieutenant general and appointment to the position of general in chief of the U.S. Army.[85] Grant, at least, came to his new assignment with more than merely promise. The victor at Forts Henry and Donelson and at Shiloh in 1862 and at Vicksburg and Chattanooga in 1863 already had convinced many Northerners that he could meet the challenge. After Grant sent

Bragg's Confederates retreating from Missionary Ridge, a Philadelphian had celebrated the general's "genius which places him in the first rank of modern soldiers. For once, we have proof that strategy means something more than an unwillingness to fight, or a fixed resolution not to move an army out of a swamp."[86]

From the start, however, Grant seemed difficult to categorize. Although he had graduated from West Point in 1843, observers recognized in him more glimmers of genius than erudition. As Brigadier General Orlando B. Willcox wrote while serving under the general in Tennessee, Grant "disregards abstract rules and formularies. . . . He scarcely seems to know whether he has violated principles laid down in the books, but unconsciously carries out new principles." Perceiving this creative spirit, Willcox logically considered Grant's ability to be "a gift; not the gift of inspiration, but the intuition of prodigious common sense, genius bounded by utility."[87] Indeed, Grant seemed bent on downplaying his intellectual prowess. Early in the war, he had enjoyed telling correspondents that he had never even read the tactics manuals he used to drill his troops. His friend and subordinate William T. Sherman, who clearly deemed himself to be intellectually superior, admitted in early 1864 that he had entertained doubts about Grant's "knowledge of grand strategy, and of books of science and history," but then he acknowledged that Grant's "common-sense seems to have supplied all this."[88]

Sherman's comment illustrates the manner in which Grant made his greatest impact on the people he met: he impressed them not through genius or intellect, but through strength of character. His modesty, simple habits (except for nagging rumors of a drinking problem), plainspokenness, and steadiness under stress suggested an inner strength to see the war through to victory. Even the editors of the military press chose at first to emphasize the strength of Grant's character rather than make premature claims for military prowess. Henry Coppee limited his comments on the eve of active campaigning in May 1864 simply to his approval of Grant's "busy energy" as he engaged in planning "with a singleness of purpose."[89] Church—and many other editors, politicians, and soldiers in the ranks—likewise chose to await further events before taking the measure of their new general in chief.

The first few months of the Overland Campaign quickly turned both Coppee and Church—and most of their regular readers—into ardent supporters of Grant. But the source of Grant's success continued to defy easy classification. His slow and costly advance toward Richmond turned some

Northerners—especially those in Democratic strongholds—against him. While Coppee and Church praised his strategic vision in ordering a concentration of effort by all Union armies, they found little creativity or boldness in his aggressive hammering of Lee's army to suggest the operation of genius. Nor could they discern in Grant's maneuvers against the Army of Northern Virginia any evidence of a plan produced by the finely honed intellect of a professionally educated soldier. Thus, they fell back again and again on Grant's personal and professional character to explain his actions. Coppee, for one, found much to admire, since Grant, more than any of his predecessors, represented Coppee's military ideal: a "strong, iron, living, busy, honest, capable, self-sustained commander, who will plan wisely, fight terribly, follow up his victories, and leave the rest to Providence."[90] The public press—at least that part of it that did not lose faith as casualty lists lengthened—adopted the same approach. As a New York journalist wrote, Grant possessed an "inconquerable tenacity of purpose. He is a soldier who cannot be shaken or daunted; whose imperturbable coolness cannot be ruffled by the most unexpected and threatening incidents."[91] Even Lincoln himself admired Grant's "perfect coolness and persistency of purpose." To a White House visitor, the president observed that his new general in chief "has the *grit* of a bulldog! . . . It is the dogged pertinacity of Grant that wins."[92]

If Grant remained a bit of a mystery, even fewer Northerners could make very much of his senior subordinate, Major General William Tecumseh Sherman, commander of the combined Union armies advancing toward Atlanta.[93] Concerned about operational security and already harboring a strong dislike of the press, Sherman essentially silenced it, denying passes to correspondents and sending most war correspondents out of his camps.[94] Thus, Northern press coverage of the march from Chattanooga to Atlanta paled in comparison with the detailed descriptions of the Overland Campaign. Indeed, Northern editors clipped much of the campaign narrative that appeared in their papers from Southern sources. Still, reports about the activities of Sherman's forces clearly showed progress. As Grant's and Sherman's campaigns had unfolded during the late spring and summer, observers of Union military affairs attributed the two men's successes to different root causes. While Grant pinned down Lee around Petersburg and held him there with unyielding tenacity, the few snippets of reliable information coming from Georgia suggested that Sherman relied upon creativity and boldness to design maneuvers and launch aggressive attacks. But when both campaigns bogged down during the summer, the familiar complaints about unfulfilled promise once again arose from the Northern public.

This low point in popular confidence in the progress of the war coincided with the peak of the heated presidential campaign. The race pitting Lincoln against his onetime general in chief George McClellan temporarily diverted public attention from the battlefield to the unfolding political spectacle. Historians of the election of 1864 have documented in detail the highly charged political environment that pervaded all elements of Northern society during that summer, and both campaigns seized upon yet another opportunity to consider Little Mac's tenure as general in chief.[95] McClellan's service provided the substance for dissection by political friends and foes alike—with entirely predictable results—but now the military publications established since his relief added new and informed voices to the fray.

Both Church and Coppee threw their support to Lincoln early on, but they generally succeeded in avoiding the personal vitriol of the partisan political press; they based their critiques of McClellan's generalship on recognized tenets propounded in the classic works of military theory. Their comparatively moderate tone did not bar hyperbole, however, nor did it signify a refusal to reach highly critical conclusions about the former general in chief. Coppee, for instance, lamented the nation's willingness early in the war "to accept a hero on trust" rather than on results, especially since McClellan had shown himself not to be a bold eagle but merely a weak "eagle chick." Creativity represented one defining trait of genius, but Coppee saw McClellan's greatest demonstration of inventiveness not in his war plans but in his "every excuse . . . except the true one, that our chicken was no eagle after all." The change-of-base maneuver from the York River to the James River during the 1862 Peninsula Campaign's Seven Days Battles—an act that McClellan and his partisans touted as incontrovertible evidence of his outstanding military skill—reminded Coppee of "a bad novel in weekly installments, with 'To be continued' grimly ominous at the end of every part." If one persisted in acknowledging genius in McClellan, he argued, one must also admit to the existence of two different kinds of genius: "The first finds the enemy, and beats him; the second finds him and succeeds in getting away." McClellan, of course, "had the second kind." Another contributor to Coppee's journal noted simply that McClellan "failed to prove his title to at least one of the indispensable qualities of a great captain," notably "the difference between the ability to plan and the ability to execute—between thought and action."[96]

However much the editors and contributors to Church's and Coppee's publications wanted to trade on the authority of the classic works on the art of war to inform their critique of McClellan's generalship, however, the Northern public accorded their judgments no greater credibility than those of any other citizen. An editor in Bangor, Maine, who supported Lincoln's reelection just as much as Church and Coppee did, nonetheless believed that he and his fellow "editorial generals" had every right to advance their own opinions and then let the common sense of the masses "weigh this pretended Napoleon in the balances, and give him his just due." He made clear that the people had learned much about the conduct of war over the past several years. "We believe in Grant and Sherman and Hancock and Farragut, because their deeds speak for them," he noted, adding: "We did believe in Gen. McClellan *in advance*. . . . We do not believe in him now because he has proved himself utterly wanting"—not in knowledge, but in courage and decisiveness.[97] Neither genius nor intellect worked for the man from Maine. Similarly, Philadelphia correspondent "Occasional"—a volunteer officer—attested that, early in the war, he and most of his West Point–educated comrades believed in McClellan's military genius, the academy men doing so chiefly "because such a belief was fashionable, and skepticism would have been a reflection upon the dignity of their own profession." Many of the graduates had changed their minds about McClellan by now, but he, for one, still believed that genius existed. As evidence, he claimed that only some innate quality in Grant, Sherman, Sheridan, and others—and not their West Point education—allowed them to gather "the harvest from soil that McClellan and Buell declared to be barren."[98] The rhetoric of the 1864 presidential campaign revealed, first, that the familiar nature-versus-nurture dichotomy on military leadership that had divided public opinion since the start of the war still had its uses; and second, among the general public—other than the readers of Coppee's and Church's publications who believed intellect to be the central trait of successful military leaders—the split showed few signs of narrowing.

McClellan's defeat and Lincoln's reelection quickly returned public attention to military operations. With Grant still besieging Petersburg, the drama of Sherman's march from Atlanta to the sea, his capture of Savannah, and the Confederate reaction to the general's bold strokes fascinated Northerners. Unaccountably, and quite out of character after nearly sixteen months of attacking the concept, Church began to apply the term "genius" freely to Sherman. By splitting his forces to send Major General George Thomas to confront Confederate General John Bell Hood's late-1864 offensive into Tennessee while still pressing on with his own advance to Savannah, Sherman, "with the instinct of genius, and the skill of a thorough-bred soldier, took the offensive, and, out of the nettle danger, plucked the flower safety." Thomas smashed Hood near Nashville in mid-December, but in Church's view, the Confederate commander in fact was "thwarted only by the genius of Sherman."[99] The public press and the military press alike cited the novelty and daring of the march to the sea. If a measure of luck "equal to one half his genius and his skill" accompanied Sherman, Church predicted, then an "inestimable victory awaits the Nation."[100] In the war's final months, it seemed that even the military press had finally found its genius, as that generation described it—and it was not the general in chief.

By early 1865, with the end of the war only weeks away, the success of the Grant-Sherman team had captured the North's collective imagination.[101] As Sherman began his march north into the Carolinas, the *Army and Navy Journal* anticipated his linkup with Grant in the most convincing demonstration of the effectiveness of the concentration strategy. As the editor reported, "whatever may be the detailed route which he might pursue," Sherman's "*ultimate* object could only be Richmond—at present the point on which the whole military and political existence of the Confederacy hangs."[102] But Lee's army surrendered before the two Union armies combined, leaving Northerners to wonder about the spectacle they missed. The Northern public continued to voice admiration for Grant's perseverance, but in an unexpected turn of events in late April 1865, they all but relieved Sherman of his crown of genius—not for a military decision, but for a political one. When he offered terms of surrender to General Joseph E. Johnston that far exceeded his authority, he set off a storm of public condemnation. "Sherman committed an enormous blunder. If it was his first, it was, nevertheless his fatal error," editor Church wrote, adding: "Where shrewd, intelligent, common-sense mediocrity walks safely, genius may plunge, slip and fall." Church was certain that "not a soldier in Sherman's Army, would have made his mistake."[103] His decision seriously undermined popular confidence in his judgment. And, in the end, if Northerners felt compelled to credit genius for the victory—and many remained entirely satisfied merely to extend the primary credit to the soldiers in the ranks who carried the fight directly to the enemy—then, by default more than from enthusiasm, Grant won the laurel.

In an eloquent summary of Northern views on generalship as they stood at the end of the conflict, war correspondent William Swinton—very well-read in the military theory of the era—testified to the endurance of popular faith in genius by offering three tests to identify it in an army's senior commander. First, the general must have the ability to direct large numbers of troops effectively over large spaces in a timely manner. Second, he must demonstrate complete self-possession in disaster. Finally, he must possess "such fertility of resources as to attain success by means or movements entirely unexpected." Good generals without military genius may pass the first two tests, Swinton argued, but "the last *is* military genius." In Swinton's mind, Grant came closer than any other Northern general to passing all three tests.[104] Popular belief in the existence of generals possessed of military genius clearly survived the national trauma of the Civil War.

At the same time, advocates of a military education system designed to cultivate the intellectual competence of army officers ended the war with little to cheer. Even before Appomattox, lively exchanges about the structure, size, and composition of the postwar U.S. Army and its officer corps filled the civilian and military press. An article penned by citizen-soldier Thomas W. Higginson in the *Atlantic Monthly*—a widely reprinted and highly praised piece—argued that the war had erased most distinctions between West Point graduates and volunteer officers. While the former still offered discipline and "specific professional training," the latter infused "the knowledge of human nature and the habit of dealing with mankind in masses—the very thing from which the younger regular officers at least has been rigidly excluded." During the war, amateurs and professionals had combined their different habits of command to lead the world's most intelligent troops to victory. Therefore, Higginson asserted, the army should continue to draw its officers from both sources.[105]

The pages of the *Army and Navy Journal* teemed with critiques of Higginson's piece. Most contributors argued that any degree of reliance upon citizen-soldier volunteers—especially as officers—established an entirely unsound foundation for the future U.S. Army. One correspondent remained convinced that "a soldier, no matter what his natural abilities, must needs learn his trade, if he do not wish to be overshadowed by men of less native but more acquired power."[106] A correspondent who signed himself as "Volunteer" actually took the side of the Regulars to assert that, from experience, he now realized that he and his peers shared two great weaknesses: an inability to "enforce implicit, *blind* obedience" and "ignorance." The paltry efforts of the "noble sons of Harvard, Yale, Amherst, and other colleges" to master the duties of lieutenants and captains entirely unimpressed him, and he now placed his trust only in educated Regular officers.[107] Plans of all kinds surfaced, including one suggesting that one-third of all vacant lieutenancies in the postwar Regular Army be set aside for the promotion of promising sergeants with at least three years of service who could pass muster with a board of examiners. The rest, the author of the plan believed, should be filled only by West Point graduates.[108]

The reaction of the public press to Higginson's article proved that a distrust of professional soldiers still thrived outside military circles. The *New York Tribune* demanded clarification. If the question asked whether it was "advisable that military officers should be educated for their vocation," then the editor would answer in the affirmative. If the query was restated, however, to ask if "a monopoly of all the commissions in our Army" should "be secured to the graduates of a single school," then "on that question we vote no."[109] A civilian reader of Church's journal, bothered by the political nature of congressional appointments to West Point, concurred with the *Tribune*'s view, arguing that any established university could produce graduates capable of passing a commissioning examination and thus open up military careers to ambitious and capable young men whose families simply lacked connections.[110] In the end, the postwar battle lines drawn over the question of educating the nation's army officers looked little different from those that existed before Fort Sumter.

The seeds of change had been planted, however, and patience rewarded those whose commitment to professional military education never wavered. They cherished a vision already laid out for them in Jomini and other classic writers on the art of war who, in their own ways, encouraged professional soldiers to work toward "an *aristocracy of education*" in their officer corps to make their army into "a living machine, to be put in motion and moved at the will of the *controlling intellect*, its commander-in-chief."[111] Regular officers visited, compared, and reported on the course of study at military schools around the world to prepare for that day when the United States was ready to take those important steps.[112] But until that day came—and the first glimmers of the new dawn took at least fifteen years to arrive—they bided their time as the citizen-soldiers who exchanged army life for the halls of government kept alive the spirit of the "heavenly born genius" for another generation.

3

LOST IN JOMINI'S SILENCE

The Human Factor in War

In September 1862 a New York journalist identified a particularly glaring weakness in the body of military literature that Northerners looked to for so many insights into strategy, tactics, and generalship. "Military pedants persist in asserting, especially of late, that the issues of modern warfare solely, or at all events mainly, depend upon scientific strategical combinations," he complained. As a result, the journalist noted, "the individual soldier counts but as a mathematical unit, occupying its place and performing its appointed duty," creating the unacceptable impression that "personal prowess, zeal, intelligence, however remarkable, prevail little or nothing in influencing the general result." Dismissing this "pompously propounded dictum" as entirely misguided, he reasserted the primacy of "individual daring, enterprise, and intelligence" in war, asserting that "no movement or maneuver taught by any soldier-sciologist from Caesar to Jomini" ever saved an army from defeat.[1]

The journalist's lament addressed an element of nineteenth-century war fighting to which few European military authorities gave any more than glancing attention. Since they wrote about the complexity of war on the highest levels and searched for—or occasionally challenged the existence of—its scientific rules and principles, they largely ignored war's human element. Indeed, in most writings on the art of war available to the Civil War generation, soldiers in the ranks existed mostly as nameless ciphers with no individual identities, wants, needs, or fears.

The most relevant nineteenth-century military idea that addressed this concern centered on the notion of "morale," or "military spirit." As Jomini wrote about it, only the army—the institution, not the individual soldiers who comprised it—possessed this spirit, and "it is the *morale* of armies . . .

more than anything else, which makes victories and their results decisive." Jomini stressed as well that only "the skill of the commander" determined the strength of his army's morale. An outstanding general inspired in his officer corps a "conviction that resignation, bravery, and faithful attention to duty" led inevitably to victory. It then became the responsibility of these subordinates to inure their soldiers "to labor and fatigue, by keeping them from stagnation in garrison in times of peace, but inculcating their superiority over their enemies" by manipulating "their enthusiasm by every means in harmony with the tone of mind, by honoring courage, punishing weakness, and disgracing cowardice."[2] Jomini did not intend by this to cultivate in his officers a paternalistic sense of responsibility for the health and welfare of each of their soldiers; instead, he offered these words as a warning that the collapse of a unit on the field of battle—regardless of cause—represented, first and foremost, a failure of command.

These ideas still resonated in European military cultures that relied upon the harsh discipline of conscript armies, but they did not suit nations like the United States that called upon citizen-soldiers to volunteer for military service. Indeed, English military writer Robert Jackson declared Americans to be not at all "susceptible of such perfection of mechanical discipline, as gives expectation of success in systematic war." From the time of the nation's founding, he wrote, Americans "floated in the wilds of liberty" that encouraged individual expression and personal responsibility.[3] They viewed their enlistment papers as a contract between themselves and the state, as represented by the officers placed in authority over them. In exchange for their voluntary service, they expected to be led by competent superiors who could balance soldierly discipline with respect for the individual. They simply could not be the kind of soldier that served in the armies Jomini and his ilk wrote about, nor could their "military spirit" spring solely from strict obedience to rules, regulations, and strict discipline. Even back in the eighteenth century, Marshal Maurice de Saxe understood that the best generals possessed "a knowledge of the human heart" and admitted that "it is much easier to take men as they are than to make them as they should be."[4] But very few military writers took up that theme. Jomini, in fact, had suggested there was little reason to do so. "There are, it is true, cases where all human resources are insufficient for the maintenance of order . . . and when their officers find it impossible to do any thing to organize them," he wrote.[5] But then, as he quickly explained, he deemed such situations "exceptional" and, like most of his contemporaries, discussed it no further.

Thus, during the massive mobilization efforts after Fort Sumter, the War Department and the U.S. Army's senior leaders focused on institutional organization as a whole rather than its thousands of citizen-soldiers who comprised its component parts. The officer-physicians of the Medical Department—the element of the U.S. Army most directly responsible for the health of the soldier in the ranks—approached their tasks in much the same way, drawing heavily upon a substantial, specialized literature on military medicine that stressed the organization and administration of brick-and-mortar hospitals or the new therapies, therapeutics, diets, and equipment that might be used in them.[6] Newly commissioned officers serving in infantry, cavalry, and artillery units learned administrative procedures that covered health-related matters as one of their unit accountability measures, but they received very little training about their responsibilities to promote the physical and mental health of the individual soldiers under their command. The 314-page *Army Officer's Pocket Companion* for 1862 counted only three pages of medical "hints"—mostly concerning sanitation and diet while in camp—and contained almost no comparable information for soldiers on active campaign.[7] Frederick Law Olmsted, a civilian serving as secretary of the new U.S. Sanitary Commission, issued a "Circular Addressed to the Colonels of the Army" to restate the importance of camp hygiene and high-quality food and, equally significant, to urge colonels to hold their company-grade officers and noncommissioned officers accountable for enforcing health-related regulations. But no War Department mandate backed Olmsted's pleas, and his suggestions could not alter the "incorrigible 'rugged individualism'" of the Union soldier.[8]

In 1862 Dr. Edward Jarvis took to the pages of the popular *Atlantic Monthly* expressly to decry the Medical Department's failure to impose stronger requirements upon officers of all ranks to protect and promote the health of the soldiers under their command. He had picked up his pen, he asserted, specifically to reject the "very common belief" that the "human body has an indefinite power of endurance, or, if it suffer from disease or fall in death, it is from causes beyond man's control." He accused the War Department of "requiring their men to do the hard work of war without a certain, full supply or sustenance. They expect from the army the largest expenditure of force, but sometimes give it the smallest means and poorest conditions of recuperating it."[9] Jarvis, of course, offered a number of suggestions to improve the army's medical care. In the end, however, only a single item on his list of needed reforms generated significant public, congressional, and army interest: an ambulance system.[10] Moreover, he only had addressed the physical health of soldiers; to the medical authorities of the era, the psychological impact of military service—especially combat—remained a closed book.

The lack of substantive action on matters directly affecting the human elements of war cannot be blamed entirely on incompetence or lack of interest on the part of commanding officers, the surgeon general's office, or the War Department. The social and medical sciences into which these concerns fall today simply did not yet exist. That does not mean, however, that scholars cannot explore the physical and psychological impact of military operations and combat on Civil War soldiers. Eric T. Dean Jr., R. Gregory Lande, and Judith Andersen, among others, already have opened up a modern dialogue on some physical and psychological dimensions of the Civil War combat experience, including evidence of drug addiction, post-traumatic stress disorder, and other conditions caused or exacerbated by a soldier's exposure to the various stressors of a lethal environment.[11] These studies, however, represent only "first words" on the subjects they address. Much of their work remains largely anecdotal in its evidentiary base and divorced from the specific Civil War experiential and conceptual foundations that give context to individual soldiers' expressions of fear, exhaustion, disorientation, despair, loss, and a wide range of stress reactions. Moreover, what Jomini and his contemporaries failed to address, and what modern scholars barely have begun to explore, is the all-important link between a military unit's mission-effectiveness levels and the physical and mental condition of that force's smallest component part: the soldier.

My point of departure for this discussion is the Army of the Potomac's Overland Campaign in Virginia between 3 May and mid-June 1864. This operation, one of the war's costliest, began when the army, commanded by Major General George G. Meade, broke winter camp around Culpeper on 3 May and began its southward march to take on General Robert E. Lee's Army of Northern Virginia. Newly promoted Lieutenant General Ulysses S. Grant, although commanding general of the entire U.S. Army, accompanied Meade's army on this campaign. Meade's force fought Lee's army at the Battle of the Wilderness on 5–6 May, at Spotsylvania from 8 May until 21 May, and at the North Anna River from 22 May until 26 May and then marched on to Bethesda Church and Cold Harbor to fight from 30 May until 6 June. The campaign ended when the army crossed the

James River on 15 June to make its first probes of the defenses around Petersburg between 16 and 22 June.

The complexity and duration of the campaign make it possible to apply three modern analytical tools to the human elements of war, each one emerging from scholarly disciplines outside the field of history. First, organizational behavior specialists have developed an expansive literature on the capacity for groups to respond to danger and risk with both positive and negative responses; it follows that modern armies now place great importance on identifying and preventing or limiting the impact of the worst of these behaviors and encouraging positive—or "adaptive"—responses to threats and the stresses they cause. Generally, studies of this sort describe this concept through two related terms: "unit identity" and "unit cohesion." Second, especially since the Vietnam era, social scientists and the medical community have studied in depth the concept of "combat stress" to describe and analyze the range of behaviors individual soldiers display in response to the wide array of stressors present in active military operations. The U.S. Army currently works from the assumption that "combat and war bring out the best and the worst in human beings."[12] In light of this, it has adopted a classification system that describes both adaptive "positive combat stress behaviors" that can help a soldier compensate and carry on with the mission and "dysfunctional combat stress behaviors" that further subdivide into "battle fatigue" and "misconduct behaviors and criminal acts."[13] Third, to appreciate the physiological underpinnings of these numerous stress responses and behaviors, a new field of study, dubbed "warrior science" by its practitioners, applies a multidisciplinary approach that draws upon sociology, psychology, biology, and kinesiology, among other sciences, to understand what actually happens to a combat soldier's body and mind in stress-inducing and potentially lethal environments. The Army of the Potomac, of course, enjoyed none of the benefits of these modern studies. The art of war, as senior commanders understood it, paid little attention to the welfare of the common soldier and did not consider the consequences to the army if the physical and mental needs of its soldiers went unmet. In this way, the silence of Jomini and his peers fostered a horrific legacy that scarred thousands of Union survivors of the Overland Campaign and filled many soldier graves.

Even as they prided themselves in their individuality, the Northern soldiers who marched south from Culpeper in early May 1864 identified themselves proudly as soldiers in the Army of the Potomac. As an astute war correspondent had noted, a Northern army is "an organic structure—with its parts, members, functions, vital spirit and animating soul. An army is something more than the sum of its individual musket-bearers . . . just as the body is more than the individual atoms that compose it. Organization—that is, organic arrangement—incorporates these atoms in the subordination of their functions and members, and animates them with a living soul."[14] On every level of military organization, from regiment through brigade, division, corps, and army, the concept of "unit identity"—usually described at the time as "esprit de corps"—rested on the bonds of shared traditions and experiences and upon recognized standards of organizational performance. Within the army's smaller units—the regiment and especially the ten companies that composed it—the existence of an even stronger, and qualitatively different, bond of "unit cohesion" provided the essential glue that sustained the individual soldier's commitment to mission and comrades, a tie secured by "a mutual trust, based on personal face-to-face interaction."[15] A strong sense of unit identity combined with tight unit cohesion helps both a soldier and an army endure the physical and mental challenges of a hostile environment.

In March 1864, however, a series of War Department–ordered institutional changes broke long-standing bonds of unit identity in the larger elements of the Army of the Potomac, entirely eliminating some organizations, drastically altering others, and creating new ones, all within six weeks of the opening of the spring campaign. By contrast, their Confederate counterpart, the Army of Northern Virginia, underwent very little organizational restructuring.

The Army of the Potomac's institutional changes began at the level of the corps, which were composed of 10,000 men or more, the army's largest component units. Since corps-level organization did not exist in the U.S. Army until early 1862, the War Department had no real understanding of potential positive or negative consequences of altering or disbanding them. The military literature of the era offered no warnings against it. Jomini, for one, even admitted the potential utility of reorganizing corps to deceive an enemy. Recent debate in the *Army and Navy Journal* neatly straddled the question. Some observers argued that "whatever honor it may be to a soldier to belong to such and such a regiment, he tells with far more pride that he belongs to 'the fighting second,' 'the bloody sixth,' or 'the gallant fifth' corps." Others believed, however, that even the best corps "should receive wholesome modification from time to time, so that each should be a large, strong, compact thunderbolt."[16] In any case, with little warning, in March 1864 War Department orders consolidated the Army of the Potomac's five corps into three. The I Corps, nearly destroyed on the first day at Gettysburg nine months earlier, merged its brigades into the V Corps. Likewise, the III Corps, which made good its heavy Gettysburg losses in the fall of 1863 with the arrival of a hard-luck command tagged "Milroy's Weary Boys" from the Shenandoah Valley, now had two of its veteran divisions sent to the II Corps and the newcomers reassigned to the VI Corps. Soon thereafter, after more than a year of detached service, Major General Ambrose Burnside's IX Corps now rejoined the Army of the Potomac, but as an attached command since Burnside outranked Meade.

As Colonel Henry L. Scott defined it in his 1861 *Military Dictionary*, "esprit de corps" literally meant "the brotherhood of a corps."[17] When word of the reorganization reached the troops, veterans of the I and III Corps clearly exhibited precisely the kind of "esprit de corps" that Colonel Scott described. In October 1863 officers with ties to the III Corps already had established the Third Corps Union as a benevolent and commemorative society.[18] Soldiers with long service in the two disbanded corps howled in protest at the order. As Private John W. Haley of the 17th Maine, a III Corps regiment, wrote: "It was a heavy blow to veterans of the old 3rd Corps to sink their identity in another body."[19] Soldiers in former I and III Corps regiments received authorization to continue wearing their original corps badges—symbols in which they took great pride—on their kepis, but many admitted they would have done so anyway.

The reassignment of the I and III Corps units required reorganizations within the three corps preparing to receive them. In Major General Winfield S. Hancock's II Corps, three veteran divisions, each with its own proud history and tight bonds, were consolidated into two, a process that required reassigning brigades and reshuffling regiments into new organizations lacking such ties and, in many cases, with different commanding officers. Major General Gouverneur K. Warren's V Corps underwent the same process as it made room for I Corps units. The three veteran divisions of Major General John Sedgwick's VI Corps also merged into two to make room for Milroy's Weary Boys. Recent changes in Burnside's IX Corps included a newly formed division of the first African American soldiers assigned to the Army of the Potomac. The cavalry corps got a new commander in Major General Philip H. Sheridan, and two of its three divisions received new commanders as part of its reorganization. Thus, the Army of the Potomac went into the Overland Campaign numerically strong—it carried a paper strength of at least 118,000 men—but, as an organization, it looked little like it had in its last major campaign in Pennsylvania in July 1863. The changes compromised unit identity on the brigade, division, and corps level, and no one knew what consequences might follow.

The Army of the Potomac experienced a second great threat in the spring of 1864, one that directly threatened unit cohesion in the smallest unit recognized on its table of organization: the regiment. Even more than his pride in his corps, a soldier defined his primary corporate identity in the army as a member of a specific regiment. Even if he served in different theaters of war or in different brigades, divisions, or corps, his identification with a regiment remained a constant. European armies long had appreciated the importance of this unit in setting standards of behavior and performance, in instilling pride, and in maintaining high morale. As French marshal Auguste Frédéric Louis Viesse de Marmont had written, a regiment "acquires a kind of social constitution, animated by a love equal to that of country and of home."[20] Especially within each of a regiment's ten companies—each starting with approximately 100 men, who were often recruited locally and already had strong familial and social ties—three years of military life had forged strong personal bonds. Survivors had shared the experience of victory and defeat, watched friends die in combat or waste away from disease, worried about comrades languishing in Southern prisons, deplored desertions, and both envied and pitied those sent home with medical discharges. Regiments left their home states in 1861 and 1862 with full ranks approximately 1,000 strong; by the spring of 1864, most counted considerably fewer than half that number. The shared bonds of affection and respect among their members demonstrate the very essence of unit cohesion. Commanding a regiment was a special charge, Colonel James A. Beaver of the 148th Pennsylvania asserted, because only on that level could a senior officer remain "in touch with his men. He knows to what extent he can rely upon them. . . . When you get farther away from the regiment, however, although responsible for the conduct of everybody under your command, you know less of what you can depend upon."[21]

During the winter before the Overland Campaign, Secretary of War Edwin M. Stanton realized that the Army of the Potomac—in reality, the whole U.S. Army—faced a looming manpower crisis. Hundreds of three-year regiments accepted into service during the spring and summer of 1861 were due to muster out by mid-1864. Although the Army of the Potomac included at least forty-eight three-year regiments raised in 1862 that had muster-out dates safely in 1865, at least 100 of its most seasoned regiments—and thousands of soldiers who had served three years under the same regimental colors—legally could terminate their service and go home by midsummer 1864. To forestall such a possibility, Stanton astutely appealed to regimental pride: if enough seasoned men in three-year regiments due to muster out reenlisted, they could keep their flags and their original numerical designations—in short, the most essential elements of their military identity. If too few reenlisted, however, their regiment would be stricken from the army roster and their flags retired. As added incentives, reenlisted soldiers could go home on leave together for a month.

Stanton's gambit to retain experienced regiments worked, but only to a point. Enough three-year men reenlisted in at least sixty-five regiments in the II, V, and VI Corps to give them veteran status. Still, the secretary's success remained incomplete. Each veteranized regiment still carried on its roster a significant minority of three-year men who refused to reenlist; they would leave for home on their original muster-out date, even in the midst of active operations. To fill both existing and anticipated gaps, each veteranized regiment—and those recruited in 1862—also received infusions of recent volunteers and conscripts, strangers believed by many veterans to be "actuated by very different motives from those that had influenced the men who had voluntarily filled the ranks before."[22] As a Pennsylvania soldier explained, the arrival of so many raw recruits "sometimes completely changed [a unit's] character temporarily, and not only the character of regiments, but even of brigades and divisions."[23] The arrival of raw recruits and the imminent departure of trusted veterans strained strong bonds built over three years even in so-called veteranized regiments.

Worse, Stanton failed to convince the men of at least thirty-eight regiments assigned to II, V, and VI Corps—including all ten regiments of the Pennsylvania Reserves serving as a full division in the V Corps—to veteranize. At some point in May, June, or July, each of these units simply would leave the line for home. Soldiers in these regiments already counted the days until their departure. Those in the Reserves openly debated which of two key days counted as their discharge date: their muster into state service in April or early May 1861, or the day in late May or early June 1861 when they were accepted into Federal service. The men of the 6th Pennsylvania Reserves plainly preferred the first; when the regiment did not muster out in late April as they had hoped, six men refused to do any additional duty, and many of their comrades believed that "their claim is just."[24] Could unit cohesion built over three years keep their soldiers committed to the mission when departure for home beckoned in as few as three weeks?

The adaptive utility of unit identity, and especially of unit cohesion, relies in part on the interplay of two additional factors: vertical and horizontal bonding. The former centers on the authority-based bonds forged between the leaders and the led that stand on a foundation of trust in officers' competence, confidence, and concern for those they lead; the latter centers on the personal bonds in small units between peers and near-peers. Beginning in the Wilderness and increasing throughout the Overland Campaign, vertical bonding weakened and frequently collapsed—due to a variety of causes and on all levels of organization—shattering the strength of a key bond that held soldiers to their mission.

The army's recent consolidation effort had created brigades, divisions, and corps much larger than units bearing the same designation in 1861–63, with some nearly doubling in size. This change triggered a subtle but important difference in the way the army's more-senior leaders commanded these units and the frequency with which they made direct contact with their soldiers. Soldiers seldom saw their army commander in the midst of battle; this explains to some degree why historians have made much of General Lee's personal intercessions at the front during this campaign.[25] But the Army of the Potomac's veterans expected to see their corps commanders sharing their dangers or ameliorating their hardships with a highly personalized command style. They did not expect to witness their senior leaders buckling under pressure; General Hancock's lingering debility from his Gettysburg wound and General Warren's increasingly erratic behavior, clearly evident by the middle of the fighting at Cold Harbor unnerved superiors and subordinates alike.[26] The men of the VI Corps genuinely lamented the loss of General Sedgwick at Spotsylvania on 9 May and never truly warmed to his successor, Major General Horatio G. Wright. Corps commanders adapted to the changed organization by adopting distant, depersonalized, and managerial command styles.[27]

Distance between the corps commanders and their soldiers put greater pressure on division and especially brigade commanders to lead by example. During the Overland Campaign, unexpected displays of incapacity or incompetence in once-trusted commanders—whether the problem was perceived or real—quickly eroded the soldiers' confidence in those to whom they entrusted their lives. At both the Wilderness and Spotsylvania, Brigadier General W. H. H. Ward, previously a solid performer of long tenure at the head of a III Corps brigade (now enlarged and relocated to II Corps) behaved erratically, possibly from strong drink, leading to his relief on 11 May. Colonel Paul T. Frank, another II Corps brigade commander, was relieved for drunkenness the same day. On three separate occasions— once at Spotsylvania and twice on 3 June at Cold Harbor—Brigadier General Joshua T. Owen was relieved after three times failing to advance his brigade or to come to the support of troops already engaged.[28] In the war's earlier days, soldiers in the Army of the Potomac might protest the relief of officers they deemed unfairly treated; none of these departures met the disapprobation of the soldiers these men had led. On 10 May at Spotsylvania, after several repulses, a unit of V Corps troops expressed outrage when a general's aide—and not the general himself—arrived with orders for yet another assault. "The whole expression of the person who brought the message seemed to say 'The general commanding is doubtful of your success,'" a Pennsylvania soldier recalled, adding that the aide then "put spurs to his horse and rode off, lest by some misunderstanding the assault should begin before he was safe."[29] Indeed, the soldiers' increasingly hostile feelings toward their senior leaders extended even to Grant, particularly after Cold Harbor, when that battle's bloody repulses convinced some of his men that he simply did not value the lives of the privates.

The weakening of vertical bonding on multiple levels of the Army of the Potomac—especially when new organizations did not have time to anneal strongly in the first place—in part contributed to the lackluster performance of Brigadier General Gershom Mott's entire division of the II Corps during the first two weeks of the Overland Campaign. Earlier in the war, this division won fame as "Kearny's Own," an accolade bestowed in 1862 when Brigadier General Philip Kearny had forged it into an effective III Corps combat force. The division lived up to its reputation on the peninsula at Second Bull Run and Chantilly—where Kearny fell at the head of his command—as well as at Chancellorsville and Gettysburg. During the reorganization of March 1864, however, the division—its seventeen three-year regiments consolidated first from three brigades to two—became the new fourth division of the II Corps. Although neither a professional soldier nor a particularly inspiring leader, Mott already possessed strong ties to perhaps half of his division as a regimental and brigade commander, but the rest did not know him. His senior subordinates—Colonels Robert McAllister and William Brewster—possessed long service in Kearny's Own, but neither had impressed sufficiently to win promotion to brigadier general, and now they commanded overly large brigades with little shared unit identity. Further complicating matters, seven of the seventeen regiments had chosen over the previous winter not to reenlist; the veterans of the old 1st Massachusetts Infantry already counted the days until their departure on 24 May, and all seven would be gone by July. A Confederate attack at the Wilderness on 5 May scattered the division badly, and neither Mott nor his brigade commanders could rally their men. Colonel McAllister admitted as much in a letter home: "Our Division did not do well."[30] On 10 May at Spotsylvania, Grant himself labeled the efforts of Mott's troops to support Colonel Emory Upton's breakthrough of the Confederate line as "feeble," noting that Upton "had gained an important advantage, but a lack in others of the spirit and dash possessed by him lost it to us."[31] A senior army staff officer used words far more blunt, writing that "the whole army would have been stronger without Mott's division."[32] Indeed, after receiving orders for an assault on 11 May and being informed that this unit would support his effort, General Wright protested to Meade: "'General, I don't WANT Mott's men on my left; they're not a support; I would rather have no troops there!'" By now, McAllister could name a specific reason for their continuing poor performance: "The troops whose term of service is just coming to a close do not fight well. I am sorry to say that in our Division we have too many of this kind."[33] The next day brought another lackluster performance, and with little fanfare, Mott's division was dissolved on 13 May, and most of its remaining men were consolidated into a single brigade attached to General David Bell Birney's division but still under Mott's command. The failure of Mott's division entirely validates an observation in the modern U.S. Army's combat stress manual that "in battle, men and units are more likely to fail catastrophically than gradually."[34]

The War Department did its best to refill Grant's thinning ranks, of course, but the reinforcements further disrupted already fragile unit identity and vertical cohesion. Corps and division commanders did not quite know what to do with the newly organized state regiments filled with raw recruits and the untested heavy artillery regiments—the latter each numbering 1,500 strong—that arrived in mid-May (the "heavies" easily identified by their red-trimmed uniforms and the crossed cannons on their caps, both signifying the artillery branch). They could be parceled out to restore the combat power of depleted brigades, but such a choice carried a serious risk: if the brigade commander fell, the untested colonel would outrank far-more-experienced lieutenant colonels and majors and thus would assume command over them. Other senior commanders simply organized these reinforcements into a new brigade and let subordinates figure out how to fit into divisions and corps with as little organizational disruption as possible.

Of course, to soldiers in the ranks, the most obvious evidence of collapsing vertical cohesion came on the regimental and (especially) company levels. The war had entered a new tactical phase, one in which soldiers defended a position fought from the protection of earthworks. Colonels, lieutenant colonels, and majors—whose position by the tactics manuals put them behind the regimental battle line during an advance—quickly realized that leading from the front more effectively guaranteed energetic obedience. As a consequence, untested units, three-year regiments preparing to muster out, and seasoned regiments that had just received large infusions of new recruits suffered especially high losses in field-grade officers. After Spotsylvania, Colonel Richard Coulter of the 11th Pennsylvania lamented the loss of veteran Major John Keenan, whose "personal exertions and example sustained his command, which I believe could not otherwise have been done, many being new men for the first time brought into action."[35] Forty of the 279 officer casualties suffered in General John Gibbon's division over the course of the campaign commanded regiments, causing the general to lament that "the bravest and most efficient officers and men were those who fell; it is always so."[36] Veteran regiments with few cohesion issues did not need their senior officers to lead from the front and even prevented them from doing so. At Spotsylvania's Mule Shoe, when Colonel Beaver of the 148th Pennsylvania tried to muscle his way to the front lines, a sergeant called to him, "Colonel, don't come up here. . . . You have no business here; we will take care of this."[37]

As the loss of colonels and majors rose, it fell to captains and lieutenants to step up from their companies to take command of entire regiments. For the enlisted men, these changes broke the most important bond, the "link between the formal organization and the fighting soldier," on the level where vertical and horizontal bonding merged and provided the greatest support for the men in ranks.[38] As a Pennsylvania soldier noted: "The men, missing the familiar forms and voices that had led them to the charge, would complain that they had not their old officers to follow."[39]

Unfortunately, not all officers adapted well to their new responsibilities. Competency boards met regularly, even at the peak of the campaign, for regimental officers charged with incompetence or cowardice. Lieutenant Colonel Rufus Dawes of the 6th Wisconsin, who sat on one such board, recalled a captain who "drank a decoction of powdered slate pencils in vinegar to render himself unfit for service." Dawes acknowledged that most cases concerned men simply broken down by exhaustion, hard work, and stress, so they judged each case on its individual merits. "Brave men were shielded" if their overall record justified it, he recalled, but "cowards met no mercy."[40]

Some of those shown leniency became part of an unusual experiment during the Overland Campaign to salvage those whose failure likely stemmed from a temporary state of physical and emotional exhaustion rather than incompetence. Selected offenders judged guilty but showing potential for rehabilitation received the arms and equipment of a private soldier and orders to join the 150th Pennsylvania Infantry. There, they became part of an informal formation nicknamed "Company Q." Major George W. Jones kept these men in the front lines and watched them closely in camp. In time, if they performed well, the charges against them were dropped and they rejoined their original units; if they wavered, they were dismissed from the service, and their names were published in official orders and often publicized in the *Army and Navy Journal*.[41] In time, most rejoined their regiments, but their very public failures still broke faith with their men.

As vertical bonding weakened, the Northern soldier placed increasing importance on horizontal bonding and, indeed, considered it to be almost essential for survival.[42] As a Philadelphian wrote, the common soldier "is strengthened for the conflict by the knowledge that sympathizing friends will care for him if wounded, or bestow the last rites if he falls."[43] When bonds of this nature broke, the cost to the army might have been small, but the toll on the men themselves was incalculable. Men who stayed the course, perhaps uncomfortable with open emotion, often relied upon recitations of raw numbers to illustrate how severely the Overland Campaign disrupted the horizontal cohesion within their regiments and companies. But the importance of those numbers came into especially clear focus when three-year regiments that did not reenlist prepared to leave for home. Individual joy often competed with an intense sense of loss, since all of these departing regiments contained at least a few veterans who chose to sign on again, even if they had to complete their service in another regiment. When the 2nd Pennsylvania Reserves headed home in early June, those few members who had decided to stay the course reflected upon the moment of departure as "one of the saddest and most trying hours of our lives. . . . We could not realize the strong attachments that had grown up between us, until the hour of separation came. . . . It was the parting of brothers."[44] The same sentiment could be found in veteranized regiments when those comrades who had chosen not to reenlist left for home. As a 3rd Michigan veteran noted, however, we "do not censure them or feel hard toward them for not re-enlisting, for we consider that they have done their share at least for awhile."[45]

While the veterans bemoaned the breaking of horizontal bonds, the recently arrived regiments did not know if the quality of their own bonds would support them under fire. The heavies, at least, had nearly two years of shared service in camp, but they did not know if those ties would carry over into combat. It was no small concern, since their baptism of fire came within days of their arrival; some regiments that arrived on 16 May participated in the final phases of the Spotsylvania fighting at Harris farm on 19 May. As one Connecticut heavy recalled, when he and his comrades first deployed, their souls "became a theatre, where the two star actors, HOPE and FEAR, supported by Imagination, Apprehension, Patriotism, Courage, Doubt, Resolution, Ambition, and a host of supernumeraries, rehearse the coming battles."[46]

The heavies acquitted themselves reasonably well in their first fights, but their losses overwhelmed them. Their horizontal bonds held, however, and they learned to trust, adapt, and soldier on. Unit cohesion made it possible for them to handle the catcalls and hazing from the veterans, who often taunted them for their clean uniforms and white gloves and took macabre pleasure in showing them badly mangled corpses.[47] As a Maine heavy artilleryman quickly learned, "The strongest ties between human beings are not cemented in safety, luxury, and comfort."[48] The newly arrived veterans of the XVIII Corps from the Army of the James received the same gruesome welcome, but they proved far more capable of handling it than the brand-new regiments of volunteers fresh from their home states with no previous service on which to base these all-important bonds.

Strong cohesion within a unit not only provides the strength to hold together its members as they strive to complete their missions; it also provides the social support that its individual members need to deal with the many stressors of the combat environment. The world of combat is very personal, and combat stress manifests itself in many different ways. One researcher, describing its disruptive potential to individual soldiers, dubbed it an "emotional and physical carnivore."[49] Dysfunctional combat stress reactions or behaviors can be triggered by one or more of a wide range of stressors experienced singly, combined, or in sequence. Two soldiers standing side by side may respond to the same stressor or stressors in entirely different ways. Its multifaceted manifestations have made it difficult for military medical professionals and their civilian counterparts to agree on a single, comprehensive definition of combat stress, which consequently has made it even more difficult to diagnose. To date, researchers have made their most significant strides simply in defining the various kinds of combat stressors and identifying the range of behaviors they may cause. As a Department of Defense combat-stress manual emphasizes, "The operative word is *'behaviors.'* People in combat experience a range of emotions, but their behavior influences immediate safety and mission success."[50]

Combat stressors fall into at least five categories: physical, cognitive, emotional, social, and spiritual. Physical stressors include a wide array of forces that affect the efficient working of a soldier's body, usually reducing his ability to execute essential tasks at least as long as the stressor exists. These include wetness or dryness, heat or cold, bright light or darkness, mud, smoke, fog, loss of sleep, malnutrition, illness or injury, noxious fumes, loud noises, bright lights, and even interactions with dangerous plants and animals. Cognitive stressors occur when a soldier possesses too much information, conflicting information, or insufficient information to make sense of the situation in which he finds himself. Doubts about the rightness or morality of his cause or ambiguity about his role in the war effort, and even conflicted loyalties—the pull of home can be as treacherous as bullets on a battlefield—can exert unexpected stress on soldiers on the front lines. Emotional stressors can include the loss of personal friends, respected leaders, and unit members to death or any cause that leads to their departure, as well as the emergence of unexpectedly strong feelings of fear, guilt, helplessness, or shame. Confronting horrific scenes of carnage and the act of killing itself can bring on especially strong emotional stress. Social stressors can stem from the growing isolation caused by absence from friends and family at home and also from the dissolution of strong bonds with comrades—through death, wounds, capture, or discharge—that previously had provided reliable group identity and emotional support. Finally, spiritual stressors might result when active combat operations cause a soldier to question or even reject his previous beliefs in the existence of a diety and, often as a consequence, lose the ability to empathize or extend to others a sense of forgiveness. Importantly, in combat, most soldiers confront—and react to—multiple stressors simultaneously, resulting in a wide range of potential combat-stress behaviors.[51]

The spring campaign of 1864 unfolded in a way that differed greatly from the Army of the Potomac's previous operations and introduced unfamiliar stressors. In previous years, campaigns began with a maneuver phase to bring the armies into contact and then culminated in a battle of a few days' duration. Then the opposing forces separated, sometimes for months, to reorganize, refill their ranks, and await the next move. For the six weeks of this campaign, however, the Army of the Potomac remained in nearly constant contact with Lee's army. As Colonel Richard Coulter of the 11th Pennsylvania described it, from the time the army left Culpeper in early May until they reached the outskirts of Petersburg in mid-June, the army "had been labored to its utmost ability, either marching, engaging with the enemy, or employed in the erection of defensive works"—almost always in a lethal environment.[52]

This accelerated pace of military activity during the Overland Campaign approximates what modern military professionals call "continuous operations." While the Civil War experience does not meet entirely the concept's parameters as currently understood—the capacity for night fighting did not exist to make actual combat a twenty-four-hour effort—the unprecedented frequency of fighting and marching by day and marching and entrenching by night, with the possibility of death always near, brings it as close as the capabilities of nineteenth-century armies permit. Indeed, at times the campaign came close to current standards for "sustained operations," during which these same soldiers and units engaged in combat, marched, and dug, with minimal opportunity to stand down for several consecutive days or, by some definitions, to get at least four hours of sleep for several consecutive nights.[53] Colonel Robert McAllister's assertion attested to the intensity and duration of their efforts that meets the latter qualification: "Work, work! Fight, fight, takes all our time; we sleep only from two to four hours a day."[54] The duration and frequency of combat in this campaign made it probable that nearly every Northern soldier felt the cumulative effect of multiple stressors.

Unlike previous campaigns, the Army of the Potomac endured no long period of maneuver before its first battle, breaking camp on 3 or 4 May and fighting Lee's army in the Wilderness on 5–6 May. Veterans confronted all the stressors that had accompanied past combats, and, as they had done before as individuals or in groups, either adapted to them or ran to escape them. Just as they did after their earlier battles, they recorded in their reports, letters, and diaries the deaths of comrades and commanders, tales of heroism, and acts of cowardice. These same sources, however, endowed the Battle of the Wilderness with a unique quality, one most notable for the unusually high number of stressors imposed by the physical environment. The heavy scrub growth that limited field of vision and restricted soldiers' ability to identify threats and maintain visual contact with comrades; the dense smoke of dozens of fires kicked up by black-powder sparks igniting dead leaves that made eyes water and breathing labored; the fires themselves that burned to death some of the wounded, triggering feelings of guilt and fear among those who could not (or refused to) render aid; the muting of sounds by the vegetation and the resulting inability to hear commands or to gauge the nearness or direction of friends or enemies—all of these differed significantly from most of their previous experience fighting in more open terrain. The novelty found its expression in unusually eloquent language in letters, diaries, and war correspondent's reports from the field and later in memoirs and unit histories. Veteran journalist William Swinton, who had accompanied Grant's headquarters at the start of the campaign, well summarized the conditions in which the soldiers fought: "The battle of the Wilderness must remain, for the present, undescribed, for the reason that it is really indescribable. . . . No man can claim that he saw this battle, and although undoubtedly it had a line and formation of its own, it would puzzle even the Commanding General to lay it down on the map. There is something horrible and yet fascinating in the mystery shrouding this strangest of battles ever fought—a battle which no man could see—and whose progress could only be followed by the ear."[55] Just as after previous battles, the Wilderness shook loose a significant number of soldiers from their regiments—and some thought this battle caused more of that behavior than usual—but the environment seemed to control the ebb and flow of the battle more than positive control by commanders. The unsettling physical battlefield provided sufficient explanation for some individual and unit failure. Surprise flank attacks coming out of deep scrub caused Mott's newly reorganized division on the Union left to run and one brigade of Milroy's Weary Boys to collapse on the Union right.[56]

The dawn of 7 May marked another change in the way the Army of the Potomac conducted active operations, one with significant consequences for the soldiers in the ranks. Soldiers recalled, usually with satisfaction, the moment when they realized that Grant planned to move the army south toward their foe rather than return to their winter encampments as they had done after other battles. That same decision, however, began the process of extending each soldier's exposure to the stressors of the battle-field and increased the likelihood that each man would confront a greater variety of them. Previous experience could not prepare them for the impact of the cumulative effect of multiple stressors on either the individual soldier or the army's overall effectiveness.

Stresses such as those imposed by the environment could not be avoided, only endured. These contributed to the emergence of a cluster of dysfunctional combat-stress behaviors collectively described as "battle fatigue." After several consecutive dry days at the start of the campaign, the marching columns churned up such immense clouds of choking dust that by 8 May the army's chief medical officer expressed his concern about the lack of "free circulation of the air" and its effect on the men.[57] Torrents of rain began to fall on 11 May and continued for the next two days. As the 121st Pennsylvania recalled it, the roads, "which had heretofore been covered several inches deep with pulverized dust," turned into quagmires "covered with an assortment of mud, ranging from the choicest thick Virginia mud to the thinnest specimen, according to the elevation or depression of the road."[58] Near-daily showers and occasional downpours prevented the mud from drying for the rest of the month. The weather did not stop the army's maneuvering; it only increased the physical exhaustion of the soldiers executing their officers' orders.[59]

One specific kind of marching, new to most soldiers in the Overland Campaign, added a new set of unfamiliar stressors, however. Regardless of the weather or combat activity during the day, large elements of the army now frequently marched to new positions at night. The effects of the unfamiliar experience quickly emerged and proved capable of altering the army's plans. During an "intensely dark" night at Spotsylvania, V Corps commander Major General Gouverneur K. Warren discovered that his marching columns, already thinning out as soldiers dropped "from exhaustion and weariness," became "disjointed and part lost their way." The woods filled with lost soldiers seeking their units, and Warren had to post mounted men at intervals to mark the route of march. As a consequence, Warren delayed a planned attack for the following day.[60] As the campaign progressed, one of Meade's staff officers who observed the operations of the army daily came to consider "fifteen miles by night equal to twenty-five by day."[61] The impact of night operations on individual soldiers could be far more dramatic, however. Some developed severe symptoms of night blindness; Private John T. Ammerman of the 148th Pennsylvania called his affliction "moon-eye," and comrades led him by the arm along the route of march, picked him up when he lost the path and fell, and helped him into place in the line of battle for early-morning assaults.[62]

Extended nighttime activity during the military operations of May 1864 entirely disrupted the sleep cycle of nearly every man in the ranks. Optimum sleep-time requirements vary individually, but any reduction in that time for even a few days creates a "sleep debt" that exacts a physical, mental, and emotional toll. Modern sleep-deprivation studies have shown that a lack of sleep for twenty-four hours can produce results on physiological and physical reaction-time tests equivalent to those registered by test subjects who were legally drunk. Restorative time for even one night's interrupted sleep can be measured in days.[63] The press of army operations in May 1864 permitted few such breaks.

Manifestations of disrupted sleep patterns take many forms, and anecdotal evidence suggests that in May and early June 1864, soldiers in the Army of the Potomac experienced a wide range of them. Sleep loss also exacerbates a number of recognized symptoms of battle fatigue, including tunnel vision; impaired hearing; and uncontrollable physical reactions to terror, panic, anger, fear, and indecision. Numerous accounts in letters, reports, and diaries confirm the appearance of such symptoms as early as the night of 7 May. Along the II Corps line of march, a herd of army mules broke loose and charged down a road along which the men had halted and collapsed, worn out from their fight in the Wilderness and the day's march. Among sleeping soldiers, "a general panic ensued . . . instantaneously, and men who had faced death and danger in every form became utterly demoralized." Afterward, the shaken men found one recent recruit in the 105th Pennsylvania lying on the ground "pleading with the rebels, for God's sake, to spare him, as he was the only support of a widowed mother."[64] The next night, a soldier in the 150th Pennsylvania reported "many alarms and many useless volleys . . . caused by the nervous tension of which not merely the pickets but all of the troops were wrought up."[65]

Sleep deprivation in a high-stress environment can cause hyperalertness as well as the inability to remain awake at all. All too frequently, jumpy pickets fired at the slightest noise or movement, forcing their desperately tired comrades to fall into line to repel the imagined threat. On a single night at Spotsylvania, reported the commanding officer of the 37th Massachusetts, "Four times . . . we were roused by alarms, and stood to arms. Not much rest in this; but we were so exhausted that we would drop asleep the moment they allowed us to lie down."[66] The author of the

19th Maine's regimental history later resorted to poetry to describe the experience:

> Intoxicated by the drugs of sleep, my eyes are heavy and yet strict
>   vigils keep;
> Imagination fills my drowsy brain with scenes of battle, fields of
>   maimed and slain;
> The stumps and bushes into phantoms grow, and shadows shape
>   themselves into the foe.[67]

Although most threats quickly evaporated, sleep deprivation nonetheless contributed to the increasing casualty list. Adjutant George W. Wilson of the 61st Pennsylvania died on the picket line early in the Spotsylvania fighting, not from a Confederate bullet but from the discharge of a weapon wielded by a New York soldier "whose mind had suddenly left him under the great pressure of hard service and loss of sleep." The tired soldier challenged Wilson as the officer approached his position, but before the adjutant could offer the countersign, the picket shot him dead. The soldier had to be removed from the front lines, now "a raving maniac."[68]

When the Army of the Potomac stopped marching—regardless of the time of day or night, the weather, or the soldiers' need for sleep—they seldom enjoyed the recuperative time required to restore their energy. From the day of their first contact with Lee's army on 5 May until they crossed the James River in mid-June, when they halted for any long period of time, they received orders to dig in. They completed this physically demanding work before they ate, slept, or took care of other personal needs. While some units of the Army of the Potomac fought behind "hasty entrenchments" at Chancellorsville and at Gettysburg, the great majority of its soldiers had not built or fought behind earthworks until the Wilderness. Ten days into the campaign, Captain John Willoughby of the 5th Pennsylvania Reserves wrote to a friend: "How we dig." He then added: "Talk of McClellan digging; we lay him in the shade. Both armies after an hour's halt are entrenched."[69]

The physical demands of digging earthworks increased as the campaign progressed. At the Wilderness, soldiers simply laid out a single line of trenches where common sense and terrain dictated, dug a shallow ditch, and piled the dirt in front of them on logs or brush felled to clear a field of fire. When the armies faced off at Cold Harbor one month later, however, they erected complex trench systems with reinforcing second and even third lines; interlocking field of fire laid out by engineering officers; and even head logs, firing slits, and transverse trenches to limit damage from falling mortar shells.[70] Brigadier General Lewis A. Grant, commander of the famed Vermont Brigade, reported that his men worked all night at Cold Harbor, after engaging the enemy during the day, to construct works "of a formidable character, consisting of no less than seven parallel lines, some of them connected by covered or protected ways."[71]

Soldiers paid a physical price beyond exhaustion for the increased level of exertion that marching followed by digging required. During winter quarters, their limited training centered on marching in formation and weapons drills, not physical conditioning. Now, as they dug, they relied upon major muscle groups in the upper body that they seldom exercised strenuously. Large-muscle groups in arms, shoulders, and central core unprepared for the intensive physical effort of digging earthworks quickly developed aerobic fatigue. The soldier's entire body suffered from insufficient oxygen. Such extreme physical exertion triggers the release into the bloodstream of myoglobin, a substance that may damage the kidneys if not flushed out quickly. Continued physical effort on this level without sufficient rest and hydration does not strengthen a body's muscles. Quite to the contrary, the stress on joints and ligaments increases, and stress fractures may appear, incapacitating the soldier from further duties.[72]

No question, the cumulative physical demands of the Overland Campaign far outran anything Northern soldiers had experienced before. On one day alone—10 May at Spotsylvania—the 148th Pennsylvania "commenced the day by changing our position and continued changing all day, occupying twelve different and distinct positions, in two or three of which we built rifle pits." The officer who recorded this litany of marches neglected to mention that, in addition, his regiment also had participated in a sharp clash with the enemy along the Po River on the Union right flank that cost it 175 men.[73] The exhaustion brought on by such a high level of activity could be alleviated only by rest, and Grant had no intention of halting his army's forward progress. On 11 May he informed President Lincoln: "I intend to fight along this line all summer." By the time the army reached the North Anna two weeks later, the chaplain of the 125th New York recalled, the ceaseless marching, fighting, and digging "were telling upon our men, in some cases almost as seriously as wounds." One of the enlisted men complained: "'O Chaplain, it is killing me.'" In the end, the chaplain noted, "It did kill him, and more than one."[74]

While the Overland Campaign revealed Grant's tenacity and stubbornness, as well as his single-minded commitment to victory, it is equally apparent that he may not have understood the price his soldiers paid in carrying out his orders, even as he insisted that they pay it. He remained focused, as most generals of his era did, on the effectiveness of his army and not on the well-being of its individual human components. He thought about his mission in institutional terms. As he later wrote: "To provision an army, campaigning against so formidable a foe through such a country, from wagons alone seemed almost impossible," but "system and discipline were both essential to its accomplishment."[75] Although Grant's orders specified that commissary trains at Culpeper carry ten days' rations, the men carry three more, and herds of beef cattle accompany the column, the soldiers, as usual, quickly ate all of their food rather than carry it. Worse, throughout the campaign, due in part to mud and rapid troop movements and equally to administrative conflicts within the Quartermaster and Commissary Departments, the trains carrying food and other essential supplies simply could not keep pace.[76] As a result, the system failed, and discipline proved wholly insufficient to compensate for its collapse. Lee's men, even with the interior line's shorter marches and a southward movement that took them closer to their logistical stores in Richmond, suffered similarly.

As a consequence, Northern soldiers went through the Overland Campaign chronically undernourished. Complaints began as early as 7 May. Captain A. W. Acheson of the 140th Pennsylvania groused to his mother that day that, in the four days since the army broke camp, "I haven't eaten enough to keep a sick kitten alive."[77] "Often we get a meal a day, but oftener a meal in two days," wrote Lieutenant Colonel Guy Watkins of the 141st Pennsylvania, a comment that many other soldiers corroborated.[78]

The nutritional quality of the food that did arrive added little to the soldiers' ability to rebound quickly from their exertions. The standard daily ration for a Northern soldier on the march required him to be issued one pound of hardtack along with ¾ pounds of salt pork or 1¼ pounds of fresh meat—usually beef—plus salt, sugar, and coffee. The caloric value of a full ration of hardtack and salt pork might exceed 4,000 calories, comparable to the recommended 3,600 calories for a modern soldier engaged in active operations. The quality of those calories, however, did not sustain long endurance. A full ration of salt pork provided over 150 percent of an active adult's daily fat intake—174 percent of his recommended saturated fat intake—and the meat and hardtack together accounted for high sodium levels. Fresh meat maintained its nutritional quality for only a short time; after only a few days, the fat cattle that departed from Culpeper with the army already had lost significant body mass and nutrients.[79] Army regulations did not call for soldiers to receive fruits or vegetables as a regular part of marching rations; on 8 June, for the first time in the campaign, Colonel John Tidball entered this telling comment into his diary: "Full ration of vegetables issued."[80] By mid-June, the U.S. Sanitary Commission began to distribute these items to the soldiers, as drivers simply steered wagons full of produce down roads near concentrations of troops while tossing potatoes, onions, and other items to all soldiers they passed.[81]

Interestingly, only the soldiers' insufficient supply of coffee raised official concerns from the army's senior medical officer. Surgeon General William A. Hammond already had noted coffee's "excellent effects" on soldiers, who, after drinking it after "long and fatiguing marches," retired for the night "happy and refreshed."[82] Morning coffee made a difference, as well. Now the Army of the Potomac's chief surgeon noted in his official report that he observed a "shock and depression of vital power" among the wounded of the II Corps on 12 May at Spotsylvania, a condition he attributed to soldiers going into action "without having had the usual morning cup of coffee."[83] Indeed, army doctors preferred that soldiers drink coffee rather than water, condemning as "pernicious" the "habit of drinking at every stream . . . and filling the canteens for continual use."[84] Soldiers who followed that advice, of course, invited dehydration and slowed the removal of intramuscular toxins built up during marching and the digging of entrenchments.

The army's logistical challenges in providing adequate food also interrupted other well-established daily routines that promoted a soldier's sense of personal confidence and well-being. Mail deliveries became so infrequent and irregular that most soldiers received no letters from home until at least 18 May.[85] The operational pace and the lack of resupply destroyed even the most fundamental efforts to maintain basic hygienic standards among soldiers of all ranks. As Lieutenant Colonel Watkins of the 141st Pennsylvania wrote on 16 May: "I have not changed clothing in three weeks, and have had my boots off but once since we started" from their winter encampment.[86] Soldiers suffered from lice, fungal infections, foot problems of all sorts, boils, skin lesions that became infected or simply would not heal, and a wide variety of related maladies. But these problems were rarely of such severity that they required hospitalization; soldiers stayed in ranks, at reduced efficiency, and endured. As tired Union soldiers approached the James River after the fighting at Cold Harbor, some built an earthwork so that guards could cover comrades bathing in the water. "It was a goodly sight to see half a dozen regiments disporting themselves in the tepid water of the James," a Connecticut soldier recalled years later, even then marveling at the "ENJOYMENT it afforded."[87]

All of these various stressors that degraded physical strength and well-being, of course, created factors of unpredictability on the battlefield that Jomini and his peers never considered when discoursing on how to win victories. But the Overland Campaign also brought with it significant changes in tactical practice that challenged the confidence and mental toughness of even the most experienced veterans. Three years of war had accustomed them to deploying to a long firing line and confronting the enemy at a range of 50 to 200 yards. Exchanges of volley fire continued until one side or the other advanced and broke the opponent's line, usually forcing his rapid withdrawal from the field of battle. Attacking enemy entrenchments, however, generally occurred in two phases. First came the assault—usually much costlier to the attackers than the defenders, and Northern troops most often took the offensive in the Overland Campaign. Second, if the assault managed to breach the Confederate line, fighting continued at close range, even hand-to-hand, a kind of intensely personal combat still a novelty for many Union soldiers. As modern studies of military aviators and other combatants who engage their enemies from a safe distance have demonstrated, physical space separating oneself from one's foe provides a kind of psychological balm that Northern soldiers closing on enemies behind earthworks lost.[88] The introduction of unfamiliar weapons, such as the field mortar that lobbed shells behind entrenchments, also presented new ways of fighting for which they had developed no mental defenses.

The frequency of combat—or anticipation of its imminence—became a unique element of the Overland Campaign, but no single day stood out more in Union soldiers' contemporary letters, diaries, and reports, and later in their memoirs and unit histories, than the brutal fighting at Spotsylvania's Bloody Angle on 12 May 1864. Superlatives separated it from all previous and later events. "It was one of the bloodiest battles, the old soldiers say, that ever the Army had," wrote Private Gideon Mellin of the 93rd Pennsylvania three days later.[89] "The fighting of this day is without a parallel in the history of this campaign, if, indeed, it has its equal in the records of the present war," reported the 5th Vermont's Captain Friend H. Barney, recalling how it "resembled a hand-to-hand fight rather than a modern battle with long-range weapons."[90] As the historian of the 15th New Jersey later summarized: "Combine the horrors of many battle-fields, bring them into a single day and night of twenty-four hours, and the one of May 12th includes them all."[91]

When an army composed of soldiers who are physically and mentally exhausted by continuous operations, sleep deprivation, and lack of food and are vulnerable to all manner of additional stresses is thrown into combat as ferocious, as long in duration, and as violent as the Mule Shoe fight became, it should not come as a surprise that contemporary sources provide examples of nearly every acknowledged combat stress–related behavior. Recent "warrior science" work, however, looks beyond the behaviors to the body's extreme physiological responses underlying them.

Colonel John Schoonover of the 11th New Jersey, for instance, recalled at the Mule Shoe a noise reported on many different Civil War battlefields: "the whirring sound of a flying ramrod."[92] Historians generally cite this common occurrence simply as evidence of a soldier's inexperience or his quite understandable "nervousness" or "fear." But how does "fear" cause a soldier to forget to remove his ramrod from his rifle barrel? Warrior scientists explain it this way: the normal resting heart rate of an adult male is sixty to eighty beats per minute. As a Civil War soldier approached the battlefield, the anticipation of combat caused a rush of adrenaline that increased his pulse rate. Most soldiers loaded their weapons with no difficulty as they prepared to engage, but once they went into action, adrenaline—inspired by any intense emotion—continued to drive up the heart rate. At 115 beats per minute, fine motor skills began to deteriorate; this helps to explain why a soldier often fumbled with his rifle's small percussion cap. As combat intensified, the pulse rate continued to rise. The physical action of withdrawing a ramrod from its housing under the rifle barrel, driving home the bullet to seat it properly, pulling the ramrod out of the muzzle, and replacing it in its housing required the use of major muscle combinations in the arms, shoulders, and back. When the heart rate exceeded 145 beats per minute, soldiers may have lost some of the large muscle control that determined the efficiency of complex motor skills, including the actions required to wield a ramrod. At that pulse rate, one of two things generally occurred. Soldiers who received regular arms training—say, the familiar drill of "loading in nine times" that included all movements of the ramrod—may have developed the muscle memory to use their rifles effectively even with a combat-induced elevated heart rate. Accounts of the fighting at the Mule Shoe teem with examples of soldiers firing continuously for hours on end or, like Sergeant Robert Kissinger of the 148th Pennsylvania, "coolly cutting off a piece of his shelter tent, putting the screw upon his ramrod and deliberately cleaning his rifle" of the mud that had befouled it, all while under enemy fire.[93] If, however, their trainers took shortcuts and did not insist upon repetitions of the actual movements required to remove, use, and replace the ramrod, soldiers instead may have developed a "training scar" that led to performance failure at a critical time. Thus, when a poorly trained soldier's heart raced too high, the likelihood that he would fire his weapon with ramrod still in the barrel increased.[94] Many ramrods flew at the Mule Shoe.

A related physiological response likely explains another common Mule Shoe experience. A New York soldier noted how frequently he observed comrades who "would drop off to sleep while lying in line of battle and the enemy's shells busting over our heads."[95] Physical exhaustion, illness, and exertion in thick mud no doubt contributed, but in this case, too, a stress-induced heart rate that spiked over 175 beats per minute can explain the occurrence. If a soldier's heart rate reached that level, he may have lost gross motor control, causing a vasoconstriction of blood vessels that limits his body's ability to get the oxygen he needs. His body simply shut down, and he fell into a sleeplike state.

Some soldiers of the Mule Shoe fight also remarked on other personal physiological reactions that they had not experienced in previous combat. Some reported impaired hearing or noted such out-of-place behaviors by their comrades as singing happy—not patriotic—songs or firing their weapons harmlessly straight up in the air. Private Henry Keiser of the 95th Pennsylvania confided to his diary after the fighting on 12 May that he had fired 160 rounds that day, and as a consequence his right arm was "almost useless tonight from the rebound of my rifle."[96]

Just as often as soldiers reported physiological responses triggered by the Mule Shoe fight, their recollections of what they saw after the fight clearly affected them emotionally. An officer had ordered Private Mellin to search a bullet-ridden corpse for identification, and when he poked into the dead soldier's uniform pocket, he came away with a handful of maggots from an unseen wound just underneath the cloth. He later wrote to his sister that "the dead lay in some places piled up like cord wood" and after a few days "became so rotten that it was impossible for any person to stand it for the smell."[97] A VI Corps surgeon visited the Mule Shoe and later wrote of seeing dead Northern soldiers, "many nothing but a lump of meat or clot of gore where countless bullets from both armies had torn them."[98] While impossible to quantify, it is not difficult for researchers to find letters written by survivors of the Mule Shoe that begin with a gory description of all they had witnessed, only to reach a point where they simply needed to stop. As Private Maurus Oesterreich of the 96th Pennsylvania wrote: "I have seen so much that I can't nor will put it in this book. I will seal this in my memory by myself."[99] Nor is it possible to quantify the soldiers who, perhaps in an effort to depersonalize the entire event, centered their commentaries not on the deaths of comrades but on the destruction of the "Spotsylvania Oak," a tree with a trunk measuring twenty-two inches in diameter felled by musket fire alone.

The unrelenting nearness of death—whether it occurred during massive assaults like that at the Mule Shoe or was inflicted by ones and twos in the trenches—increasingly caused soldiers to manifest a range of different behaviors. Some strong individuals simply relied upon their mental toughness to accept that "some comrades fell in battle, little noted by the world, but greatly missed by their companions as well as by the loved ones at home."[100] A far more troubling reaction, however—especially to their comrades—was evident among some individuals who grew so inured to conditions that they showed a growing lack of concern about death and loss, even to the point of developing an indifference to real danger. By the time they reached the North Anna, men of the 3rd Michigan ignored nearby gunfire—"only some kind of hard skirmishing . . . which, in ordinary campaigns would be called hard fighting," as they described it—because "we are so used to it now that we don't pretend to make any more bowing to the bullets, and only when a huge shell comes slowly through the air do we bow our heads in meekness."[101] At Cold Harbor, the men of the 5th Maine rarely heeded gunfire unless the balls "were flying very thick; and with this feeling of indifference acquired through long continued exposure, if there was anything to be done in their temporary camp, went right to work to do it as if the enemy were miles away."[102]

Although Civil War armies had no systematic way to recognize and alleviate these various expressions of battle fatigue, many soldiers fell back on the practical expedient—and the foundation of treatment in the U.S. Army today—of simply giving themselves a break from the stressors for a short period. Sometimes duty assignments made this possible. Lieutenant Colonel Dawes expressed his delight when his 6th Wisconsin was detached for guard posting behind the lines for a few hours after the fighting at Cold Harbor ended. "It does seem pleasant to get even for a few hours out of the presence of death, suffering and danger," he admitted to his wife, adding: "Our spirits rise wonderfully."[103]

But not every soldier who left the line did so with official sanction. The

Overland Campaign saw a jump in the frequency of misconduct stress behavior and illegal actions, and malingering ranked high among them. Every regiment, a Connecticut soldier recalled, had a few "REAL sneaks, shirks, and dead-beats" who always seemed to turn up at "some distant hospital, detailed as nurses, or reported unfit for duty by reason of varicose veins, general debility or chronic something or other."[104] Such activity occurred during and after every battle, but during the Overland Campaign, it grew to such proportions that Brigadier General Marsena Patrick, the Army of the Potomac's chief provost marshal, greatly enlarged the cavalry detachments guarding the major roads to the army's rear area and the piers where men faking wounds tried to board ships transporting sick and injured soldiers to Northern hospitals. The guards performed their duty so aggressively that "it was said that of the two it was safer to go forward and engage the enemy, than to go back and be sabred to the front by the provost guard."[105] Every day, doctors examined the wounds of each patient in their hospital and made lists of those ready to return to duty. Massachusetts physician J. Franklin Dyer noted that at Cold Harbor, he never sent these men back to their regiments without a provost marshal escort, so certain was he that many would run at the first opportunity that "it is useless to send them except under guard."[106]

Some soldiers desperate to leave the front turned to self-inflicted wounds as a means to escape. Corporal Stephen G. Babcock of the 126th New York stopped one man preparing to shoot himself in the hand and turned him in. "No hospital for him!" the regimental historian later gloated, adding that "the order was to send the offender to the front, where he could get wounded in a less reprehensible manner."[107] The Army of the Potomac's chief surgeon, Thomas McParlin, noted after Spotsylvania a sharp increase in the number of soldiers reaching his hospitals with so much blackened skin around wounds that he became convinced that "the injury was self-inflicted either by design or accident." Worse, many of these men then misapplied tourniquets, making "their hands and forearms swollen and livid" and likely leading to gangrene, amputations, or even death.[108] Indeed, Private Henry Colby of the 2nd Connecticut Heavy Artillery shot himself in the hand at North Anna and died three weeks later.[109]

The formation of Company Q illustrated an adaptive way to deal with the unauthorized departures from the ranks of junior officers, but the substantial jump in this same behavior by enlisted men elicited a far stricter response. At the end of the first two weeks of the Overland Campaign, Grant and Meade expedited court-martial proceedings for soldiers accused of leaving ranks and especially for those who deserted in the face of the enemy. Private John Starbird of the 19th Massachusetts was tried for leaving ranks under fire at the Wilderness and again on 10 May at Spotsylvania and found guilty of the latter incident. Since Starbird was a repeat offender, General Meade quickly approved his execution by firing squad on 21 May. The army was on the move, however, so instead of the usual practice of massing the division to which Starbird belonged to witness his death, the private simply faced his executioners in a field near a road where all passing regiments could march by his bullet-riddled corpse. A Philadelphia soldier who witnessed the "example of military severity" doubted it would deliver the intended message, however, realizing that while generals expected unquestioning discipline at all times, "a soldier may act with questionable courage on one occasion and redeem himself on another."[110]

Deserters usually left ranks singly or in small groups. Far more troubling, the Army of the Potomac experienced a sharp rise in collective acts of purposeful insubordination that resulted in keeping whole units off the firing line. At Spotsylvania, one entire company of a Pennsylvania regiment deliberately disobeyed their own officers' orders and simply left the skirmish line as a group to make coffee. The brigade officer of the day peremptorily ordered them back to the skirmish line, but not a single man acknowledged or responded to the command. Only when Lieutenant Colonel Franklin P. Harlow of the 7th Massachusetts gave them a choice either to return "or be shot in their tracks, for leaving their posts in face of the enemy" did any of the men show the slightest inclination to move.[111]

The Vietnam generation gave the most extreme expression of this behavior a name: combat refusal. During the Overland Campaign, those most likely to refuse to fight—or at least to threaten to—were veteran soldiers with sufficient battle experience to evaluate a tactical situation and make up their own minds about whether or not they trusted their officers' decisions. In assessing his brigade's poor performance on 10 May at Spotsylvania, Brigadier General Alexander S. Webb explained that "the men had had time to examine the enemy's line," and, as a result, "convinced themselves that the enemy was too strongly positioned to be driven out by assault." Their resulting effort, Webb admitted, "could hardly be termed a charge."[112] A few days later, Sergeant Charles Frey of the 150th Pennsylvania noted in his diary that the men in his regiment simply stopped when they saw no promise of success in their efforts, ignoring officers who "stormed back and forth in a useless effort to make the troops advance further."[113]

Both the seriousness and frequency of dysfunctional combat stress behaviors and criminal acts increased as the campaign continued. Logistical failures combined with combat stress to fuel a spike in pillaging that kept Provost Marshal Patrick busy on the road to the North Anna River taking into custody "marauders & house plunderers." When he went to Grant's headquarters to report, he learned that the general's own staff "were, themselves, engaged in sheep stealing, fowl stealing, and the like."[114] If Grant's men lacked sympathy for Patrick's concerns, Meade and his staff at least seemed to agree that the army's discipline had begun to fail badly. One of Meade's staff officers suggested imposing a harsh penalty to stop "outrages on the inhabitants," even attempting to prevent "the grosser acts" by hanging the guilty from trees along the route of march. "I think I would do it myself, if I caught any of them," he added.[115] A few of General Hancock's II Corps division commanders took measures to stop their troops from committing such acts, but it still remained a significant problem for Patrick. As he recorded in his diary on 13 June, "I found the 6' Corps ravaging the whole Country & killing Cattle Sheep etc. with perfect abandon, while the houses are burning with the 5' Corps Head Quarters in hailing distance."[116]

Over the course of the six weeks between the breaking of winter camp and the crossing of the James River, the Army of the Potomac suffered at least 54,929 men killed, wounded, and missing. Union field hospitals admitted an unprecedented 22,596 sick and wounded in May alone.[117] The impact of the losses in just one division—that of Brigadier General John Gibbon's II Corps command—demonstrates clearly the intersection of operational imperatives and the human element of war. The adaptive factors of unit identity and unit cohesion had served Gibbon's men well at the start of the Overland Campaign. Good fortune had blessed them during the army reorganization. Gibbon himself had commanded the division for nearly a year, and the March realignments only slightly altered the structure of his three brigades; familiar brigade commanders reinforced a strong sense of unit identity. The division left winter camp on 3 May with 6,799 men. In the middle of the fighting at Spotsylvania, Gibbon received two new regiments—including one of heavy artillery—each numbering over 1,500 men, and then he added the 765 soldiers of Colonel Frank A. Haskell's green 36th Wisconsin Infantry, assigning each unit to a different veteran brigade. In early June, he received 323 additional men, his total strength over the course of the campaign reaching 11,062. By the end of July—the point at which most division commanders had received their brigade commanders' accounts of the Overland Campaign on which to base their own reports—he had lost 77 officers and 971 enlisted men killed, a total of 1,046. He lost an additional 202 officers and 3,825 enlisted men wounded, a total of 4,027. Thus, in killed and wounded alone, he lost 5,073, or 46 percent of his total strength. His division took most of those losses between 3 May and 22 June, some of the largest suffered by his new heavy artillery regiment. These totals do not include soldiers listed as prisoners or simply as "missing," veterans who departed after their enlistment had expired, noncombat casualties sent to the rear due to illness or exhaustion, or those who simply walked away for a few days—or forever. Over the course of the campaign, the division's vertical cohesion became entirely disrupted. Gibbon's three brigades—and briefly a fourth when the two large regiments first arrived—went through seventeen different commanders. Three died in battle, six fell with wounds, and General Owen was dismissed. Forty regimental commanders fell.

Although Gibbon relied upon the only quantifiable method available to him to illustrate the impact of recent operations upon his command, he clearly had come to appreciate the link between the impact of combat stress upon his soldiers and the press of army operations. In mid- and late June in the opening phases of the Petersburg Campaign, his once-reliable division suddenly collapsed on the battlefield. After six weeks of continuous operations, worn-out regiments, brigades, divisions, and even entire corps throughout the entire Army of the Potomac did the same thing. To explain the failure, Gibbon turned to his casualty list, asserting that these numbers "show why it is that the troops, which at the commencement of the campaign were equal to almost any undertaking, became toward the end of it unfit for almost any."[118]

Gibbon did not make the discovery alone. Major General David B. Birney, another II Corps division commander, also attributed early reverses at Petersburg to, among other things, "the extraordinary losses among the commanding, staff, and other officers in this command" during the Overland Campaign and the organizational disruptions caused by "the large proportion of new troops assigned to this corps to replace veterans."[119] Brigadier General Francis C. Barlow officially reported that his troops could not meet a Confederate attack early in the Petersburg Campaign "with vigor and courage and determination" since his front-line brigades "are too unsteady, from loss of commanding and other officers and other causes, to be much depended on in circumstances requiring much nerve and determination." Two days later, he reiterated that, due to loss of officers and exhaustion, three of his four brigades "cannot just now be relied on to meet critical emergencies with much determination and spirit."[120] Even General Meade realized what had occurred. When called to testify before the Joint Committee on the Conduct of the War about the frequent failure of his army to crack the Petersburg line in June and July 1864, he asserted, after reviewing recent operations: "The condition of the army was in some measure unfavorable for all operations of this kind. The men did not fight at that time with the vim with which they fought when we first crossed the Rapidan."[121] Across the trench lines, Lee's army had begun to experience the same decline.[122]

At this juncture, it is useful to consider what sustained the soldiers who still remained in ranks? Once again, adaptive combat-stress behaviors can help provide an answer. For instance, the Overland Campaign witnessed a high number of selfless acts of personal courage; at least seventy-seven Union soldiers won Medals of Honor for gallantry between 5 May and 15 June 1864 in operations connected with the Army of the Potomac's operations.[123] A strong group and personal reliance on religious faith, strengthened by regimental chaplains and U.S. Christian Commission speakers who regularly held well-attended worship services or distributed religious literature during the winter and early spring of 1864, also helped.[124]

Another apparent source of strength came from a continuing commitment to the Union's war aims. As James M. McPherson's masterful work on soldier motivation has suggested, Union soldiers fought for some combination of "cause and comrades."[125] In the study of adaptive combat-stress factors, unit cohesion and its vertical and horizontal components comprise elements of a broader concept called "social cohesion." This notion, of course, illustrates McPherson's "comrades" element. Social scientists, however, also recognize a related bond labeled "task cohesion," which equates more directly to McPherson's "cause" element.[126] During and immediately after the Overland Campaign, despite the decline in "social cohesion," the surviving members of the Army of the Potomac appear to have retained a high degree of "task cohesion." The men might not have approved of the cost of final victory, and some complained about the lack of tactical prowess in the officers charged with achieving it, but many simply refused to lose faith in the purpose behind their work. Soldier diaries and letters teem with comments such as that of Captain Alexander W. Acheson after Cold Harbor, who assured his mother: "We've got the 'Johnnies' pretty well belabored now and it will soon be to their interest to acknowledge the fact that they are 'licked.' . . . They confidently expected us to fall back over the river after the Wilderness fight, as did Burnside, Hooker, and Meade, but 'That's played out.'"[127] Postwar memoirs are even more adamant in confirming the enduring strength of the veteran soldiers' commitment during the midsummer of 1864. As a company in the 148th Pennsylvania chose to remember the period after the Overland Campaign: "Many were worn and enfeebled by service, disease and wounds. Many were placed on special detail which involved absence from the company. Many were lost from the company by disease, by death, transfer and discharge, because of inability to perform active service in the field. But those who remained were ever ready for duty."[128]

Jomini had written that "the *morale* of an army . . . has an influence upon the fate of a war; and this seems to be due to a certain physical effect produced by the moral cause." The impetuous attack of 20,000 men "thoroughly enlisted in their cause" invariably produced a more powerful effect than "forty thousand demoralized or apathetic men."[129] But that no longer held true for the Army of the Potomac. Although the military spirit of the individual survivors remained strong, the severe losses within units—measured both in numbers and in cohesive strength—had to be addressed on every level of organization. "The soul of war is a power unseen, bound up with the interests, convictions, and the passions of men," wrote journalist William Swinton. "Had not success elsewhere come to brighten the horizon [in the fall of 1864], it would have been difficult to have raised new forces to recruit the Army of the Potomac, which, shaken in its structure, its valor quenched in blood, and thousands of its best officers killed and wounded, was the Army of the Potomac no more."[130]

While some of the army's senior leaders now perceived the important link between the operations of an army and the human factors of war, such understanding did not result in a quick burst of reform that changed the way the officers and their men discharged their duties. Rethinking such interrelationships had to await the return of peace. A medical officer, observing the effects of accumulated combat stressors upon soldiers in Sherman's armies undergoing similar experiences in Georgia, did offer some astute suggestions for future consideration, however: "The most important of all reforms . . . is in the state and condition of the common soldier." Indeed, he argued, "it is of absolute importance that line and company officers be taught to take an interest in the physical well-being of the men." Failure to do so portended consequences well beyond the company and regiment. "The want of intelligent care and conservation of the private soldier has had more to do with the prolongation of the war and the mishaps which have occurred than any one or any series of causes combined," he concluded.[131]

The changes the surgeon lobbied for did not formally find a place among officer responsibilities or become institutionalized in its leadership manuals until the World War I era. Nonetheless, some senior officers learned lessons they deemed worthy of immediate inculcation. In early 1866, Brigadier General August V. Kautz, a veteran commander of cavalry, infantry, and African American soldiers, prepared a new handbook for army officers that drew upon four years of hard-fought war to describe in detail the duties of officers at each grade. For the first time, in explicit terms, he acknowledged the importance of social cohesion to the army: "Men have not the same confidence in strangers that they have in their messmates." He rejected as outmoded the notion that "a knowledge of tactics is . . . all that is necessary" to command troops, reminding officers that tactics "is only the means of acquiring discipline, and attaining control of the troops." An officer had to see to his command's "harmony, comfort, and discipline." To cement the bond, Kautz advised each officer to give his "personal attention" to "the private affairs of his men," without becoming meddlesome. If the officer "takes no interest in their joys or sorrows" then, if he is obeyed at all, "he will be obeyed as prisoners in a prison obey their keepers," with neither energy nor enthusiasm. All this heralded a new way of thinking about the responsibilities of officership. Kautz had taken just a first cautious step, however. By embracing the human element of war, he crossed into intellectual territory that Jomini and most other military writers in vogue at the start of the Civil War had slighted. But Kautz also gave that advice expressly to lieutenants and captains.[132] Closing the link between the private in the ranks and the general who planned his battles still lay far in the future.

EPILOGUE

The news of Appomattox ignited waves of celebration throughout the North, a joy soon muted by the assassination of the commander in chief and a growing awareness that the surrender of Lee's army alone did not constitute the end of hostilities. Still, Northerners took great interest in bestowing victory laurels upon those deemed responsible for winning the war. A generosity of spirit made it easy to heap the greatest measure of praise on the men in ranks—all of them—for their courage, commitment, and endurance. Even General Grant saved the final paragraph in his last campaign report to praise his soldiers. His fairness told plainly: "It has been my fortune to see the armies of both the West and the East fight battles, and from what I have seen I know there is no difference in their fighting qualities. All that it was possible for men to do in battle they have done. . . . The splendid achievements of each have nationalized our victories" and restored the "supremacy of law over every foot of territory belonging to the United States."[1] From those who chose to individualize their honors, Grant won the lion's share.

Such weighty events demanded deeper analysis, of course. To many, the interplay of "how" and "why" the Union armies won mattered much more than simply "who" commanded. The publication of Grant's final report drew little public attention, but regular readers of the *Army and Navy Journal* scrutinized it intensely in an effort to tease out the war's greatest military lessons. According to one reader, Grant won because he had rejected the practice commonly espoused in antebellum military literature that called for "seizing great strategical points, of moving upon grand key-positions in the South." Instead, Grant had made enemy armies his objective. The writer labeled this as "the lose-all or win-all method" and expressed his pleasure that "with General Grant it has been the win-all." Although the general's hammering of the Confederates had resulted in "fearful attrition" for both armies, Grant's persistence gave him "immortality in military annals, and have placed him side by side with those great soldiers, Wellington and Suvarov."[2]

But the correspondent did not merely intend to celebrate Grant. He also identified five specific points for future study: the strength of a military strategy based on "concentration and cooperation"; the need to raise mass armies to utterly shatter the enemy, "in opposition to the 'strategy' taught in the schools"; the effectiveness of focusing on defeating armies "in opposition to the theory of seizing strategic points"; a reliance upon Grant's hammering rather than Sherman's flanking; and, finally, the allowance of great latitude to trusted subordinates. Most of these points, of course, outright rejected the essence of the ideas advanced by Jomini and most of the other military authors generally accepted as the world's greatest authorities at the start of the war.[3]

But would Grant replace Jomini as the American soldiers' acknowledged master of the art of war? It did not seem likely. Grant's success may not have resulted from a purposeful application of any given set of principles drawn from antebellum military theory, but neither did he posit a new set of theorems of his own. Indeed, few saw Grant's intellect as a decisive factor in winning the war. As journalist-turned-historian J. T. Headley admitted, the difficulties facing the Union's top military commanders "would have staggered the genius of Napoleon, or the skill of Wellington, even at the close of their long experience and training." Both Grant and Sherman, he astutely noted, had entered the war as mere "children" whom field experience alone—not their West Point education or any degree of personal study—had prepared for their increasing responsibilities. The nation had been lucky that they "were fortunately kept where they could grow to the new and strange condition of things." Only "circumstances"— and not intellectual nurturing—had developed in Grant the wisdom, sagacity, integrity, and humility necessary to lead the U.S. Army to victory.[4] Few looked to Grant, the cadet who frequented the West Point library primarily to read novels, as a military theorist of note.

Nonetheless, the Civil War continued to shape the intellectual development of the U.S. Army for years to come, just as it gave new direction to the nation as a whole. Still, four years of costly war did not make it a simple task to identify and prioritize the army's most pressing needs, suggest potential solutions, win War Department and congressional acceptance—and funding—and then institute change. The process became both continuous and contentious. With soldiers disagreeing among themselves over the army's greatest lessons and future course, and with growing evidence that the antebellum split between "professionals" and "amateurs"— especially citizen-soldiers who continued to serve their country in high public office—still endured, even Grant observed that the only time the army enjoyed any peace was when it was at war.[5]

Still, some changes began quickly enough. In the first five years after Appomattox, the army—at least that part of it not engaged in the novel experience of occupation duty and experiments in civil government in the former Confederacy—began to reorganize a much smaller peacetime establishment. The officer corps, and the small number of civilians still interested after the crisis of war ended, freely offered their opinions on military matters both large and small. They debated such issues as the appropriate number of companies in a regiment: should there be ten, as in most volunteer regiments during the war, or would the army be better served by regiments of twelve companies, making it possible to divide a regiment into three four-company battalions for garrison duty?[6] Experimentation with new weapons—from different types of breech-loading, repeating rifles and carbines for the infantry and cavalry to breech-loading, rifled cannon and smokeless powder for artillery—also commanded much attention. Many officers had decried the waste of lives in frontal assaults against enemy earthworks during the war, and the return of peace finally made it possible to revise the tactics of the three combat arms. Brevet Major General Emory Upton—who in four years had jumped from newly commissioned second lieutenant to general-officer rank—requested permission as early as January 1866 to present to the secretary of war (or a board he convened) a new, more open, and more flexible system of infantry tactics based on the "principle of fours." Upton hoped to eliminate reliance on the close-ranked battle line of the war years and the casualties such a formation invariably suffered in an attack.[7] Upton's plan did not win acceptance, but his ideas impressed General Sherman. The general ordered Upton to West Point to begin an overhaul of the tactics governing all three of the army's combat arms. Indeed, the next time the U.S. Army confronted a conventional army in battle during the Spanish-American War, the tightly packed infantry ranks of the Civil War years largely had disappeared, and the army's emphasis on firepower and maneuverability had increased substantially.[8]

In the immediate postwar years, however, the War Department and the army's senior leaders gave little attention to two important and interrelated issues for which the experience of four years of war simply had not produced consensus: the development of a uniquely American body of military theory to guide the planning and fighting of the nation's future wars and the standards of preparation and performance required of officers entrusted with the authority of command. In many ways, the latter challenge seemed more capable of resolution than the former. The dramatic reduction in the size of the army in 1865 gave the War Department an opportunity to fill officer vacancies in Regular regiments with battle-tested veterans; officers who had served as generals of U.S. Volunteers now reverted to their permanent (and sometimes significantly lower) U.S. Army ranks, while the War Department could select from an expansive pool of battle-proven volunteers to fill remaining slots. This fortuitous situation in the 1860s created a bottleneck of middle-aged and older Civil War veterans in the 1870s, 1880s, and beyond that blocked the advancement of ambitious and capable junior officers commissioned after 1865. By the mid-1870s, an element of "young Turk" reformers emerged within the army, calling for a wide range of highly controversial personnel changes, from the establishment of a mandatory retirement age to a merit-based promotion system that eliminated once and for all the old seniority system. Just as it had before the war, military education became an important element of any proposal for merit-based advancement.

The young Turks' vision fit comfortably into the even broader reformist movement that was breaking over large segments of educated American society in the postwar years. Members of a great number of occupational specialties that relied primarily upon intellectual authority rather than physical skills demanded acceptance of their status as discrete professions. Doctors, attorneys, scientists, educators, librarians, and practitioners of various newly emerging academic disciplines all made their cases, invariably pointing to their educational requirements for admission, standards of ethical behavior and performance, and advancement based upon evidence of continuous intellectual development. The army's reform element adopted the same tactics. To that end, leaders pushed for the development of a progressive, career-long officer-education system in which West Point stood simply as a starting point.[9]

Military-education reformers did not appreciate that they were preaching to a nation tired of thinking about war, however. Moreover, the rise of the Grand Army of the Republic and its ardent advocacy of the American volunteer soldier made it impossible to obtain much of a hearing—or funding—in Congress, where so many former citizen-soldiers now held the reins of political power.[10] As a consequence, the army undertook much of its reform effort from the inside. By the mid-1880s, it had adopted stricter requirements for commissioning, developed promotion examinations for officers seeking promotion at least through the rank of captain, and established a mandatory retirement age of sixty-four. Other signs of institutional maturity began to appear, as well. While the *United States*

Service Magazine ceased publication in 1868, the *Army and Navy Journal* continued to thrive. In 1879 it was joined by the *Journal of the Military Service Institution of the United States*; individual professional journals for infantrymen, cavalry, and artillerymen began publication by the end of the century. Officers had ready access to the journals in newly established post libraries, and junior officers met to discuss their content in informal post seminars called lyceums.

Even the long-desired system of schools for advanced officer education began to take shape. After Upton completed his revision of the tactics of the combat arms, Sherman sent him on a global tour of military schools. After Upton published his report in 1878 as *The Armies of Asia and Europe*, Sherman named him commandant of the new Artillery School at Fortress Monroe, a school for senior lieutenants and captains.[11] Upton, for one, insisted that he would not run a mere finishing school to hone the tactical skills of battery commanders. Since artillery most often supported infantry in battle, he armed his officers with rifles on the drill field to help them appreciate the reach and the limitations of foot soldiers' capabilities. In the classroom, he used artillery deployments from the Civil War campaigns in which he served instead of imaginary textbook scenarios to inject a note of realism and practicality into their lessons.

Upton's program inspired emulation, of course, and in 1881 the Infantry and Cavalry School opened at Fort Leavenworth. The establishment of the new schools spawned great interest in the officer corps. What should the curricula of the new schools emphasize? Some argued in support of very practical training in the tactics of the students' particular branch at a level appropriate to their rank and experience. Others, of course, saw these schools as the most appropriate locus for officers to enter upon an increasingly sophisticated study of the art of war that would not merely prepare them to execute the duties of their current posting but also ready them for greater responsibilities in future assignments. These advocates, in short, envisioned the kind of school system already thriving in many European military cultures, one that was consistent with the vision that Jomini and other military writers had advanced.

The latter approach won out. The new institutions stressed problem-solving that required thought, analysis, and solutions written in a newly standardized format that governed the preparation of a commander's order to execute a movement. By the end of the decade, graduation from any of these branch schools officially became part of an officer's professional record, appropriate notice appeared in key army publications such as the *Army Register*, and promotion and assignment boards viewed such achievement positively.

As more and more graduates from the army's new midcareer schools excelled in their new postings, the service's professional culture swung decisively in favor of the educated officer. Pockets of skepticism still lingered, of course. Most of the doubters could be found among the onetime citizen-soldiers whose Civil War combat records won them their direct commissions into the postwar Regular Army despite their lack of a West Point education. These men often regarded the new army schools as irrelevant or even frivolous. They tended to agree with the fellow citizen-soldier who had proclaimed at war's end: "Education is desirable, commendable, and should be promoted; but the experience of the past five years shows that educated military men are not all able military men." What American army officers needed "as much as anything else, is a department of '*horse sense.*'"[12] Even twenty years later, these same officers still complained that too much schooling eroded physical heartiness; they bemoaned the injustice of denying a commission to an ambitious and fit man because he could not explain "who fought at the battle of Bladensburg or matters of equal import." Even as late as 1898, reactionary officers such as Colonel George S. Anderson still complained that "we are all too old to have wisdom crammed down our throats like food down the necks of Strasburg geese."[13]

The sudden outbreak of the Spanish-American War, however, caught the new education system unprepared to meet all the army's immediate needs. While midcareer officers clearly benefited from their new education opportunities, the army still had not opened a school for its more senior officers, those who might fill billets as generals or senior staff officers in time of war. Thus, when the Spanish-American War began, the army—just as in 1861—had no pool of educated soldiers prepared to take on the responsibilities of high command. President William McKinley consequently reverted to the expedient Lincoln had relied upon, filling general officer vacancies in his new army of U.S. volunteers from sources outside the Regular Army, most notably the commissioning of former Civil War generals—Union and Confederate alike—who had not worn a uniform since 1865. As a result, the brief war against Spain affected far more important institutional change in a much shorter time than the conflict of 1861–65 ever achieved. Thanks to the initiative and energy of Secretary of War Elihu Root—who drew inspiration from Colonel Upton's final work, *The Military Policy of the United States*—the U.S. Army War College, the service's capstone educational institution for its most promising majors and lieutenant colonels, opened its doors in Washington, D.C., in 1901. Moreover, Root assigned it to the most appropriate slot in the army table of organization that he could devise: he made it part of the newly established General Staff, an organizational improvement that Jomini and his era of military theorists—and many critics during the Civil War—had long recommended.[14] As the center for war planning and education, the General Staff quickly became the intellectual center of the army. The era of the "heaven-born" general in the U.S. Army finally had ended.

But the Spanish-American War did nothing to solve one of the thorniest questions of all: which of the masters of military thought would become the voice of intellectual authority in the U.S. Army? Jomini's stock had sunk. No other strategic thinker—European or American—had emerged as a likely successor. The army found no equivalent to the U.S. Navy's Captain Alfred Thayer Mahan—Dennis Hart Mahan's son—whose *Influence of Sea Power upon History* already commanded attention and respect in the world's greatest navies. Thus, the U.S. Army's ambiguous relationship with military theory continued into the twentieth century. During the remainder of the nineteenth century, as the various new army schools opened, their curricula did not feature subcourses devoted to the theory of the art of war or the devising of military strategy. Even the Army War College did not include lectures or discussions of the strategic thought of any specific military theorist on a regular basis. The U.S. Army had no place for Jomini, but it also did not identify a replacement whose ideas might provide intellectual guidance to the nation's future strategic leaders.

The U.S. Army officer schools did recognize, however, the value of a generalized concept of "principles of war." Not all officers accepted their validity—Captain James Chester, a vocal critic, rejected the utility of "immutable scientific deductions" drawn from military history, arguing they could be upset by "any greasy mechanic" in a single day—but such men became a shrinking minority.[15] To sharpen critical thinking skills, the faculty at the Leavenworth schools developed two different approaches to the study of war that spread throughout the army education system, each proceeding from a belief that "the secrets of the art of war are to be found on the pages of military history."[16] The first, called the "applicatory method" by its originator, Captain Eben Swift, required military students in the late nineteenth century to study in depth a military campaign—most often from the Civil War—and draw out the military principles it illustrated; a correct answer, however, presumed the student identified the one chosen by the instructor for emphasis. Later, in the early twentieth century, the army schools switched to the use of the "source method," which required students to read after-action reports and other primary documents to reconstruct their own battle narrative and illustrate those principles of war they believed their research had uncovered; the intellectual rigor of this approach truly challenged students to think for themselves. Students attending the Army War College in the years leading up to World War I used this second method in the preparation of essays on Civil War campaigns intended to serve as the basis for an official U.S. Army history of that conflict. Neither of the two methods, however, worked from a War Department–authorized, commonly understood list of principles of war.[17]

On the eve of the American entry into World War I, the U.S. Army apparently considered the issue settled. Definitively ending its intellectually amorphous approach to the study of the art of war, the General Staff borrowed from British and French practice to include a list of ten "combat principles" in its 1914 edition of its *Field Service Regulations* and sixteen numbered paragraphs for the use of mounted forces in the same year's *Cavalry Service Regulations* to advance the process of setting down a single set of principles to direct officers' thinking and planning. Even if that list was not based on a fully developed theoretical foundation of its own making and included very little of relevance to high-level, strategic decision making, the U.S. Army finally decided upon an intellectual direction that some officers had begun to seek before Fort Sumter.[18] Its reliance on numbered principles suggested that the spirit of Jomini and the Military Enlightenment still lived.

As the schools worked through their uncomfortable relationship between military theory and strategy and generalship during the years between the Civil War and World War I, they did little to address the gap left open by the antebellum military classics: the importance of the human element—sometimes called the moral element—of war and its impact on army operations. An army of a republic that relied upon citizen-soldiers in time of war needed to pay close attention to the topic. The value of the individual ranked high among Americans' strongest cultural values. Northerners of the nineteenth century never viewed the exigencies of war as an acceptable explanation for excessive loss of life, especially among their kinsmen who volunteered to serve in the army's ranks. Additionally, as Drew Gilpin Faust has explained, Americans of the Victorian era possessed very strong beliefs about the importance of a "Good Death" that eased passage into eternal life with spiritual preparation and the comfort of loved ones. In the "sudden and almost unnoticed death of the soldier slain in the disorder of battle, [and] the unattended deaths of unidentified diseased and wounded men denied these consolations," she noted, the Civil War could "have provided the material for an exemplary text on how not to die."[19] War's dehumanizing effects became a common fear voiced in eulogies, in sermons, and in the rich hospital literature, a theme only occasionally tempered by promise of redemption.[20]

The Overland Campaign, studied here, represented only one hard-fought campaign that added greatly to the human cost of the Northern war effort. Even though Grant's hammering of Lee's forces ranked him "with that class of generals who have been named Thor-strikers," as journalist William Swinton asserted, he had exacted a high price in blood for each forward step.[21] Earlier in the war, after Fredericksburg, Abraham Lincoln had decried the "awful arithmetic of the fight," but he noted "if the same battle were to be fought over again, every day, through a week of days, with the same relative results, the army under Lee would be wiped out to its last man, the Army of the Potomac would still be a mighty host, [and] the war would be over." All he needed was a general who "can face the arithmetic," since "the end of the war will be at hand when he shall be discovered."[22] Lincoln had found that general in Grant. Grant's single-minded purpose revealed itself to surgeon John H. Brinton, a friend who spent a night at army headquarters during the fighting at Spotsylvania and who later recounted the general's reaction to his chief of staff's daily casualty report. When told of his army's great loss and exaggerated estimates of even greater Confederate losses, Grant simply had nodded and said, "Then we are still gaining on them, still a little ahead."[23] It was fortunate for Grant that such a comment did not become part of the public record.

The repercussions of the cost of the Overland Campaign and the reverses of the midsummer of 1864 had extended beyond the army to the Northern home front. As journalist Swinton noted, "war is sustained quite as much by the moral energy of a people as by its material resources," and "the former must be active to bring out and make available the latter." No other six-week period so seriously compromised the integrity of the Army of the Potomac as did those bloody days from 3 May to 22 June 1864. A string of failures that followed in the aftermath—especially the Battle of the Crater on 30 July and several repulses and incomplete successes in breaking Lee's defenses in August and September—so seriously eroded Northern hopes for ultimate victory that Lincoln prepared for defeat at the polls in November. During the summer and fall, a number of three-year regiments—those that enlisted in the fall of 1861 and chose not to re-enlist when Secretary of War Stanton offered to veteranize them the previous winter—left for home. Some remaining veteran regiments had lost so many of their men that army headquarters ordered them to be consolidated with other equally battered units from their home state to create a single viable command, continuing a process that broke for good the most prized bond of a soldier's unit identity. Some regiments received entirely new companies that were forwarded to the front already bearing a letter designation that had been reassigned from a battle-depleted unit previously disbanded or consolidated with another. Newly raised and untested Pennsylvania regiments, bearing numerical designations in the 190s and 200s, and high-numbered regiments from other loyal states appeared on the army's table of organization in the latter half of 1864 and early 1865 to refresh the army's numbers, if not its soul. As journalist Swinton concluded: "Had not success elsewhere come to brighten the horizon, it would have been difficult to have raised [these] new forces to recruit the Army of the Potomac, which, shaken in its structure, its valor quenched in blood, and thousands of its ablest officers killed and wounded, was the Army of the Potomac no more."[24]

Still, victory ultimately did bless the Union cause. While the Union soldier in the ranks entered the pantheon of national heroes—his image in granite and bronze adorning thousands of war memorials on courthouse lawns and town squares across the loyal states—few but the survivors themselves knew the physical, emotional, and psychological toll exacted from them on the field of battle. Generals did not write about it in their memoirs. It seemed somehow out of place to talk about such distasteful matters in volumes celebrating a victory. Victorian mores and masculine sensibilities required them to bear their burden in silence. A grateful nation provided "soldiers' homes" for those who could not cope and pensions to help injured veterans find their way in life. Otherwise, with the exception of the prisoner-of-war experience, the human cost of war as experienced by the soldier in the ranks remained an unwritten chapter of the conflict.

The professional officers who led the Union armies during the Civil War represented a military culture that measured progress exclusively by positive mission completion. Institutional success trumped the loss of individual lives. Thus, Grant's expression of genuine regret for the high casualties suffered in the failed 3 June 1864 charge at Cold Harbor remains notable for its exceptional nature. Even a full decade after Appomattox, the top-down perspective employed by generals showed through clearly when Sherman considered the nature of various levels of army organization. When he wrote about regiments, he asserted that colonels should "have a personal acquaintance with every officer and man in his command"—not to get to know them, but so they could learn to respect him and to develop "a feeling of pride and affection" for him that would cause them to "naturally look to him." Sherman viewed captains in much the same way. Considering the company level of organization to be "the true unit of discipline," Sherman was convinced that a "good captain makes a good company." He despised the notion of allowing private soldiers to elect their officers—a hallmark of the Civil War's volunteer regiments—and considered their inevitably self-interested choice of a captain to be the "best reason why he should be appointed by the colonel."[25]

Less than a decade after Appomattox, however, the world's major armies slowly began to revise their thinking about the human factors in war. During the Franco-Prussian War, French colonel Charles-Jean-Jacques-Joseph Ardant du Picq published a thin volume entitled simply *Battle Studies*. Written over the course of the previous decade, this work became du Picq's only major contribution to military theory; a Prussian shell killed him near Longeville-lès-Metz in August 1870. He set himself apart from other military writers from the start, noting: "For me as a soldier, the smallest detail caught on the spot and in the heat of action is more instructive than all the Thiers and the Jominis in the world. They speak, no doubt, for the heads of states and armies but they never show me what I wish to know—a battalion, a company, a squad, in action."[26]

In his discussion of modern battle, du Picq decried the consistency with which theory-bound generals forgot a simple truth: while the "art of war is subjected to many modifications by industrial and scientific progress," the one thing that remains constant is "the heart of man." Victory in battle, he argued, "is a matter of morale." Regardless of leadership, organization, discipline, and tactics, "the human heart in the supreme moment of battle is the basic factor." The army certainly needed to rely upon discipline to "make men fight in spite of themselves," but it also had an obligation to promote within the ranks of its smaller components what du Picq labeled "unity"—his term for unit cohesion. "The soldiers themselves have emotion," he noted. "The sense of duty, discipline, pride, the example of their officers and above all their coolness, sustain them and prevent their fear from becoming terror." But, in du Picq's mind, the soldier-officer bond became exponentially stronger when the organization of an army took man's social nature into account. A military culture that acknowledged as important elements in war a soldier's "respect for and confidence in his chiefs; [his] confidence in his comrades and fear of their reproaches and retaliation if he abandons them in danger; [and] his desire to go where others do without trembling more than they" and applied this understanding to organization and leadership greatly increased its likelihood of victory.[27]

Interestingly, du Picq had supported his most enduring conclusions with at least a few comments on the progress of the American Civil War. His observations did not flatter the U.S. Army. "The Americans have shown us what happens in modern battle to large armies without cohesion," he wrote. Civil War battles merely threw huge mass armies against each other to no decisive end and with excessive loss of life. "The theory of the strong battalions is a shameful theory," du Picq wrote, noting that "it does not reckon on courage but on the amount of human flesh." Numbers eclipsed individual quality, and, to du Picq's way of thinking, "quality alone produces real effect." If soldiers did not believe that their commanders valued their lives, they could not be counted upon to give their best, even in an emergency. To that end, du Picq considered it imperative that the army fulfill its responsibilities to meet the soldiers' basic needs or, especially in a republic, face the wrath of an angry citizenry. In this regard, du Picq praised the American people, who, through the action of the Sanitary Commission and Christian Commission, went "themselves to see how their soldiers were treated and," when they observed a need unmet by the government, "provided for them themselves." He doubted that French citizens would do the same.[28]

Du Picq's work illustrated one expression of the rise of Military Romanticism that, in the last half of the nineteenth century, partially eclipsed in influence the Military Enlightenment school that Jomini had represented. As described by historian John A. Lynn, this intellectual approach "identified war as a human phenomenon ruled by psychology and will" rather than by reason-based rules and principles.[29] Clausewitz's *On War* stands out as Military Romanticism's most influential masterwork. But just as the U.S. Army showed little interest in adopting Jomini or any other classic from the Military Enlightenment to guide its own thinking about war, it showed no greater interest in the works of this new school of military thought. While *Battle Studies* quickly drew the attention of all the major armies in Europe, American military professionals only learned of du Picq's work during World War I. The first edition edited for U.S. Army use did not appear in print until 1921, the great lapse of time largely attributable, the translators noted, to the service's continuing "scarcity of thinking men with military training."[30]

At the outbreak of the American Civil War, the military culture of the U.S. Army had taken only its first few unsteady steps toward institutional maturity. Until 1861, when the nation required the army's services, good fortune and tactical skill had fended off attackers and asserted American authority outside its borders. The army had learned to fight battles and—as the Mexican-American War demonstrated—conduct individual independent campaigns. It even demonstrated signs of developing a logistical capacity to support a large force in active operations. But the army—and the government it served—had not yet accumulated the intellectual wherewithal to know how to plan for grand-scale war, mobilize the nation's resources to support it, and conduct it to a successful end. At the start of the conflict, the concept of strategy existed in the minds of the Union's senior political and military leaders only as a theoretical abstraction—if it existed at all. The search for a general with sufficient vision—regardless of whether innate genius or rigorous study provided the spark—to grasp that complex concept, transform theory into a suitable plan of operations to accomplish Lincoln's war aims, and then oversee its execution defied an easy solution. As a consequence, thousands of loyal Union men, most of whom freely volunteered to serve in their nation's hour of trial, died on the battlefield, in overcrowded and unsanitary hospitals, and in prison pens as Northern military and political leaders sought a way forward. In earlier crises, Americans looked to the inspiration of both the heavens and the past to provide guidance as it entered into uncharted waters, but Jomini and the entire body of antebellum military thought he represented provided far less useful guidance than the Civil War generation required for the dimensions of the challenge they faced.

When Jomini died in 1869, notice of his death appeared in newspapers around the globe. Americans did not mourn his passing. Indeed, he had come to mean little more than empty promise and intellectual fraud. As a New Yorker sardonically proclaimed:

Jomini will be remembered gratefully by War Correspondents, who "crammed" for elaborate reports of battles by reading his books; who profoundly impressed his readers and diverted attention from their own ignorance by affecting a familiarity with "Jomini"; who approved or condemned strategic movements on the authority of "Jomini"; and who disguised the poverty of knowledge of engagements and the consequent helplessness to convey an intelligent understanding of them to others, in copious reference to "Jomini."[31]

Not all would judge him quite so harshly. Nor would most confess so freely the limited degree to which the Civil War generation truly engaged with his ideas or found them genuinely useful. But Jomini's fall underscored with finality that, even in victory, Americans remained neophytes in understanding the complexity of war.

ACKNOWLEDGMENTS

I would like to thank the Penn State Department of History, especially Professor A. G. Roeber, for supporting the research effort required to produce this work. Likewise, I would like to thank Director William A. Blair, as well as all the faculty, graduate students, donors, and supporters of the George and Ann Richards Civil War Era Center, who listened to my ideas, offered useful insights, and provided a lively and collegial environment in which to pursue my research. The College of Liberal Arts at Penn State University also provided essential support, including a timely sabbatical that allowed me to transform the lectures into a polished manuscript.

Special thanks go to Colonel Tom and Barbara Vossler, my Gettysburg family, for all manner of moral and logistical support, especially during the particularly challenging time following my father's passing away in March 2011. Tom's insightful reading of the entire manuscript, sharpened by his thirty years of service as an infantry officer, cannot be surpassed. Dusty and Thor helped, too.

My deepest gratitude goes to Steven and Janice Brose, whose unstinting support of the scholarly endeavors of the Richards Center makes them very special folks indeed. This volume began as a series of lectures that they endowed, and all of us at the Richards Center hope they will continue to take a great sense of satisfaction from their tangible contribution to cutting-edge scholarship in nineteenth-century American history.

NOTES

Abbreviations

ALP	Abraham Lincoln Papers, Library of Congress, Washington, D.C.
ANJ	*Army and Navy Journal*
NYH	*New York Herald*
NYT	*New York Times*
OR	U.S. War Department, *War of the Rebellion: A Compilation of the Official Records of the Union and Confederate Armies*. 128 vols. Washington, D.C.: Government Printing Office, 1880–1901
PI	*Philadelphia Inquirer*
PP	*Philadelphia Press*
SFB	*San Francisco Daily Evening Bulletin*
USAMHI	U.S. Army Military History Institute, U.S. Army Heritage and Education Center, Carlisle, Pa.
USSM	*United States Service Magazine*

Introduction

1. Hittle, *Jomini and His Summary of the Art of War*, 2.

2. There is no truly scholarly modern biography of Jomini written in English. According to historian Azar Gat, the oldest of the three extant French-language biographies of Jomini—one written by Swiss colonel Ferdinand Lecomte, who will appear briefly in these pages—remains the most useful. See Gat, *A History of Military Thought*, 109n3. The most useful English-language reviews of Jomini's work, in addition to Gat's assessment, remain Brinton, Craig, and Gilbert, "Jomini"; and Shy, "Jomini." See also Alger, *Antoine-Henri Jomini*.

3. See Lynn, *Battle*, especially chap. 4. See also Howard, "Jomini and the Classical Tradition in Military Thought," 5–9.

4. Gat, *A History of Military Thought*, 45–55. See also Palmer, "Frederick the Great, Guibert, Bülow."

5. From Jomini's 1804 *Treatise on the Art of War*, quoted in Gat, *A History of Military Thought*, 114. See also Brinton, Craig, and Gilbert, "Jomini," 81.

6. Lloyd, *The History of the Late War in Germany*, 139.

7. Gat, *A History of Military Thought*, 69–80.

8. Quoted in Williams, "The Military Leadership of North and South," 44.

9. Charles von Hapsburg, *Principles of War*, 1–2. See also Gat, *A History of Military Thought*, 104, 128.

10. Hittle, *Jomini and His Summary of the Art of War*, 42.

11. Ibid., 43; Jomini, *The Art of War*, 61–63. The 1862 Lippincott printing is the edi-

tion that was readily available to most Civil War officers after the first year of the war. All references to this work cited in this volume have been taken from the 1862 edition.

12. Jomini, *The Art of War*, 61–63.

13. Donald, *Lincoln Reconsidered*, 86–88.

14. Williams, "The Military Leadership of North and South," 42, 46–47. See also Williams, "The Return of Jomini—Some Thoughts on Recent Civil War Writing."

15. Weigley, *The American Way of War*, 83.

16. Harsh, "Battlesword and Rapier," 133.

17. See Jones, "Jomini and the Strategy of the American Civil War"; and Alger, *The Quest for Victory*, 34–55. Alger, however, still tends to view Jomini's ideas as the primary intellectual driving force of the era. See also Marszalek, "Where Did Winfield Scott Find His Anaconda?"

18. See, for instance, such works as Hattaway and Jones, *How the North Won*; Beringer, Hattaway, Jones, and Still, *Why the South Lost the Civil War*; Dougherty, *Civil War Leadership and Mexican War Experience*; Stoker, *The Grand Design*; and Swain, "'The Hedgehog and the Fox': Jomini, Clausewitz, and History."

19. See Hsieh, *West Pointers and the Civil War*, 6–7, for a particularly trenchant discussion of this phenomenon.

20. Morrison, *"The Best School in the World,"* 96–97.

21. Donald, *Lincoln Reconsidered*, 89.

22. Moten, *The Delafield Commission and the American Military Profession*, 59. For a traditional view, see Hagerman, *The American Civil War and the Origins of Modern Warfare*, 8.

23. Quoted in Hagerman, *The American Civil War and the Origins of Modern Warfare*, 23.

24. U.S. Congress, *Report of the Committee Appointed to Examine the Organization, System of Discipline, and Course of Instruction of the Military Academy*, 183.

25. Ibid., 191. Carl von Decker's work was abridged and translated into English by Major Inigo Jones of Prince Albert's Hussars and published in London in 1848. See Decker, *The Three Arms*.

26. Hattaway and Jones, *How the North Won*, 12.

27. See Cunliffe, *Soldiers and Civilians*, 19–27, for an explanation of the professional, antiprofessional, and antimilitarist mind-sets in antebellum America.

28. See Skelton, *An American Profession of Arms*, 238–59.

29. U.S. Congress, *Report of the Committee Appointed to Examine the Organization, System of Discipline, and Course of Instruction of the Military Academy*, 108.

30. See, for instance, the debate over French and British tactical manuals in Crackel, "The Battle of Queenston Heights, 13 October 1812," 33–56.

31. "West Point 'Horse Sense,'" *ANJ* 3 (31 March 1866): 505; Hagerman, *The American Civil War and the Origins of Modern Warfare*, 14.

32. Delafield, *Report on the Art of War in Europe in 1854, 1855, and 1856*, 1–3.

33. See Shy, "Jomini," 173.

34. See Lynn, *Battle*, 192–214; and Gat, *A History of Military Thought*, 141–58.

35. Mahan, *An Elementary Treatise on Advanced-Guard, Out-Post, and Detachment Service of Troops*, 31.

Chapter 1

1. "The Education of Generals," *ANJ* 1 (5 September 1863): 26.

2. These widely reprinted items may be found in Townsend, *Anecdotes of the Civil War in the United States*, 249–56. Townsend served on Scott's staff at the start of the war.

3. *NYH*, 13 April 1861.

4. Jomini, *The Art of War*, 59.

5. Neff, *Justice in Blue and Gray*, 29.

6. Jomini, *The Art of War*, 12–34.

7. Ibid., 45.

8. Scott, *Military Dictionary*, 574. See also Bartholomees, "A Survey of the Theory of Strategy," 13–14.

9. For a further discussion of the "ends-ways-means" approach to the study of strategy, see Lykke, "Toward an Understanding of Military Strategy," 3–7.

10. *OR*, series 1, vol. 1, 338–39. See also Sears, *The Civil War Papers of George B. McClellan*, 13.

11. Nicolay and Hay, *Abraham Lincoln*, 4:300.

12. *OR*, series 1, vol. 1, 178.

13. Marszalek, "Where Did Winfield Scott Find His Anaconda?," 79. See also Dougherty, *Civil War Leadership and Mexican War Experience*, 64–68.

14. *Napoleon's Maxims of War*, 5. Whether or not Scott approved this publication is unclear; the absence of Scott's rank suggests that the publisher took liberties.

15. Steece, *A Republican Military System*, 23.

16. Joseph Gardner Swift to Abraham Lincoln, 8 May 1861, ALP.

17. "Action," *PI*, 5 May 1861.

18. See, for instance, *PI*, 13 June 1861; *Lowell (MA) Daily Citizen and News*, 14 June 1861; and *NYH*, 16 June 1861.

19. Jomini, *The Art of War*, 79.

20. Nicolay and Hay, *Abraham Lincoln*, 4:303–4.

21. Ropp, "Anacondas Anyone?"

22. Jomini, *Treatise on Grand Military Operations*, xix–xx. Samuel Beckley Holabird penned his preface in May 1861.

23. "National Encouragement to the Novelties of Inventors," *PI*, 17 July 1861.

24. *Napoleon's Maxims of War*, 22.

25. "True War Cry—Hasten Slowly," *Wisconsin Daily Patriot*, 20 July 1861.

26. "On to Richmond," *Portland (ME) Daily Advertiser*, 20 July 1861.

27. "True as Gospel," *Lowell (MA) Daily Citizen and News*, 1 July 1861.

28. "Action," *PI*, 5 May 1861.

29. *Pittsfield (MA) Sun*, 25 July 1861; clipped from the *Albany (NY) Atlas and Argus*.

30. Carl Schurz to Abraham Lincoln, 6 August 1861, ALP.

31. McClellan, *The Armies of Europe*, 9, 12, 28, 32.

32. *OR*, series 1, vol. 5, 6–8.

33. *OR*, series 1, vol. 5, 9–11.

34. "Inactivity of the American Army," *NYT*, 9 January 1862.

35. Original in *New York Post*; reprinted as "Approaching Movements," *New Hampshire Sentinel*, 16 January 1862, and as "The Break of Day—Gen. McClellan's Strategy," *Lancaster (PA) Intelligencer*, 21 January 1862.

36. *Springfield (MA) Republican*, 25 January 1862.

37. Lincoln, *What Lincoln Read*, 69. It appears that the president's oldest son, Robert, checked out Jomini's *Operations Militaire* on 1 March 1865, but the editor misspelled the author's name as "Domini" (95).

38. Lincoln to Buell, 13 January 1862, in Basler, *The Collected Works of Abraham Lincoln*, 5:98. Emphasis in original.

39. *OR*, series 1, vol. 8, 508–11.

40. "Another Attack on Gen. McClellan," *Richmond (VA) Daily Dispatch*, 25 March 1862.

41. Quoted in McPherson, *Tried by War*, 76. See also McPherson's comments on the possible apocryphal nature of this familiar event.

42. Burlingame and Ettlinger, *The Complete Civil War Diary of John Hay*, 36.

43. Jomini, *The Art of War*, 5–6.

44. Jomini, *The Political and Military History of the Campaign of Waterloo*.

45. Duparcq, *Elements of Military Art and History*, 3.

46. Ibid., 9, 171–85.

47. Marmont, *The Spirit of Military Institutions* (1864 reprint), 23, 28.

48. Marmont, *The Spirit of Military Institutions* (1862 edition), vi.

49. Ford, *War Letters*, 199.

50. Schalk, *The Art of War*, vii–viii.

51. Ibid., 11. See Alger, *The Quest for Victory*, 52–53, for a rare mention of Schalk's work by a historian, as well as for a typical assessment that Schalk—like so many other writers—simply repackaged Jomini without accounting for differences.

52. Schalk, *The Art of War*, 25–54, especially 25–28.

53. Emil Schalk to Abraham Lincoln, 23 June 1862, ALP.

54. See McPherson, *Tried by War*, 101–3, on criticism of Stanton by McClellan's friends.

55. Quoted in Hattaway and Jones, *How the North Won*, 238.

56. See Marszalek, *Commander of All Lincoln's Armies*, 135–54, for a sound assessment of Halleck's first six months as general in chief.

57. Welles, *Diary of Gideon Welles*, 1:122.

58. Quoted in Marszalek, *Commander of All Lincoln's Armies*, 149.

59. Emil Schalk to Abraham Lincoln, 23 September 1862, ALP.

60. See Hattaway and Jones, *How the North Won*, 239, 250–51, 286, 288–89, 293, 689, for a positive assessment of the Lincoln-Halleck team based primarily on Halleck's ability to convince Lincoln to adopt a strategy that called for concentration in the west—as the more promising theater of war—to avoid an unproductive siege of Richmond.

61. Entry for 15 December 1862, in Gurowski, *Diary for November 18, 1862, to October 18, 1863*, 30.

62. *New York Evening Post*, 16 April 1863.

63. *Boston Daily Advertiser*, 12 November 1862.

64. "The Scattering Policy," *Milwaukee Sentinel*, 18 April 1863.

65. Quoted in "The Diary of Count Gurowski," *ANJ* 1 (20 February 1864): 405.

66. Ford, *War Letters*, 33–34.

67. "From Gen. Rosecrans' Army," *PP*, 10 November 1862.

68. Schalk, *Campaigns of 1862 and 1863*.

69. See "New Publications," *PP*, 9 April 1863.

70. Ibid.

71. "The War," *PI*, 6 April 1863. Emphasis in original.

72. "Theory of the War," *New York Evening Post*, 14 April 1863; reprinted in the *Daily National Intelligencer* (Washington, D.C.) 16 April 1863.

73. "The News," *PI*, 20 April 1863.

74. Duncan, *Blue-Eyed Child of Fortune*, 351.

75. Entry of 18 March 1863, in Gurowski, *Diary from November 18, 1862, to October 18, 1863*, 173.

76. "Mr. Emil Schalk on the Last Operation on the Rappahannock, and the Causes of Its Failure," *PP* (published the Saturday before). Reprinted in the *Boston Daily Advertiser*, 11 May 1863; the *NYH*, 11 May 1863; and widely throughout the North.

77. "Shall We Abandon the Coast?," *North American and United States Gazette* (Philadelphia), 21 April 1863.

78. "Strategy—Emil Schalk," *NYT*, 24 June 1863.

79. Pilsen, *Reply of Lieut.-Col. Pilsen*, 1.

80. "Schalk!," in Harte, *Stories and Poems and Other Uncollected Writings*, 356–57. The poem originally appeared in the *Golden Era*, July 19, 1863.

81. Chesney, *A Military View of Recent Campaigns in Virginia and Maryland*, 2. For more on Chesney, see Luvaas, *The Military Legacy of the Civil War*, 100–105.

82. Lecomte, *The War in the United States*, 5. For more on Lecomte, see Luvaas, *The Military Legacy of the Civil War*, 86–91.

83. Szabad, *Modern War*, 130.

84. "The Lesson of the Disaster on the Rappahannock—The Blunders of Two Campaigns," *NYH*, 12 May 1863.

85. Jomini, *The Art of War*, 163.

86. De Peyster, *Winter Campaigns*, 4. For more on de Peyster's life during the Civil War, see Allaben, *John Watts de Peyster*, 2:58–67.

87. De Peyster, *Practical Strategy*, 2, 4, 6, 9, 50, 59.

88. "The Campaign in Virginia," *North American and United States Gazette* (Philadelphia), 11 November 1863.

89. "Practical Strategy," *ANJ* 1 (17 October 1863): 115.

90. Bigelow, *William Conant Church and the "Army and Navy Journal,"* 106–7.

91. "Information Wanted," *ANJ* 1 (26 September 1863): 67–68.

92. "The Military Situation," *ANJ* 1 (10 October 1863): 97.

93. See Hattaway and Jones, *How the North Won*, 455–56, for a particularly insightful dialog between Halleck and Lincoln over reinforcing Rosecrans.

94. Welles, *Diary of Gideon Welles*, 1:384.

95. "The Lessons of Rosecrans' Repulse," *ANJ* 1 (26 September 1863): 72.

96. "The Initiative of War," *ANJ* 1 (17 October 1863): 120.

97. "Successive and Rapid Blows," *ANJ* 1 (7 November 1863): 164.

98. "The Anaconda Policy," *ANJ* 1 (31 October 1863): 152.

99. "The Coming Campaign of General Grant," *ANJ* 1 (7 November 1863): 168.

100. "General Halleck on the Conduct of the War," *ANJ* 1 (19 December 1863): 264. Emphasis in original.

101. *Amherst (NH) Farmer's Cabinet*, 7 January 1864.

102. "The Lieutenant General," *ANJ* 1 (19 March 1864): 504.

103. "The Spring Campaign," *ANJ* 1 (20 February 1864): 408; "Bickerings in the North," *Richmond (VA) Examiner*, 6 May 1864. Emphasis in original.

104. "Editor's Special Department," *USSM* 1 (April 1864): 412–13.

105. Grant, *Personal Memoirs of U.S. Grant*, 1:38–40, 2:130–31, 142–43; "Concentration," *ANJ* 1 (7 May 1864): 616.

106. McPherson, *Tried by War*, 213.

107. Quoted in ibid, 214.

108. "The Truth Cannot Be Told," *Cincinnati Daily Enquirer*, 4 May 1864; "On to Richmond," *NYH*, 1 June 1864; "Concentration," *PI*, 4 June 1864; "Speech of Sen. Pomeroy," *NYH*, 5 June 1864.

109. See, for instance, Meade, *The Life and Letters of General George Gordon Meade*, 2:197, 202; Simpson and Berlin, *Sherman's Civil War*, 664, 667.

110. "The Last Man Called For," *Republican Compiler*, 25 July 1864.

111. Review of Dufour's *Strategy and Tactics* in *Atlantic Monthly* 14 (August 1864): 259–60.

112. "Public Opinion Concerning the War," *ANJ* 2 (24 September 1864): 72.

113. "The Shenandoah Campaign," *ANJ* 2 (1 October 1864): 88.

114. "The City," *PP*, 18 October 1864.

115. "Gen. Johnston's Career," *New Orleans Daily True Delta*, 13 August 1864; reprinted from the *NYT*.

116. *Wisconsin Daily Patriot*, 2 June 1864.

117. "General Sherman's Grand Movement," *NYH*, 23 November 1864.

118. "The Western Campaigns," *ANJ* 2 (10 December 1864): 248. See also McPherson, *Tried by War*, 251–52.

119. "Strength of the Enemy," *ANJ* 2 (19 November 1864): 201.

120. "Sherman's Grand March," *ANJ* 2 (3 December 1864): 232.

121. "Sherman at Savannah," *ANJ* 2 (17 December 1864): 264.

122. "Fruits of Sherman's Campaign," *ANJ* 2 (31 December 1864): 297.

123. "The Mustering of the Forces," *ANJ* 2 (25 March 1865): 488.

124. *Boston Daily Advertiser*, 21 April 1865.

125. "Things at the East," *SFB*, 3 May 1865.

126. "Speech of General Sherman at St. Louis," *ANJ* 2 (5 August 1865): 791.

127. "On Tactics in General," *ANJ* 2 (27 May 1865): 626.

128. "Jomini as a Military Man," *ANJ* 2 (12 August 1865): 806.

129. "On the Science of War," *ANJ* 2 (29 July 1865): 774.

130. "The War as a Military School," *North American and United States Gazette* (Philadelphia), 24 October 1864.

Chapter 2

1. "Popular Appreciation of Military Education," *ANJ* 1 (21 November 1863): 200.

2. See Goss, *The War within the Union High Command*, 24–50. See also Wood, *Civil War Generalship*, 50.

3. For some preliminary ideas on this topic, see Reardon, "From Genius to Intellect."

4. Lloyd, *The History of the Late War in Germany*, 58.

5. [Benton], *Thirty Years' View*, 186.

6. Jomini, *The Art of War*, 39, 51.

7. Halleck, *Elements of Military Art and Science*, 383, 405.

8. Jomini, *The Art of War*, 50–51.

9. Ibid., 298–99. Emphasis in original.

10. Ibid., 50, 53. Emphasis in original.

11. Ibid., 51.

12. For the best scholarly biographies of Scott, see Johnson, *Winfield Scott*; Eisenhower, *Agent of Destiny*; and Peskin, *Winfield Scott and the Profession of Arms*.

13. Keyes, *Fifty Years' Observations of Men and Events*, 39. See also Peskin, *Winfield Scott and the Profession of Arms*, 11. Peskin ultimately assessed Scott's intellectual prowess as that of a debater, not as a genuine scholar.

14. For an argument that suggests Scott was inspired by Jomini during his Mexican-American War experience, see Pohl, "The Influence of Antoine Henri de Jomini on Winfield Scott's Campaigns in the Mexican War," 85–110.

15. "The Great Victory," *Lancaster (PA) Intelligencer*, 25 June 1861.

16. "Wisdom, Patience and Firmness," *American Presbyterian*, 13 June 1861; "Young Blood," *New Hampshire Sentinel*, 24 October 1861.

17. Quoted in Peskin, *Winfield Scott and the Profession of Arms*, 245.

18. "Fun among the Soldiers," *Lebanon (PA) Advertiser*, 19 June 1861.

19. "Dissatisfaction of the Soldiers of the Regular Army, *PI*, 15 June 1861.

20. "Another Blunder and the Lesson It Teaches," *NYH*, 19 June 1861.

21. "Let Us Have No More Paper Generals," *PI*, 14 June 1861. Emphasis in original.

22. "Study of the Art of War," *PI*, 17 May 1861.

23. "The Recent Achievements of McClellan and Siegel the Result of Military Education," *PI*, 15 July 1861.

24. *PI*, 26 August 1861.

25. "Politics and Soldiering," *Springfield (MA) Weekly Republican*, 10 August 1861.

26. "Military Appointments," *PI*, 24 July 1861.

27. The best scholarly biography of McClellan remains Sears, *George B. McClellan: The Young Napoleon*. See also Rafuse, *McClellan's War*, for useful insights. McClellan's personal memoir, *McClellan's Own Story*, remains interesting for its coverage of the war through lenses only McClellan himself could bring to bear on it.

28. "Gen. McClelland's Military Genius," *Huntingdon (Pa.) Globe*, 30 July 1861.

29. "Important from Washington," *PI*, 24 July 1861.

30. *Wisconsin Daily Patriot*, 1 November 1861; reprinted from the *New York Tribune*.

31. See Tap, *Over Lincoln's Shoulder*, chaps. 2 and 3, for the committee's early work.

32. Ellet, *The Army of the Potomac and Its Mismanagement*, 16.

33. See Glatthaar, *Partners in Command*, 237–42.

34. Reprinted in the *Richmond Daily Dispatch*, 4 February 1862.

35. "Letter from 'Occasional,'" *PP*, 12 February 1862.

36. Quoted in "Political Attack on West Point," 51.

37. Gurowski, *Diary for March 4, 1861, to November 12, 1862*, 127–28.

38. "Regulars and Volunteers," *SFB*, 1 February 1862; reprinted from the *New York World*.

39. *PI*, 18 January 1862.

40. *PI*, 7 May 1862; *PP*, 31 May 1862.

41. Barnard, *The Peninsular Campaign and Its Antecedents*, 5.

42. Joinville, *The Army of the Potomac*, 4.

43. Wilkes, *McClellan*, 16.

44. "What Is to Be Decided at Richmond," *Deseret (UT) News*, 30 July 1862.

45. Denslow, *Fremont and McClellan*, 26.

46. Ibid., 27.

47. *OR*, series 1, vol. 11, 73–74.

48. Denslow, *Fremont and McClellan*, 29.

49. "The Virtue There Is in an 'If,'" *NYH*, 9 April 1862.

50. Richards, *A Brief History of the Rebellion*, 11.

51. Quoted in McPherson, *Tried by War*, 102.

52. Tap, *Over Lincoln's Shoulder*, 165.

53. "A General for the West," *PI*, 7 November 1861; *Albany (NY) Journal*, 13 December 1861.

54. *NYH*, 16 November 1861.

55. "Letter from St. Louis," *SFB*, 21 July 1862. See also Marszalek, *Commander of All Lincoln's Armies*, 118–19.

56. *PP*, 31 May 1862; *PI*, 7 May 1862.

57. "From Boston," *Springfield (MA) Republican*, 26 July 1862.

58. *OR*, series 2, vol. 17, 150.

59. See Sears, *Controversies and Commanders*, 131–66.

60. Quoted in Hattaway and Jones, *How the North Won*, 263.

61. "Gen. Meade," *New Haven Daily Palladium*, 3 August 1863; reprinted from the *Cincinnati Gazette*. "General Meade," *New Haven Palladium*, 19 October 1863; reprinted from the *Springfield (MA) Republican*.

62. De Peyster, *Practical Strategy*, 4.

63. "Wool on Military Genius," *NYH*, 7 May 1863.

64. *OR*, series 2, vol. 23, 518.

65. "Great Generals," *ANJ* 1 (4 April 1863): 77.

66. "Able Generalship," *ANJ* 1 (11 July 1863): 250.

67. Bigelow, *William Conant Church and the "Army and Navy Journal,"* 106–7.

68. "Our Military Commanders," *ANJ* 1 (29 August 1863): 10.

69. "Practical and Impractical Strategy," *ANJ* 1 (31 October 1863): 147.

70. "Jomini's Life of Napoleon," *USSM* 2 (August 1864): 128–29.

71. "Corps D'Armee," *ANJ* 1 (24 October 1864): 137.

72. C. W. Tolles, "Reorganization," *USSM* 2 (August 1864): 159–61.

73. "The Army of the Cumberland," *SFB*, 25 July 1863; reprinted from the *NYT*.

74. "Responsibilities of the Staff," *ANJ* 2 (13 February 1864): 393.

75. "Major General William T. Sherman," *USSM* 2 (September 1864): 255.

76. Webster, *Free Military School for Applicants for Commands of Colored Troops*, 3–12.

77. Quoted in Tap, *Over Lincoln's Shoulder*, 47.

78. See Boynton, *The History of West Point*. To avoid direct connection to the Civil War years, he ended his treatment in 1852.

79. "West Point," *North American Review* 97 (April 1864): 535.

80. Seymour, *Military Education*, 3.

81. "Concerning West Point and Its Graduates—A History and an Argument," *Milwaukee Sentinel*, 31 May 1864; reprinted widely from the *North American Review*.

82. Review of Boynton's *History of West Point*, *Atlantic Monthly* 13 (February 1864): 260.

83. "West Point," *North American Review* 97 (April 1864): 535, 540–41, 543.

84. "A Word about West Point," *ANJ* 1 (19 December 1863): 245.

85. On Grant, see McFeely, *Grant: A Biography*; Simpson, *Ulysses S. Grant*; and Waugh, *U.S. Grant*. Grant's own memoirs remain an excellent source on his views of the conduct of the war.

86. "The Value of the Victory," *PP*, 1 December 1863.

87. Orlando B. Willcox to Wife, 17 January 1864, in Scott, *Forgotten Valor*, 499.

88. Sherman to Grant, 10 March 1864, in Simpson and Berlin, *Sherman's Civil War*, 603.

89. Editorial note, *USSM* 1 (May 1864): 526.

90. "Lieutenant General Grant," *USSM* 1 (June 1864): 564.

91. "The Tactics and Characteristics of Grant and Lee," *Milwaukee Sentinel*, 16 May 1864; reprinted from the *New York World*.

92. Quoted in McPherson, *Tried by War*, 219.

93. On Sherman, see Marszalek, *Sherman: A Soldier's Passion for Order*; and Hirshson, *The White Tecumseh*. British military author B. H. Liddell Hart's *Sherman: Soldier, Realist, American* remains a very useful source. Sherman's two-volume memoirs, like Grant's own, remain essential reading for students of Civil War strategy and generalship.

94. See Andrews, *The North Reports the Civil War*, 552–84.

95. See especially Neely, *The Union Divided*, 80–88.

96. "General McClellan's Campaigns," *USSM* 1 (May 1864): 504, 516.

97. *Bangor (ME) Daily Whig and Courier*, 10 September 1864.

98. *PP*, 23 September 1864.

99. "Strength of the Enemy," *ANJ* 2 (19 November 1864): 200; "The Western Campaigns," *ANJ* (10 December 1864): 248.

100. "Sherman's Grand March," *ANJ* 2 (3 December 1864): 232.

101. For more on the Grant-Sherman team, see Glatthaar, *Partners in Command*, 135–62. See also Flood, *Grant and Sherman*.

102. "War and Peace," *ANJ* 2 (4 February 1865): 376.

103. "Sherman's Treaty," *ANJ* 2 (29 April 1865): 568.

104. See "Nebulae," *Galaxy* 1 (1866): 748–49.

105. Thomas W. Higginson, "Regular and Volunteer Officers," *Atlantic Monthly* 14 (September 1864): 348–57.

106. Untitled, *ANJ* 2 (24 September 1864): 72.

107. Volunteer, "Volunteer Officers," *ANJ* 2 (24 September 1864): 69.

108. Regular Graduate, "The Army and Its Training," *ANJ* 2 (8 April 1865): 518.

109. Undated *New York Tribune* article quoted in "Military Education and Military Appointments," *ANJ* 2 (17 June 1865): 675.

110. Vigo, "The Permanent Army," *ANJ* 2 (22 July 1865): 758.

111. Volunteer, "Volunteer Officers," 69. Emphasis in original.

112. See, for instance, "European Military Systems," *ANJ* 2 (20 May 1865): 611; and "Military Schools of the World," *ANJ* 2 (1 July 1865): 706–7.

Chapter 3

1. "Daring in War," *Brooklyn Daily Eagle*, 2 September 1862.

2. Jomini, *The Art of War*, 56–57, 162–63.

3. Jackson, *A Systematic View of the Formation, Discipline and Economy of Armies*, 79.

4. De Saxe, "My Reveries," 190–92.

5. Jomini, *The Art of War*, 59.

6. See Duncan, *The Medical Department of the United States Army in the Civil War*, for an overview of Union medical service. Unfortunately, Duncan says little about medical conditions at the start of the war. Adams, *Doctors in Blue*, 3–23, presents a fuller overview.

7. Craighill, *The 1862 Army Officer's Pocket Companion*, 253–55.

8. Adams, *Doctors in Blue*, 18.

9. Edward Jarvis, "The Sanitary Condition," 485–86.

10. See, for instance, Bowditch, *A Brief Plea for an Ambulance System for the Army of the United States*; Palfrey, *The Ambulance System*; and Balch, *Have We the Best Possible Ambulance System?*

11. See Dean, *Shook over Hell*, especially chap. 3; Lande, *Madness, Malingering, and Malfeasance*; and Judith Andersen, "'Haunted Minds': The Impact of Combat Exposure on the Mental and Physical Health of Civil War Veterans, in Schmidt and Hasegawa, *Years of Change and Suffering*, 143–58.

12. Department of the Army, *U.S. Army Combat Stress Control Handbook*, 48.

13. Ibid., 42.

14. "The Army of the Cumberland," *SFB*, 25 July 1863; reprinted from the *NYT*.

15. Department of the Army, *U.S. Army Combat Stress Control Handbook*, 52–54; Henderson, *Cohesion*, 4.

16. Jomini, *The Art of War*, 262; "Corps D'Armee," *ANJ* 1 (24 October 1863): 137.

17. Scott, *Military Dictionary*, 262.

18. "The Third Corps Union," *ANJ* 1 (17 October 1863): 114.

19. Silliker, *The Rebel Yell and the Yankee Hurrah*, 139.

20. Marmont, *The Spirit of Military Institutions* (1864 reprint), 50.

21. Muffly, *The Story of Our Regiment*, 116.

22. Ward, *History of the 106th Pennsylvania Volunteers*, 290.

23. Ibid., 290.

24. Benjamin Ashenfelter to "Father Churchman," 23 April 1864, Harrisburg Civil War Round Table Collection, USAMHI.

25. See, for instance, Power, *Lee's Miserables*, 44–46; and Glatthaar, *General Lee's Army*, 365, 369, 375.

26. Lowe, *Meade's Army*, 189. On the decline of corps-level command in Lee's army, see Glatthaar, *General Lee's Army*, 374–75; and Power, *Lee's Miserables*, 43–44, 54.

27. See Henderson, *Cohesion*, 108.

28. See Rhea, *The Battles for Spotsylvania Court House and the Road to Yellow Tavern*, 138, 243–44; Rhea, *To the North Anna River*, 396, 414; and Rhea, *Cold Harbor*, 202. See also *OR*, series 1, vol. 36, 435.

29. Banes, *History of the Philadelphia Brigade*, 243.

30. Robertson, *The Civil War Letters of General Robert McAllister*, 416. See also Rhea, *The Battle of the Wilderness*, 190–200.

31. Grant, *Personal Memoirs of Ulysses S. Grant*, 2:224.

32. Agassiz, *Meade's Headquarters, 1863–1865*, 208.

33. Robertson, *The Civil War Letters of General Robert McAllister*, 417.

34. Department of the Army, *U.S. Army Combat Stress Control Handbook*, 10.

35. *OR*, series 1, vol. 36, 598.

36. *OR*, series 1, vol. 40, 367.

37. Muffly, *The Story of Our Regiment*, 124.

38. Henderson, *Cohesion*, 108.

39. Quoted in Banes, *History of the Philadelphia Brigade*, 286.

40. Dawes, *Service with the Sixth Wisconsin Volunteers*, 300.

41. Chamberlin, *History of the One Hundred and Fiftieth Regiment Pennsylvania Volunteers*, 239.

42. For a particularly interesting study on the importance of cohesion within a company and the variables that affect it, see Costa and Kahn, *Heroes and Cowards*, 94–119.

43. Banes, *History of the Philadelphia Brigade*, 238.

44. Woodward, *Our Campaigns*, 255.

45. Crotty, *Four Years Campaigning in the Army of the Potomac*, 138.

46. Vaill, *History of the Second Connecticut Volunteer Heavy Artillery*, 49.

47. Wilkeson, *Recollections of a Private Soldier in the Army of the Potomac*, 85.

48. Shaw, *The First Maine Heavy Artillery*, 124.

49. Grossman with Christensen, *On Combat*, 4.

50. Department of the Army, *Combat Stress*, 2. The army version of this book is FM-6-22.5; the Marine Corps edition is MCRP 6-11C; the navy edition is NTTP 1-15M.

51. See Nash, "The Stressors of War," for a fuller discussion.

52. *OR*, series 1, vol. 36, 597.

53. See Department of the Army, *U.S. Army Combat Stress Control Handbook*, 106–7, for a fuller explanation of these terms. I offered some preliminary observations about

the combat stress indicators that follow in "A Hard Road to Travel: The Impact of Continuous Operations on the Army of the Potomac and Army of Northern Virginia in May 1864."

54. Marbaker, *History of the Eleventh New Jersey Volunteers*, 184.

55. "The Battle of the Wilderness," *ANJ* 1 (14 May 1864): 629.

56. See Rhea, *The Battle of the Wilderness*, which is the best modern study of this battle.

57. *OR*, series 1, vol. 36, 226.

58. Survivors Association, *History of the 121st Regiment Pennsylvania Volunteers*, 75.

59. See Krick, *Civil War Weather in Virginia*, 123–31; and Winters, *Battling the Elements*, 99–106.

60. *OR*, series 1, vol. 36, 541.

61. Agassiz, *Meade's Headquarters*, 140.

62. Muffly, *The Story of Our Regiment*, 154.

63. Grossman with Christensen, *On Combat*, 22–24.

64. Scott, *History of the One Hundred and Fifth Regiment of Pennsylvania Volunteers*, 252–53.

65. Chamberlin, *History of the One Hundred and Fiftieth Pennsylvania Volunteers*, 226–27.

66. Bowen, *History of the Thirty-Seventh Regiment, Mass., Volunteers*, 169.

67. Smith, *The History of the Nineteenth Regiment of Maine Volunteer Infantry*, 185.

68. Brewer, *History of the Sixty-First Regiment Pennsylvania Volunteers*, 90.

69. Captain John Willoughby to Simpson, 13 May 1864, in Cpl. James Randolph Simpson and Sgt. George Simpson Papers, Civil War Miscellaneous Collection, USAMHI.

70. See Hess, *In the Trenches at Petersburg*, especially chaps. 1 and 2.

71. *OR*, series 1, vol. 36, 709.

72. Department of the Army, *U.S. Army Combat Stress Control Handbook*, 30–31.

73. Muffly, *A History of Our Regiment*, 120.

74. Simons, *A Regimental History*, 212.

75. Grant, *Personal Memoirs of Ulysses S. Grant*, 2:127.

76. See "The Staff: Re-organization of the Quartermaster's and Commissary Department," *ANJ* 1 (26 March 1864): 514.

77. A. W. Acheson to Mother, May 7, 1864, in Fulcher, *Family Letters in a Civil War Century*, n.p.

78. Craft, *History of the One Hundred Forty-First Regiment, Pennsylvania Volunteers*, 200.

79. For calories for hardtack, see http://baking.food.com/recipe/civil-war-hardtack-142600 (1 June 2011). For calories for salt pork, see http://www.fitday.com/WebFit/nutrition/All_Foods/Meat_Beef_Pork_Misc_/Pork_salt_cooked.html (1 June 2011). See also U.S. Army Research Institute of Environmental Medicine, *Nutrition for Health and Performance*, 18.

80. *OR*, series 1, vol. 36, 513.

81. Bryan, *History of the Thirty-Seventh Massachusetts*, 238.

82. Hammond, *A Treatise on Hygiene*, 550.

83. *OR*, series 1, vol. 36, 231.

84. Hammond, *A Treatise on Hygiene*, 226.

85. See Henry Keiser Diary, entry for 18 May 1864, Harrisburg Civil War Round Table, USAMHI. See also Jerome Cutler to "My Dear Emily," 19 May 1864, in Cutler, *Letters of Jerome Cutler*, during his enlistment in the 2nd Vermont Infantry.

86. Craft, *History of the One Hundred Forty-First Pennsylvania*, 200.

87. Vaill, *History of the Second Connecticut Heavy Artillery*, 70.

88. See Grossman with Christensen, *On Combat*, 202–3.

89. Gideon Mellin to Sister, 15 May 1864, Pennsylvania Save the Flags Collection, USAMHI.

90. *OR*, series 1, vol. 36, 715.

91. Haines, *History of the Fifteenth Regiment New Jersey Volunteers*, 172.

92. Marbaker, *History of the Eleventh New Jersey*, 175.

93. Muffly, *The Story of Our Regiment*, 124.

94. Grossman with Christensen, *On Combat*, 31,

95. Washburn, *A Complete Military History and Record of the 108th Regiment N.Y. Vols.*, 74.

96. Henry Keiser Diary, 12 May 1864, Harrisburg Civil War Round Table Collection, USAMHI.

97. Gideon Mellin to Sister, 15 May 1864, Pennsylvania Save the Flags Collection, USAMHI.

98. Hyde, *Following the Greek Cross*, 202.

99. Maurus Oesterreich Diary, entry for 13 May 1864, Harrisburg Civil War Round Table Collection, USAMHI.

100. Vautier, *History of the 88th Pennsylvania Volunteers in the War for the Union*, 187.

101. Crotty, *Four Years Campaigning in the Army of the Potomac*, 135.

102. Bicknell, *History of the Fifth Regiment Maine Volunteers*, 331–32.

103. Dawes, *Service with the Sixth Wisconsin Volunteers*, 284.

104. Vaill, *History of the Second Connecticut Heavy Artillery*, 351.

105. Survivors Association, *History of the Fifth Massachusetts Battery*, 817.

106. Dyer, *The Journal of a Civil War Surgeon*, 164. The problem of malingers is a common concern for Dyer during the Overland Campaign. See also Lande, *Madness, Malingering, and Malfeasance*, 131–56, for the impact of malingering on cohesion.

107. Willson, *Disaster, Struggle, Triumph*, 275.

108. *OR*, series 1, vol. 36, 231.

109. Vaill, *History of the Second Connecticut Heavy Artillery*, 205.

110. Many regimental histories recount this event. See, for instance, Smith, *History of the Nineteenth Regiment, Maine Volunteers*, 172–73; and Banes, *History of the Philadelphia Brigade*, 256–59.

111. Hutchinson, *History of the Seventh Massachusetts Volunteer Infantry*, 186.

112. *OR*, series 1, vol. 36, 437.

113. Chamberlin, *History of the One Hundred Fiftieth Pennsylvania*, 237.

114. Sparks, *Inside Lincoln's Army*, 375–76.

115. Agassiz, *Meade's Headquarters*, 117.

116. Sparks, *Inside Lincoln's Army*, 383.

117. For a breakdown of Union casualties, see U.S. Army Surgeon General, *The Medical and Surgical History of the War of the Rebellion*, 1:329.

118. *OR*, series 1, vol. 36, 434.

119. *OR*, series 1, vol. 40, 327.

120. *OR*, series 1, vol. 40, 329.

121. Quoted in Gibbon, *Personal Recollections of the Civil War*, 229–30.

122. See, for instance, Glatthaar, *General Lee's Army*, 371–78, 414–15.

123. See examples in Beyer and Keydel, *Deeds of Valor*.

124. Haskell, "A Brief Address to Our Soldiers on the Importance of their Mission."

125. See McPherson, *For Cause and Comrades*, esp. chap. 1. The literature on Civil War soldier motivation is rich and extensive. Gerald Linderman's *Embattled Courage*, esp. 34–61, accepts the primacy of the "comrades" approach. Earl J. Hess, in *Liberty, Virtue, and Progress*, 56–80, makes a strong case for cultural values—including political ideology—as particularly strong motivation for citizen-soldiers.

126. See Wong, Kolditz, Millen, and Potter, *Why They Fight*; and McCoun, Kier, and Belkin, "Does Social Cohesion Determine Motivation in Combat?"

127. Alexander W. Acheson to Mother, 5 June 1864, Alexander W. Acheson Papers, Pennsylvania Save the Flags Collection, USAMHI.

128. Muffly, *The Story of Our Regiment*, 710.

129. Jomini, *The Art of War*, 294.

130. Swinton, *The Campaigns of the Army of the Potomac*, 495.

131. *OR*, series 2, vol. 38, 534–35.

132. Kautz, *The 1865 Customs of Service for Officers of the Army*, 223, 226, 242–44.

Epilogue

1. Grant, *Personal Memoirs of Ulysses S. Grant*, 2:632.

2. "Genl. Grant's Report," *ANJ* 3 (16 December 1865): 261.

3. Ibid., 262.

4. Headley, *Grant and Sherman*, 34–36.

5. Grant's observation was noted in Fry, "Origins and Progress of the Military Service Institution of the United States," 29.

6. See Sherman, *Memoirs of General William T. Sherman*, 2:383–85.

7. See Upton to Adjutant General E. D. Townsend, 13 January 1866, in Michie, *The Life and Letters of Emory Upton*, 191–93.

8. For the best study on this transition, see Jamieson, *Crossing the Deadly Ground*.

9. For a summary of this movement, see Reardon, *Soldiers and Scholars*, chap. 1.

10. One of the most influential books of the last quarter of the nineteenth century was John A. Logan's *The Volunteer Soldier of America*. His title and his dedication to the "immortal host of citizen-soldiers and sailors" clearly reflects his sentiments.

11. See Upton, *The Armies of Asia and Europe*.

12. "Military Common Sense," *ANJ* 3 (17 March 1866): 473.

13. Quoted in Reardon, *Soldiers and Scholars*, 23–24.

14. For the early histories of these institutions, see Hunt and Lorence, *History of Fort Leavenworth*; Nenninger, *The Leavenworth Schools and the Old Army*; Pappas, *Prudens Futuri*; and Ball, *Of Responsible Command*.

15. Chester, "Some of the Artillery Difficulties Likely to Be Encountered in the Next Maritime War," 557–58.

16. U.S. War Department, "Report of the Assistant Commandant of the U.S. Army Staff College, 1906," 21.

17. See Reardon, *Soldiers and Scholars*, 125–44.

18. See Alger, *The Quest for Victory*, 110–11.

19. Faust, *This Republic of Suffering*, 8–9.

20. *Notes of Hospital Life from November, 1861, to August 1863*, xi–xii.

21. Swinton, *The Campaigns of the Army of the Potomac*, 494.

22. Quoted in Boritt, *Lincoln and the Economics of the American Dream*, 271.

23. Brinton, *Personal Memoirs of John H. Brinton*, 273.

24. Swinton, *The Campaigns of the Army of the Potomac*, 495.

25. Sherman, *Memoirs of General William T. Sherman*, 2:385.

26. Du Picq, *Battle Studies*, 5.

27. Ibid., 120, 122, 131.

28. Ibid., 111–12, 133–34, 214.

29. Lynn, *Battle*, 193.

30. Du Picq, *Battle Studies*, 5.

31. *Brooklyn Daily Eagle*, 8 April 1869.

BIBLIOGRAPHY

Primary Sources

Archival Sources

Carlisle, Pa.
    U.S. Army Military History Institute, U.S. Army Heritage and Education Center
        Civil War Miscellaneous Collection
            Corporal James Randolph Simpson and Sergeant
                George Simpson Papers
            Harrisburg Civil War Round Table Collection
                Benjamin Ashenfelter Letters
                Henry Keiser Diary
                Maurus Oesterreich Diary
            Pennsylvania Save the Flags Collection
                Alexander Acheson Papers
                Gideon Mellin Letters
Washington, D.C.
    Library of Congress
        Abraham Lincoln Papers

Government Documents

Delafield, Richard. *Report on the Art of War in Europe in 1854, 1855, and 1856.* 36th Cong., 2nd sess. Senate Ex. Doc. No. 59. Washington, D.C.: George W. Bowman, 1860.

Department of the Army. *Combat Stress.* Washington, D.C.: Pentagon Publishing, 2000.

———. *U.S. Army Combat Stress Control Handbook.* Guilford, Conn.: Lyons Press, 2003.

U.S. Army Research Institute of Environmental Medicine. *Nutrition for Health and Performance.* Technical note TN01/4. N.p., 2001.

U.S. Army Surgeon General. *The Medical and Surgical History of the War of the Rebellion.* 15 vols. Washington, D.C.: Government Printing Office, 1870.

U.S. Congress. *Report of the Committee Appointed to Examine the Organization, System of Discipline, and Course of Instruction of the Military Academy.* 36th Cong., 2nd sess. Senate Misc. Document 3. Washington, D.C., 1861.

U.S. War Department. "Report of the Assistant Commandant of the U.S. Army Staff College, 1906." In *Annual Report of the Commandant of the U.S. Army School of* the Line and Staff School, 1906, 21. Washington, D.C.: Government Printing Office, 1907.

———. *War of the Rebellion: A Compilation of the Official Records of the Union and Confederate Armies.* 128 vols. Washington, D.C.: Government Printing Office, 1880–1901.

Newspapers and Periodicals

Albany (NY) Atlas and Argus
Albany (NY) Journal
American Presbyterian
Amherst (NH) Farmers Cabinet
Army and Navy Journal
Atlantic Monthly
Bangor (ME) Daily Whig and Courier
Boston Daily Advertiser
Brooklyn Daily Eagle
Cincinnati Daily Enquirer
Daily National Intelligencer (Washington, D.C.)
Deseret (UT) News
Galaxy
Hallowell (ME) Gazette
Huntingdon (PA) Globe
Lancaster (PA) Intelligencer
Lebanon (PA) Advertiser
Lowell (MA) Daily Citizen and News
Macon (GA) Telegraph
Milwaukee Sentinel

New Hampshire Sentinel
New Haven Daily Palladium
New Orleans Daily True Delta
New York Evening Post
New York Herald
New York Times
New York Tribune
North American and United States Gazette (Philadelphia)
North American Review
Pennsylvania Daily Telegraph
Philadelphia Inquirer
Philadelphia Press
Pittsfield (MA) Sun
Portland (ME) Daily Advertiser
Richmond (VA) Daily Dispatch
Richmond (VA) Examiner
San Francisco Daily Evening Bulletin
Springfield (MA) Weekly Republican
United States Service Magazine
Wisconsin Daily Patriot

Works on Military Theory

Chesney, Charles Cornwallis. *A Military View of Recent Campaigns in Virginia and Maryland.* London: Smith, Elder & Co., 1863.

Decker, Carl von. *The Three Arms; or Division Tactics of Decker.* Translated by Inigo Jones. London: Parker, Furnivall, and Parker, 1848.

De Peyster, John Watts. *Practical Strategy, as Illustrated by the Life and Achievements of a Master of the Art, the Austrian Field Marshal Traun.* Catskill, N.Y.: Joseph Joesbury, 1863.

———. *Winter Campaigns: The Test of Generalship.* New York: Charles G. Stone, 1862.

De Saxe, Maurice. "My Reveries upon the Art of War." In *Roots of Strategy: The Five Greatest Military Classics of All Time,* edited by T. R. Phillips. Harrisburg, Pa.: Stackpole Books, 1985.

Dufour, G. H. *Strategy and Tactics*. Translated by William P. Craighill. New York: D. Van Nostrand, 1864.

Duparcq, Édouard de la Barre. *Elements of Military Art and History*. Edited by George W. Cullum. New York: D. Van Nostrand, 1862.

Du Picq, Charles-Jean-Jacques-Joseph Ardant. *Battle Studies*. 8th ed. Translated by John N. Greeley and Robert C. Cotton. New York: Macmillan Co., 1921.

Halleck, H. Wager. *Elements of Military Art and Science; or, Course of Instruction in Strategy Fortification, Tactics of Battles. . . .* 3rd ed. New York: D. Appleton, 1862.

Hammond, William Alexander. *A Treatise on Hygiene: With Special Reference to the Military Service*. Philadelphia: J. B. Lippincott, 1863.

Hapsburg, Charles von. *Principles of War*. Translated by Daniel I. Radakovich. Ann Arbor, Mich.: Nimble Books LLC, 2009.

Jackson, Robert. *A Systematic View of the Formation, Discipline and Economy of Armies*. 1804. Reprint, Memphis, Tenn.: General Books, 2010.

Jomini, Antoine-Henri. *The Art of War*. Translated by G. H. Mendell and W. P. Craighill. Revised edition. Philadelphia: J. B. Lippincott, 1862.

———. *The Political and Military History of the Campaign of Waterloo*. Translated by Stephen Vincent Benet. New York: D. Van Nostrand, 1862.

———. *Treatise on Grand Military Operations V1: Or a Critical and Military History of the Wars of Frederick the Great*. Translated by Samuel Beckley Holabird. New York: D. Van Nostrand, 1865.

Lecomte, Ferdinand. *The War in the United States: Report to the Swiss Military Department: Preceded by a Discourse to the Federal Military Society Assembled at Berne, Aug. 18, 1862*. New York: D. Van Nostrand, 1863.

Lloyd, Henry. *The History of the Late War in Germany; between the King of Prussia, and the Empress of Germany and Her Allies*. London: S. Hooper, 1781. Facsimile edition, 2011.

Mahan, Dennis Hart. *An Elementary Treatise on Advanced-Guard, Out-Post, and Detachment Service of Troops. . . .* New edition. New York: John Wiley, 1861.

Marmont, Auguste Frédéric Louis Viesse de. *The Spirit of Military Institutions*. Translated and edited by Henry Coppee. Philadelphia: J. P. Lippincott, 1862.

———. *The Spirit of Military Institutions*. Translated and annotated by Colonel Frank Schaller. Reprint of Confederate edition. Columbia, S.C.: Evans & Cogswell, 1864.

McClellan, George B. *The Armies of Europe: Comprising Descriptions in Detail of the Military Systems of England, France, Russia, Prussia, Austria, and Sardinia, Adapting Their Advantages to All Arms of the United States*. Philadelphia: J. B. Lippincott, 1861.

Napoleon's Maxims of War. New York: Gregory of Walker Street, 1861.

Schalk, Emil. *The Art of War: Written Expressly for and Dedicated to the U.S. Volunteer Army*. Philadelphia: J. B. Lippincott, 1862.

———. *Campaigns of 1862 and 1863, Illustrating the Principles of Strategy*. Philadelphia: J. B. Lippincott, 1863.

Scott, H. L. *Military Dictionary: Comprising Technical Definitions; Information* on Raising and Keeping Troops; Actual Service, Including Makeshifts and Improved Matériel; and Law, Government, Regulation, and Administration Relating to Land Forces. New York: D. Van Nostrand, 1861.

Szabad, Emeric. *Modern War: Its Theory and Practice.* New York: Harper & Brothers, 1863.

Works by Civil War–Era Figures

Balch, Frank. *Have We the Best Possible Ambulance System?* Boston: Walker, Wise & Company, 1864.

Barnard, J. G. *The Peninsular Campaign and Its Antecedents, as Developed by the Report of Maj. Gen. George B. McClellan, and Other Published Documents.* New York: D. Van Nostrand, 1864.

[Benton, Thomas Hart]. *Thirty Years' View: Or, A History of the Workings of the American Government for Thirty Years, from 1820 to 1850.* New York: D. Appleton & Co., 1858.

Bowditch, Henry I. *A Brief Plea for an Ambulance System for the Army of the United States. . . .* Boston: Ticknor & Fields, 1863.

Boynton, Edward C. *The History of West Point.* New York: D. Van Nostrand, 1863.

Brinton, John H. *Personal Memoirs of John H. Brinton, Civil War Surgeon, 1861–1865.* Reprint edition. Carbondale: Southern Illinois University Press, 1996.

Craighill, William P., ed. *The 1862 Army Officer's Pocket Companion.* New York: D. Van Nostrand, 1862.

Denslow, Van Buren. *Fremont and McClellan, Their Political and Military Careers Reviewed.* Yonkers, N.Y.: Office of the Semi-Weekly Clarion, 1862.

Ellet, Charles, Jr. *The Army of the Potomac and Its Mismanagement, Respectfully Addressed to Congress.* Washington, D.C.: n.p., 1861.

Ford, Worthington Chauncey, ed. *War Letters, 1862–1865, of John Chipman Gray, Major, Judge Advocate, and John Codman Ropes, Historian of the War.* Boston: Houghton Mifflin, 1927.

Gibbon, John. *Personal Recollections of the Civil War.* New York: G. P. Putnam's Sons, 1928. Reprint, Dayton, Ohio: Morningside Press, 1988.

Grant, Ulysses S. *Personal Memoirs of Ulysses S. Grant.* New York: Charles L. Webster and Company, 1885–86. Facsimile ed., New York: Bonanza Books, 1974.

Gurowski, Adam. *Diary for March 4, 1861, to November 12, 1862.* Boston: Lea and Shepard, 1862.

———. *Diary for November 18, 1862, to October 18, 1863.* New York: Carleton, 1864.

Harte, Bret. *Stories and Poems and Other Uncollected Writings.* Reprint edition. Vancouver: Read Books, 2008.

Haskell, T. N. "A Brief Address to Our Soldiers on the Importance of Their Mission, during the Present Crisis." In *Soldier's Armor of Strength,* by Pilgrim John, 18–25. Brooklyn, N.Y.: D. S. Holmes, 1863.

Hasson, Alexander B. *Our Military Experience and What It Suggests.* Baltimore: Cushing and Bailey, 1863.

Headley, Joel T. *Grant and Sherman: Their Campaigns and Generals*. New York:
    E. B. Treat & Co., 1865.

Jarvis, Edward. "The Sanitary Condition of the United States Army." *Atlantic
    Monthly* (October 1862): 463–97.

Joinville, Prince de. *The Army of the Potomac: Its Organization, Its Commander, and
    Its Campaigns*. Translated and annotated by William Henry Hurlbert. New York:
    Anson D. F. Randolph, 1862.

Kautz, August V. *The 1865 Customs of Service for Officers of the Army*. Philadelphia:
    J. B. Lippincott & Sons, 1866.

Keyes, Erasmus D. *Fifty Years' Observations of Men and Events, Civil and Military*.
    New York: Charles Scribner's Sons, 1884.

Logan, John A. *The Volunteer Soldier of America*. Chicago: R. S. Peale, 1887.

McClellan, George B. *McClellan's Own Story*. New York: Charles L. Webster, 1887.

Meade, George Gordon. *The Life and Letters of General George Gordon Meade*. 2 vols.
    New York: Charles Scribner's Sons, 1913.

Michie, Peter Smith, ed. *The Life and Letters of Emory Upton*. New York:
    D. Appleton, 1885.

Nicolay, John, and John Hay. *Abraham Lincoln: A History*. 10 vols. New York: The
    Century Company, 1904.

Notes of Hospital Life from November, 1861, to August, 1863. Philadelphia: J. B.
    Lippincott, 1864.

Palfrey, Francis Winthrop. *The Ambulance System*. Boston: Crosby and Nicholas,
    1864.

Pilsen, John. *Reply of Lieut.-Col. Pilsen to Emil Schalk's Criticisms of the Campaign
    in the Mountain Department, under Maj.-Gen. J. C. Fremont*. N.p., June 1863.

Richards, G. W. *A Brief History of the Rebellion, and a Life of Gen. McClellan
    Containing Some Facts Never before Published*. Philadelphia: J. McGee, 1862.

Seymour, Truman. *Military Education: A Vindication of West Point and the Regular
    Army*. N.p., 1864.

Sherman, William T. *Memoirs of General William T. Sherman*. 2 vols. New York:
    D. Appleton, 1875.

Steece, Tecumseh. *A Republican Military System*. New York: John A. Gray & Green,
    1863.

Swinton, William. *The Campaigns of the Army of the Potomac*. 1882. Reprint, New
    York: Smithmark, 1995.

Townsend, Edward D. *Anecdotes of the Civil War in the United States*. New York:
    D. Appleton Co., 1884.

Upton, Emory. *The Armies of Asia and Europe*. New York: D. Appleton Co., 1878.

Webster, Thomas. *Free Military School for Applicants for Command of Colored
    Troops*. Philadelphia: King & Baird, Printers, 1863.

Welles, Gideon. *Diary of Gideon Welles, Secretary of the Navy under Lincoln and
    Johnson*. 3 vols. Boston: Houghton Mifflin, 1911.

Wilkes, George. *McClellan: From Balls Bluff to Antietam*. New York: Sinclair Tousey,
    1863.

Unit Histories and Soldier Letters

Agazzis, George R., ed. *Meade's Headquarters, 1863–1865: Letters of Colonel Theodore Lyman from the Wilderness to Appomattox.* 1922. Reprint, Salem, N.H.: Ayer Company Publishers, 1970.

Banes, Charles. *History of the Philadelphia Brigade.* Philadelphia: J. B. Lippincott & Sons, 1876.

Bicknell, George W. *History of the Fifth Regiment Maine Volunteers.* Portland, Maine: Hall L. Davis, 1871.

Bowen, James Lorenzo. *History of the Thirty-Seventh Regiment, Mass. Volunteers, in the Civil War of 1861–1865.* Holyoke, Mass.: Clark W. Bryan and Company, 1884.

Brewer, A. T. *History of the Sixty-First Regiment Pennsylvania Volunteers, 1861–1865.* Pittsburgh: Art Engraving and Printing, 1911.

Chamberlin, Thomas. *History of the One Hundred and Fiftieth Regiment Pennsylvania Volunteers, Second Regiment, Bucktail Brigade.* Philadelphia: F. McManus, Jr., & Co., 1905.

Craft, David. *History of the One Hundred Forty-First Regiment, Pennsylvania Volunteers, 1862–1865.* Towanda, Pa.: Reporter-Journal Printing Company, 1885.

Crotty, Daniel G. *Four Years Campaigning in the Army of the Potomac.* Grand Rapids, Mich.: Dygert Bros. & Co., 1874.

Cutler, Jerome. *Letters of Jerome Cutler, Waterville, Vermont, during His Enlistment in the Union Army, 2nd Regiment Vermont Volunteers, 1861–1864.* Bennington, Vt.: privately printed, 1990.

Dawes, Rufus R. *Service with the Sixth Wisconsin Volunteers.* 1890. Reprint, Dayton, Ohio: Morningside Press, 1991.

Duncan, Russell, ed. *Blue-Eyed Child of Fortune: The Civil War Letters of Colonel Robert Gould Shaw.* Athens, Ga.: University of Georgia Press, 1992.

Dyer, J. Franklin. *The Journal of a Civil War Surgeon.* Edited by Michael B. Chesson. Lincoln, Neb.: University of Nebraska Press, 2003.

Fulcher, Jane M., ed. *Family Letters in a Civil War Century.* Avella, Pa.: n.p., 1962.

Haines, Alanson A. *History of the Fifteenth Regiment New Jersey Volunteers.* New York: Jennings and Thomas, 1883.

Hutchinson, Nelson V. *History of the Seventh Massachusetts Volunteer Infantry.* Taunton, Mass.: Regimental Association, 1890.

Hyde, Thomas W. *Following the Greek Cross, or Memories of the Sixth Army Corps.* 1894. Reprint, Columbia: University of South Carolina Press, 2005.

Lowe, David W., ed. *Meade's Army: The Private Notebooks of Lt. Col. Theodore Lyman.* Kent, Ohio: Kent State University Press, 2007.

Marbaker, Thomas. *History of the Eleventh New Jersey Volunteers.* Trenton, N.J.: MacCrellish & Quigley, 1898.

Muffly, J. W., comp. *The Story of Our Regiment: A History of the 148th Pennsylvania Volunteers.* Des Moines, Iowa: Kenyon Printing, 1904.

Robertson, James I., Jr., ed. *The Civil War Letters of General Robert McAllister.* New Brunswick, N.J.: Rutgers University Press, 1965.

Scott, Kate M. *History of the One Hundred and Fifth Regiment of Pennsylvania Volunteers*. Philadelphia: New-World Publishing Company, 1877.

Scott, Robert Garth, ed. *Forgotten Valor: The Memoirs, Journals, and Civil War Letters of Orlando B. Willcox*. Kent, Ohio: Kent State University Press, 1999.

Sears, Stephen W., ed. *The Civil War Papers of George B. McClellan*. New York: Ticknor and Fields, 1989.

Shaw, Horace H. *The First Maine Heavy Artillery*. Portland, Maine: n.p., 1903.

Silliker, Ruth L., ed. *The Rebel Yell and the Yankee Hurrah: The Civil War Journal of a Maine Volunteer*. Camden, Maine: Down East Books, 1985.

Simons, Ezra D. *A Regimental History: The One Hundred Twenty-Fifth New York State Volunteers*. New York: Ezra D. Simons, 1888.

Simpson, Brooks D., and Jean V. Berlin, eds. *Sherman's Civil War: Selected Correspondence of William T. Sherman, 1860–1865*. Chapel Hill: University of North Carolina Press, 1999.

Smith, John Day. *The History of the Nineteenth Regiment of Maine Volunteer Infantry, 1862–1865*. Minneapolis, Minn.: Great Western Printing Company, 1909.

Sparks, David S., ed. *Inside Lincoln's Army: The Diary of Marsena Rudolph Patrick, Provost Marshal General of the Army of the Potomac*. New York: Thomas Yoseloff, 1964.

Survivors Association. *History of the Fifth Massachusetts Battery*. Boston: Luther E. Cowles, 1901.

———. *History of the 121st Regiment Pennsylvania Volunteers*. Philadelphia: Burk & McFetridge, 1893.

Vaill, Theodore F. *History of the Second Connecticut Volunteer Heavy Artillery*. Winsted, Conn.: Winsted Printing Company, 1868.

Vautier, John D. *History of the 88th Pennsylvania Volunteers in the War for the Union, 1861–1865*. Philadelphia: J. B. Lippincott, 1894.

Ward, Joseph R. C. *History of the 106th Pennsylvania Volunteers*. Philadelphia: F. McManus, Jr. & Co., 1906.

Washburn, George H. *A Complete Military History and Record of the 108th Regiment N.Y. Vols. from 1863 to 1894*. Rochester, N.Y.: n.p., 1894.

Wilkeson, Frank. *Recollections of a Private Soldier in the Army of the Potomac*. New York: G. P. Putnam's Sons, 1887.

Willson, Arabella M. *Disaster, Struggle, Triumph: The Adventures of 1000 "Boys in Blue," from August, 1862, to June 1865*. Albany, N.Y.: The Argus Company, 1870.

Woodward, Evan Morrison. *Our Campaigns: The Second Regiment Pennsylvania Reserve Volunteers. . . .* Edited by Stanley W. Zamoski. 1865. Reprint, Shippensburg, Pa.: Burd Street Press, 1995.

Secondary Sources

Books

Adams, George Worthington. *Doctors in Blue: The Medical History of the Union Army in the Civil War*. New York: Henry Schuman, 1952.

Alger, John I. *Antoine-Henri Jomini: A Bibliographical Survey* West Point, N.Y.: U.S. Military Academy Library, 1975.

———. *The Quest for Victory: The History of the Principles of War*. Westport, Conn.: Greenwood Press, 1986.

Allaben, Frank. *John Watts de Peyster*. 2 vols. New York: Frank Allaben Genealogical Company, 1908.

Andrews, J. Cutler. *The North Reports the Civil War*. Pittsburgh: University of Pittsburgh Press, 1955.

Ball, Harry P. *Of Responsible Command: A History of the U.S. Army War College*. Carlisle Barracks, Pa.: Alumni Association of the U.S. Army War College, 1983.

Basler, Roy P., ed. *The Collected Works of Abraham Lincoln*. New Brunswick, N.J.: Rutgers University Press, 1953.

Beringer, Richard E., Herman Hattaway, Archer Jones, and William N. Still Jr. *Why the South Lost the Civil War*. Athens: University of Georgia Press, 1986.

Beyer, W. F., and O. F. Keydel, eds. *Deeds of Valor: How America's Civil War Heroes Won the Congressional Medal of Honor*. Detroit: Perrien-Keydel, 1903.

Bigelow, Donald Nevius. *William Conant Church and the "Army and Navy Journal."* New York: AMS Press, 1852.

Boritt, Gabor S. *Lincoln and the Economics of the American Dream*. Memphis: Memphis State University Press, 1978.

Burlingame, Michael, and John R. Turner Ettlinger. *Inside Lincoln's White House: The Complete Civil War Diary of John Hay*. Carbondale: Southern Illinois University Press, 1997.

Costa, Dora L., and Matthew E. Kahn. *Heroes and Cowards: The Social Face of War*. Princeton, N.J.: Princeton University Press, 2008.

Cunliffe, Marcus. *Soldiers and Civilians: The Martial Spirit in America, 1775–1865*. Boston: Little, Brown and Company, 1968.

Dean, Eric T., Jr. *Shook over Hell: Post-Traumatic Stress, Vietnam, and the Civil War*. Cambridge, Mass.: Harvard University Press, 1997.

Donald, David Herbert. *Lincoln Reconsidered: Essays on the Civil War Era*. 2nd ed., enlarged. New York: Vintage Books, 1961.

Dougherty, Kevin. *Civil War Leadership and Mexican War Experience*. Jackson: University Press of Mississippi, 2007.

Duncan, Louis. *The Medical Department of the United States Army in the Civil War*. Reprint edition. Gaithersburg, Md.: Olde Soldier Books, 1994.

Eisenhower, John S. D. *Agent of Destiny: The Life and Times of General Winfield Scott*. Norman: University of Oklahoma Press, 1999.

Faust, Drew Gilpin. *This Republic of Suffering: Death and the American Civil War*. New York: Alfred A. Knopf, 2008.

Flood, Charles Bracelen. *Grant and Sherman: The Friendship That Won the Civil War*. New York: Harper Perennial, 2006.

Gat, Azar. *A History of Military Thought: From the Enlightenment to the Cold War*. New York: Oxford University Press, 2001.

Glatthaar, Joseph T. *General Lee's Army: From Victory to Collapse*. New York: Free Press, 2008.

———. *Partners in Command: The Relationships between Leaders in the Civil War.* New York: Free Press, 1994.

Goss, Thomas J. *The War within the Union High Command: Politics and Generalship during the Civil War.* Lawrence: University Press of Kansas, 2003.

Grossman, Dave, with Loren W. Christensen. *On Combat: The Psychology and Physiology of Deadly Conflict in War and Peace.* 3rd ed. N.p.: Warrior Science Publications, 2008.

Hagerman, Edward. *The American Civil War and the Origins of Modern Warfare: Ideas, Organization, and Field Command.* Bloomington: Indiana University Press, 1988.

Handel, Michael I. *Masters of War: Classical Strategic Thought.* 3rd revised and expanded edition. Portland, Ore.: Frank Cass, 2002.

Hattaway, Herman, and Archer Jones. *How the North Won: A Military History of the Civil War.* Urbana: University of Illinois Press, 1983.

Henderson, William Darrell. *Cohesion: The Human Element in Combat.* Washington, D.C.: National Defense University Press, 1985.

Hess, Earl J. *In the Trenches at Petersburg: Field Fortifications and Confederate Defeat.* Chapel Hill: University of North Carolina Press, 2009.

———. *Liberty, Virtue, and Progress: Northerners and Their War for the Union.* New York: New York University Press, 1988.

Hirshson, Stanley P. *The White Tecumseh: A Biography of General William T. Sherman.* New York: Wiley, 1998.

Hittle, J. D. *Jomini and His Summary of the Art of War.* Harrisburg, Pa.: Telegraph Press, 1947.

Hseih, Wayne Wei-Siang. *West Pointers and the Civil War: The Old Army in War and Peace.* Chapel Hill: University of North Carolina Press, 2009.

Hunt, Elvid, and Walter E. Lorence. *History of Fort Leavenworth, 1827–1937.* 2nd ed. Fort Leavenworth, Kans.: Command and General Staff College Press, 1937.

Jamieson, Perry D. *Crossing the Deadly Ground: United States Army Tactics, 1865–1899.* Tuscaloosa: University of Alabama Press, 1994.

Johnson, Timothy D. *Winfield Scott: The Quest for Military Glory.* Lawrence: University Press of Kansas, 1998.

Krick, Robert K. *Civil War Weather in Virginia.* Tuscaloosa: University of Alabama Press, 2007.

Lande, R. Gregory. *Madness, Malingering, and Malfeasance: The Transformation of Psychiatry and the Law in the Civil War Era.* Washington, D.C.: Potomac Books, 2003.

Liddell Hart, B. H. *Sherman: Soldier, Realist, American.* New York: Dodd, Mead & Company, 1929. Reprint, New York: DaCapo Press, 1993.

Lincoln, Rufus Rockwell. *What Lincoln Read.* Washington, D.C.: Pioneer Publishing Company, 1932.

Linderman, Gerald. *Embattled Courage: The Experience of Combat in the American Civil War.* New York: Free Press, 1987.

Luvaas, Jay. *The Military Legacy of the Civil War: The European Inheritance.* Chicago: University of Chicago Press 1959.

Lynn, John A. *Battle: A History of Combat and Culture*. New York: Westview Press, 2003.

Marszalek, John F. *Commander of All Lincoln's Armies: A Life of General Henry W. Halleck*. Cambridge, Mass.: Harvard University Press, 2004.

———. *Sherman: A Soldier's Passion for Order*. New York: Free Press, 1992.

McFeely, William S. *Grant: A Biography*. New York: W. W. Norton, 1981.

McPherson, James M. *For Cause and Comrades: Why Men Fought in the Civil War*. New York: Oxford University Press, 1997.

———. *Tried by War: Abraham Lincoln as Commander in Chief*. New York: Penguin, 2008.

Morrison, James L., Jr. *"The Best School in the World": West Point, the Pre–Civil War Years, 1833–1866*. Kent, Ohio: Kent State University Press, 1986.

Moten, Matthew. *The Delafield Commission and the American Military Profession*. College Station: Texas A&M University Press, 2000.

Neely, Mark E., Jr. *The Union Divided: Party Conflict in the Civil War North*. Cambridge, Mass.: Harvard University Press, 2002.

Neff, Stephen C. *Justice in Blue and Gray: A Legal History of the Civil War*. Cambridge, Mass.: Harvard University Press, 2010.

Nenninger, Timothy K. *The Leavenworth Schools and the Old Army: Education, Professionalization, and the Officer Corps of the United States Army, 1861–1918*. Westport, Conn.: Greenwood Press, 1978.

Pappas, George S. *Prudens Futuri: The U.S. Army War College, 1901–1967*. Carlisle Barracks, Pa.: Alumni Association of the U.S. Army War College, 1967.

Peskin, Alan. *Winfield Scott and the Profession of Arms*. Kent, Ohio: Kent State University Press, 2003.

Power, J. Tracy. *Lee's Miserables: Life in the Army of Northern Virginia from the Wilderness to Appomattox*. Chapel Hill: University of North Carolina Press, 1998.

Rafuse, Ethan Sepp. *McClellan's War: The Failure of Moderation in the Struggle for the Union*. Bloomington: Indiana University Press, 2005.

Reardon, Carol. *Soldiers and Scholars: The U.S. Army and the Uses of Military History, 1865–1920*. Lawrence: University Press of Kansas, 1990.

Rhea, Gordon C. *The Battle of the Wilderness, May 5–6, 1864*. Baton Rouge: Louisiana State University Press, 1994.

———. *The Battles for Spotsylvania Court House and the Road to Yellow Tavern, May 7–12, 1864*. Baton Rouge: Louisiana State University Press, 1997.

———. *Cold Harbor: Grant and Lee, May 26–June 3, 1864*. Baton Rouge: Louisiana State University Press, 2002.

———. *To the North Anna River: Grant and Lee, May 13–25, 1864*. Baton Rouge: Louisiana State University Press, 2000.

Schmidt, James M., and Guy R. Hasegawa. *Years of Change and Suffering: Modern Perspectives on Civil War Medicine*. Roseville, N.H.: Edinborough Press, 2009.

Sears, Stephen W. *George B. McClellan: The Young Napoleon*. New York: Ticknor & Fields, 1988.

———. *Controversies and Commanders: Dispatches from the Army of the Potomac*. Boston: Houghton Mifflin, 1999.

Simpson, Brooks D. *Ulysses S. Grant: Triumph over Adversity, 1822–1865.* New York: Houghton Mifflin, 2000.

Skelton, William B. *An American Profession of Arms: The U.S. Army Officer Corps, 1784–1861.* Lawrence: University Press of Kansas, 1992.

Stoker, Donald. *The Grand Design: Strategy and the U.S. Civil War.* New York: Oxford University Press, 2010.

Tap, Bruce. *Over Lincoln's Shoulder: The Committee on the Conduct of the War.* Lawrence: University Press of Kansas, 1998.

Waugh, Joan. *U.S. Grant: American Hero, American Myth.* Chapel Hill: University of North Carolina Press, 2009.

Waugh, John C. *Lincoln and McClellan: The Troubled Partnership between the President and His General.* New York: Palgrave Macmillan, 2010.

Weigley, Russell F. *The American Way of War: A History of United States Military Policy and Strategy.* Bloomington: Indiana University Press, 1977.

Winters, Harold A. *Battling the Elements: Weather and Terrain in the Conduct of War.* Baltimore: Johns Hopkins University Press, 1998.

Wong, Leonard, Thomas A. Koldiz, Raymond A. Millen, and Terrence M. Potter. *Why They Fight: Combat Motivation in the Iraq War.* Carlisle Barracks, Pa.: Strategic Studies Institute, 2003.

Wood, W. J. *Civil War Generalship: The Art of Command.* Cambridge, Mass.: DaCapo Press, 2000.

Articles and Essays

Bartholomees, J. Boone. "A Survey of the Theory of Strategy." In *U.S. Army War College Guide to National Security Issues.* Vol. 1, *Theory of War and Strategy,* 13–44. Carlisle Barracks, Pa.: U.S. Army War College, 2010.

Brinton, Crane, Gordon Craig, and Felix Gilbert. "Jomini." In *Makers of Modern Strategy: Military Thought from Machiavelli to Hitler,* edited by Edward Mead Earle, Gordon Alexander Craig, and Felix Gilbert, 77–92. Princeton, N.J.: Princeton University Press, 1943.

Chester, James B. "Some of the Artillery Difficulties Likely to Be Encountered in the Next Maritime War." *Journal of the Military Service Institution of the United States* 19 (1898): 556–73.

Crackel, Theodore J. "The Battle of Queenston Heights, 13 October 1812." In *America's First Battles, 1775–1965,* edited by Charles E. Heller and William A. Stofft, 33–56. Lawrence: University Press of Kansas, 1986.

Fry, James B. "Origins and Progress of the Military Service Institution of the United States." *Journal of the Military Service Institution of the United States* 1 (1979): 20–31.

Harsh, Joseph L. "Battlesword and Rapier: Clausewitz, Jomini, and the American Civil War." *Military Affairs* 38 (December 1974): 133.

Howard, Michael. "Jomini and the Classical Tradition in Military Thought." In *The Theory and Practice of War,* edited by Michael Howard, 3–30. Bloomington: Indiana University Press, 1965.

Jones, Archer. "Jomini and the Strategy of the American Civil War." *Military Affairs* 38 (December 1970): 127–31.

Lykke, Arthur F., Jr. "Toward an Understanding of Military Strategy." In *Military Strategy: Theory and Application*, 3–7. Carlisle Barracks, Pa.: U.S. Army War College, 1986.

Marszalek, John F. "Where Did Winfield Scott Find His Anaconda?" *Lincoln Herald* 89 (Summer 1987): 77–81.

McCoun, Robert J., Elizabeth Kier, and Aaron Belkin. "Does Social Cohesion Determine Motivation in Combat?" *Armed Forces and Society* 32 (July 2006): 646–54.

Nash, William. "The Stressors of War." In *Combat Stress Injury: Theory, Research, and Management*, edited by Charles R. Figley and William Nash, 18–29. New York: Routledge, 2007.

Palmer, R. R. "Frederick the Great, Guibert, Bülow." In *Makers of Modern Strategy: Military Thought from Machiavelli to Hitler*, edited by Edward Mead Earle, Gordon Alexander Craig, and Felix Gilbert. Princeton, N.J.: Princeton University Press, 1943. Reprinted in *Makers of Modern Strategy: From Machiavelli to the Nuclear Age*, revised edition, edited by Peter Paret, Gordon Craig, and Felix Gilbert. Princeton, N.J.: Princeton University Press, 1986.

Pohl, James W. "The Influence of Antoine Henri de Jomini on Winfield Scott's Campaigns in the Mexican War." *Southwest Historical Quarterly* 77 (July 1972): 75–110.

"Political Attack on West Point." *Blue and Gray Magazine* 9 (December 1991): 51.

Reardon, Carol. "From Genius to Intellect: Unorthodox Union Army Officers in the American Civil War." In *Military Heretics: The Unorthodox in Policy and Strategy*, edited by B. J. C. McKercher and A. Hamish Ion, 57–82. Westport, Conn.: Praeger, 1994.

———. "A Hard Road to Travel: The Impact of Continuous Operations on the Army of the Potomac and the Army of Northern Virginia in May 1864." In *The Spotsylvania Campaign*, edited by Gary W. Gallagher, 170–202. Chapel Hill: University of North Carolina Press, 1998.

Ropp, Theodore. "Anacondas Anyone?" *Military Affairs* 27 (Summer 1963): 71–76.

Shy, John W. "Jomini." In *Makers of Modern Strategy: From Machiavelli to the Nuclear Age*, revised edition, edited by Peter Paret, Gordon Craig, and Felix Gilbert, 143–85. Princeton, N.J.: Princeton University Press, 1986.

Swain, Richard M. "'The Hedgehog and the Fox': Jomini, Clausewitz, and History." *Naval War College Review* 43 (Autumn 1990): 98–109.

Williams, T. Harry. "The Military Leadership of North and South." In *Why the North Won the Civil War*, edited by David Herbert Donald, 44. New York: Simon & Schuster, 1960.

———. "The Return of Jomini—Some Thoughts on Recent Civil War Writing." *Military Affairs* 39 (December 1975): 204–6.

INDEX

Bülow, Adam Heinrich Dietrich von, 3–4, 5, 8
Burgoyne, Gen. John, 70
Burnside, Maj. Gen. Ambrose E., 35, 73–74, 95, 122
Butler, Maj. Gen. Benjamin F., 60

Cameron, Simon, 24, 26, 27
Campaigns of 1862 and 1863, Illustrating the Principles of Strategy (Schalk), 37–38
Casey, Maj. Gen. Silas, 79
Cavalry Service Regulations (U.S. Army, 1914), 132
Chancellorsville, Battle of, 38, 39, 40, 74, 99, 109
Chandler, Zachariah, 64, 70
Chantilly, Battle of, 99
Chaplains, 104, 110, 121
Character, as a leadership parameter, 57, 66–69, 74–75, 82–83, 86, 101–3, 126
Chase, Salmon P., 35
Chattanooga, Tenn., battle at, 46, 81
Chesapeake v. Leopard incident, 59
Chesney, Charles Cornwallis, 40–41
Chester, Capt. James, 131
Chickamauga, Battle of, 44, 45, 75
Chief of staff: of the U.S. Army, 46–47; on senior commanders' staffs, 78
Chippewa, Battle of, 59
Church, William Conant, 17, 80, 88; on Halleck, 44, 46; takes over journal, 44, 76; on the nature of war, 45; on concentration, 46, 48; on progress of the war, 49, 50, 51; on military education, 76, 78; on Grant, 82, 83; on McClellan, 85. See also *Army and Navy Journal*
Civil War Centennial, 22–23
Clausewitz, Carl von, 4, 7, 18, 41, 136
Coffee, 112
Colby, Pvt. Henry, 117
Cold Harbor, Battle of, 14, 48, 50, 92, 98, 99, 109–10, 112, 116, 117, 121–22, 134–135

Combat refusal, 118
Combat stress and stressors, 92, 93, 96, 103–4, 114–15, 121, 122–23; types of stressors, 104
Company-grade officers (lieutenants and captains), 88, 101–2, 117, 122–23, 128, 129, 135
Company Q, 102, 117
Competency boards, 101–2
Concentration: as a military principle, 3–4, 5, 7, 26; Lincoln and Halleck on, 28, 29; Schalk on, 32–33, 36–39; as key element of late-war Union strategy, 41, 45, 46, 48, 51, 69, 126
Confederate Veteran magazine, 6
Confiscation Act, 70, 71
Connecticut regiments: 2nd Heavy Artillery, 117
Conscripts and conscription, 34, 71, 97
Continuous operations, 105, 114
Coppee, Henry, 32, 44, 46, 47, 48, 77, 78, 80, 82, 83, 85. See also *United States Service Magazine*
Corinth, Miss., Halleck's advance upon, 33, 34, 39
Cornwallis, Gen. Charles, 70
Corps, of Army of the James, XVIII, 103
Corps, of Army of the Potomac: I, 95; II, 94, 95, 97, 99, 108, 112, 119–20; III, 95, 99; V, 94, 95, 97, 99, 107, 119; VI, 94, 95, 97, 98, 115, 119; IX, 95
Coulter, Col. Richard, 101, 105
Coup d'oeil, 10, 56, 79
Courage: as essential to good leadership, 42, 58, 68, 75, 83; as human factor in combat, 90, 98–99, 101–2, 105, 117, 118, 120
Craighill, Lt. William P., 30
Crater, Battle of the, 49, 133–34
Crimean War, 12, 25
Cullum, Brig. Gen. George W., 31

D. Van Nostrand (publishing house), 30
Davis, Jefferson, 8, 11, 22
Dawes, Lt. Col. Rufus, 101–2, 116

Dean, Eric T., Jr., 92
Decatur, Stephen, 76
Decker, Carl von, 9, 41
Delafield, Maj. Richard, 11
Delafield Commission, 10–11, 25
Democratic Party, 50, 61, 64, 65, 66, 83
Department of the Missouri, 29
De Peyster, John Watts, 41–42, 75, 77
De Saxe, Marshal Maurice, 59, 90
DiCesnola, Col. L. P., 52–53
Disease, 14, 67, 91, 96, 112, 122
Donald, David Herbert, 6, 7, 8, 9
Dufour, Gen. G. H., 49, 52
Duparcq, Édouard De La Barre, 31, 52
Du Picq, Charles-Jean-Jacques-Joseph
    Ardant, 135–36
Dyer, Surg. J. Franklin, 117
Dyer, William R., 44, 76
Dysfunctional combat stress behaviors,
    103, 107, 117–19

Elementary Treatise on Advanced-
    Guard, Out-Posts, and Detachment
    Service of Troops (Mahan), 11
Elements of Military Art and History
    (Duparcq), 31
Elements of Military Art and Science
    (Halleck), 11, 28, 34, 71
Ellet, Charles, 64
Emancipation Proclamation, 34, 71, 72,
    73
Entrenchments, 109–10, 112–13, 116, 127
Essai général de tactique (Guibert), 2–3
European military thought: during ante-
    bellum period, 2–5, 7–8; Austrian, 4,
    19, 53; limitations of, 9, 15, 23, 52–53,
    90, 126; inspiration drawn from, 17,
    132; wartime publication of, 30–32,
    49, 50–51; British, 40–41; Hungarian,
    41; Swiss (excluding Jomini), 41, 49
Executions, military, 117
Eylau, Battle of, 2

Fair Oaks, Battle of, 30, 67
Farragut, Adm. David G., 85

Faust, Drew Gilpin, 132
Field-grade officers (major, lieutenant
    colonel, and colonel), 91, 100, 131,
    135
Field Service Regulations (U.S. Army,
    1914), 132
Food and nutrition, 111–12, 114
Fort Fisher, N.C., 51
Fort Leavenworth, 129, 131
Fort Pillow, battle at, 47
Fortress Monroe, 60, 66, 129
Forts Henry and Donelson, 29, 34, 72, 81
Fort Sumter, 17, 18, 23, 58, 63, 91, 132
Fort Wagner, 38
Franco-Prussian War, 135
Frank, Col. Paul T., 99
Franklin, Battle of, 50
Fredericksburg, Va., 38, 70; Battle of, 35,
    42, 73–74, 132
Frederick the Great, 1, 3, 57, 59
Fremont, Maj. Gen. John C., 29, 40, 64,
    72
French Revolution, 74
Frey, Sgt. Charles A., 118
Fuller, J. F. C., 7–8

Gaines Mill, Battle of, 69
Gat, Azar, 2, 141 (n. 2)
Gates, Gen. Horatio, 66
General in chief, of the U.S. Army, 23,
    25, 46
General officers: preference for men of
    genius, 5, 10–12, 65–66, 76, 80, 85,
    130; preference for educated soldiers,
    11–12, 61–62, 75–77, 80–81, 87–88;
    tensions between professionals and
    amateurs, 55–56; and morale, 90; and
    command styles, 98; public percep-
    tions at the end of the war, 126–27
General staff, 19, 57, 131
Genius: faith in as key to successful gen-
    eralship, 5, 10–12, 37, 56–57, 60, 61,
    65–66, 80–85; rejection of as key to
    successful generalship, 11–12, 61–62,
    76–77, 80–81, 87–88; Scott and,

59–61; McClellan and, 65, 67–68; Halleck and, 73; Sherman and, 85–86; Grant and, 86–87, 123–26

Gettysburg, battle and campaign, 40, 43, 44, 74, 75, 76, 99, 109

Gibbon, Brig. Gen. John, 101, 119–20

Gillmore, Brig. Gen. Quincy, 42, 81

Glatthaar, Joseph T., 65

Goss, Thomas J., 55

Grand Army of the Republic, 128

Grant, Brig. Gen. Lewis A., 110 Grant, Lt. Gen. Ulysses S., 6, 14, 29, 46, 73; as general in chief, 46–47, 50, 81–86; supporters of, 46–47, 80, 81; and military theory, 47, 53; and Lincoln, 49; rise of, 66; critics of, 72; character of, 82; genius of, 87; in Overland Campaign, 92, 99, 100, 106, 110–11, 117–18, 119, 134; assessment of Union war effort, 125–26; postwar assessments of, 126, 133

Gray, John Chipman, 32, 37

Grebel, Lt. John T., 60

Greene, Gen. Nathanael, 66

Grundsätze der Stratgie (Archduke Charles), 4

Guibert, Jacques Antoine Hippolyte Comte de, 2–3

Gurley, John A., 65

Gurowski, Count Adam, 36, 38, 66

Haley, Pvt. John W., 95

Halleck, Maj. Gen. Henry Wager, 7, 11, 19, 21, 28, 29, 31; critics of, 32, 33, 36, 37, 39, 44–45, 46–47, 48; as general in chief, 34–36, 46, 71–74, 145 (n. 93); on military education, 57–58; character of, 72–73; as military author, 77

Hammond, William A., 112

Hancock, Maj. Gen. Winfield S., 85, 95, 98, 119

"Hard war" policy, 34, 35, 71, 72

Harlow, Lt. Col. Franklin P., 118

Harpers Ferry, W.Va. 59

Harris, Sitwell, 44, 76

Harris Farm, Battle of, 103

Harrison's Landing, 67, 69

Harsh, Joseph, 7

Haskell, Col. Frank A., 119

Hattaway, Herman, 9, 36

Hatteras Island, N.C., battle at, 27

Hay, John, 20, 22, 29

Headley, J. T., 126

Heavy artillery regiments, 100, 103, 119, 120

Higginson, Thomas W., 87, 88

History of the French Revolution (Thiers), 21

Hittle, Brig. Gen. J. D., 1, 4, 5, 6

Holabird, Col. Samuel B., 23

Hood, Gen. John Bell, 50, 85, 86

Hooker, Maj. Gen. Joseph, 38, 39, 74, 76, 122

Horizontal bonding or cohesion, 98, 101, 102, 103, 121

Human factors in war, 13–14, 31–32, 67, 89–123, 132–136

Hurlbert, William Henry, 67–70

Hygiene, 14, 91, 112–13

Infantry and Cavalry School, 129

Influence of Sea Power upon History (A. T. Mahan), 131

Interior and exterior lines, 3, 5, 33, 39, 44, 46

Irving, Washington, 42

Island No. 10, 33

J. B. Lippincott (publishing house), 25, 30, 32, 34

Jackson, Andrew, 10, 56, 57

Jackson, Robert, 90

Jackson, Lt. Gen. Thomas J. "Stonewall," 37

Jacksonian Democracy, 10, 56

James River, crossing of, 93, 112–13, 119

Jarvis, Dr. Edward, 91–92

Jena, Battle of, 2

Johnston, Gen. Joseph E., 9, 47, 50, 86

Joint Committee on the Conduct of the War, 27, 29, 30, 34, 64, 65, 70, 71, 73, 74, 80, 120

Jomini, Antoine-Henri: biography of, 1–2; ideas of, 2–5, 18, 19; as intellectual godfather of the Civil War military strategy, 5–8, 28; Civil War–era critics of, 8, 9, 23, 31, 33, 39, 41, 44, 50, 52–53, 126, 135; modern challenges to Jomini's intellectual preeminence, 8–10; works of, republished during the Civil War, 30, 31, 77; on army organization, 57, 78, 88, 129, 131; on character, 58; on generalship, 58, 71; ignores human elements of war, 89–90, 91, 122–23; death and post–Civil War legacy of, 132, 137–38. *See also individual works by Jomini*

Jones, Archer, 7, 9, 36

Jones, Maj. George W., 102

Journal of the Military Service Institution of the United States, 129

Julian, George, 64

Kautz, Brig. Gen. August V., 123

Kearny, Maj. Gen. Philip, 99

Keenan, Maj. John, 101

Keiser, Pvt. Henry, 115

Kennesaw Mountain, battle at, 49

Kissinger, Sgt. Robert, 114–15

Lande, R. Gregory, 92

Lecomte, Maj. Ferdinand, 41, 141 (n. 2)

Lee, Gen. Charles, 66

Lee, Gen. Robert E., 14, 38, 39, 44, 47, 50, 51, 63, 68, 73, 74, 86; in Overland Campaign, 92, 98

Liddell Hart, Sir B. H., 8

Life of Napoleon (Jomini; Halleck, translator), 77

Lincoln, Abraham, 6, 18, 19; war aims of, 24, 26, 27; and appointments of generals in chief, 25, 29, 46, 61–62, 64, 66, 71, 81; and McClellan, 26–29, 30, 62–63, 69; military education and background of, 28, 33–34; and making of military strategy, 29, 34, 38, 39, 44, 47, 48, 132; and Schalk, 33–34, 35; and Halleck, 34, 72–73, 145 (n. 93); and "hard war," 35, 36; and Grant, 47–48, 49, 82, 83, 110; reelection of, 50, 84–85; and appointments of generals, 55, 60, 61, 62, 73–74, 130; and removal of generals, 74–75

Lincoln, Robert, 144 (n. 37)

Lloyd, Henry Humphrey Evans, 3–4, 5, 56

Longstreet, Lt. Gen. James, 44

Lundy's Lane, Battle of, 59

Lynn, John A., 2, 136

Lyon, Brig. Gen. Nathaniel, 62

Mahan, Alfred Thayer, 131

Mahan, Dennis Hart, 7, 8, 11, 14, 21, 41, 69, 131

Maine regiments: 5th Infantry, 116; 17th Infantry, 95; 19th Infantry, 109

Malingering, 117

Manassas Junction, 24, 27. *See also* Bull Run: First Battle of; Bull Run: Second Battle of

Manual (Thiébault), 21

Marmont, Auguste Frédéric Louis Viesse de, 13, 31–32, 96

Marszalek, John F., 7, 21, 35, 36

Massachusetts regiments: 1st Infantry, 100; 7th Infantry, 118; 19th Infantry, 118; 37th Infantry, 108; 54th Infantry, 38;

McAllister, Col. Robert, 99–100, 105

McClellan, Maj. Gen. George B., 6, 12, 20, 25–26, 47; strategic thought of, 20, 26, 28–29; inaction of, 27–28, 64–65, 66; during Peninsula Campaign, 30, 67–70; military critics of, 32, 33, 37, 67–69; friends of, 49, 50;

political critics of, 49–50, 84; as general in chief, 62–66, 69; relieved, 66; and presidential campaign of 1864, 67, 80, 84–85

McDowell, Brig. Gen. Irvin, 24, 29, 38, 62, 70

McKinley, William, 130

McParlin, Surg. Thomas, 117

McPherson, James M., 28, 47–48, 121

Meade, Maj. Gen. George G.: and Gettysburg, 43, 44, 47, 48–49, 74–75, 81; and Overland Campaign, 92, 95, 107, 117–18, 119–20, 122

Mechanicsville, Battle of, 69

Medal of Honor, 120

Mellin, Pvt. Gideon, 113, 115

Mendell, Capt. George H., 30

Meridian Campaign, 47

Mexican-American War, 18, 59, 71, 137

Michigan regiments: 3rd Infantry, 103, 116

Military Dictionary (H. L. Scott), 19–20, 95

Military education, 11–12, 57, 59, 64, 76, 78–80, 88, 128–30

Military Enlightenment, 2, 13, 132, 136

Military Order of the Loyal Legion, 6

Military Policy of the United States (Upton), 130–31

Military Romanticism, 13, 136

Military surgeons, 91, 92, 115, 117, 122–23, 133

Milroy's Weary Boys, 95, 106

Missionary Ridge, battle at, 82

Mississippi River and river valley, 20, 21, 22, 24, 52; McClellan and, 26; Halleck and, 29

Mobile Bay, Union naval victory at, 49

Modern War: Its Theory and Practice, (Szabad), 41

Morale, 13, 89–90, 113, 122, 135

Mordecai, Maj. Alfred, 12

Morrison, James L., 8

Mortars, 110, 113

Morton, Capt. James St. Clair, 8

Mott, Brig. Gen. Gershom, 99–100, 106

Mule Shoe at Spotsylvania, 113–16

Napoleon Club, 8

Napoleon's Maxims ("Scott"), 21

Nashville, battle at, 50, 86

Naval blockade, 20, 21, 22, 39

Neff, Stephen C., 19

Nelson, Adm. Horatio, 76

New Jersey regiments: 11th Infantry, 114; 15th Infantry, 113–14

New York Evening Post, 36, 38

New York Herald, 18, 41, 48, 61, 70

New York regiments: 125th Infantry, 110; 126th Infantry, 117

New York Times, 27, 39–40, 50

New York Tribune, 22, 48, 88

Ney, Marshal Michel, 1

Nicolay, John, 20, 22

Night operations, 107–108

Noncombatants, 18, 25, 26, 66, 69, 73

North American Review, 30, 81

North Anna, Battle of, 14, 48, 92, 110, 116, 119

Oesterreich, Pvt. Maurus, 116

Olmsted, Frederick Law, 91

Olustee, battle at, 47

On War (Clausewitz), 4, 136

Overland Campaign, 12–14, 82–83, 92–123, 133–34

Owen, Brig. Gen. Joshua T., 99, 120

Patrick, Brig. Gen. Marsena, 117, 119

Peninsula Campaign, 30, 33, 34, 37, 50, 66–68, 69–70, 84

Pennsylvania regiments: 11th Infantry, 101, 105; 61st Infantry, 109; 95th Infantry, 113, 115; 96th Infantry, 116; 105th Infantry, 108; 121st Infantry, 107; 140th Infantry, 111; 141st Infantry, 111, 112; 148th Infantry, 96, 101, 107–8, 110, 114, 122; 150th Infantry,

Sigel, Brig. Gen. Franz, 62, 66
Skelton, William B., 10
Sleep deprivation, 108–9, 114
Slocum, Maj. Gen. Henry W., 78
Social cohesion, 121, 123
Source method of instruction, 132
Southern Historical Society Papers, 5
Spanish-American War, 127, 130, 131
Spirit of Military Institutions (Marmont), 13, 31–32
Spotsylvania, Battle of, 14, 48, 92, 98–99, 100, 107, 108–10, 112, 133
Spotsylvania Oak, 116
Stanton, Edwin M., 29, 34, 35, 70, 75, 96–97, 134
Starbird, Pvt. John, 118
Stone, Brig. Gen. Charles P., 63, 64, 65
Stones River, battle at, 35, 42
Strategy: definitions of, 4–5, 19–20, 24, 31, 32–33; interpretations of, 4–5, 31, 32–33; American interest in study of, 9, 45–52, 137; Scott and, 18, 21–25; misinterpretations of, 24, 43, 49–50; McClellan and, 25–26, 29; wartime publication on, 30, 31–33, 37–40, 49; Schalk and, 32–33, 37–39; de Peyster and, 42–43; Meade and, 43. See also *Army and Navy Journal*; *United States Service Magazine*
Strategy and Tactics (Dufour), 49
Summary of the Art of War (Jomini), 1, 4, 9, 19, 30
Sustained operations, 105
Swift, Capt. Eben, 131
Swift, Brig. Gen. John Gardner, 22
Swinton, William, 86–87, 106, 122, 133, 134
Szabad, Emeric, 41

Tactics of the Three Arms (Decker), 9
Tap, Bruce, 64
Task cohesion, 121
Thiébault, Gen. Paul, 21
Thiers, M. A., 21, 135
Third Corps Union, 95

Thomas, Maj. Gen. George H., 50, 81, 85, 86
Tidball, Col. John, 112
Tolles, Lt. Col. C.W., 78
Trans-Mississippi theater, 33
Traun, Otto Ferdinand, Count von Abensperg und, 42
Treatise on Grand Operations, A (Jomini), 1, 3, 4, 23
Trumbull, Lyman, 65–66
Tullahoma Campaign, 42–43, 73–75

Union League, 49
Unit cohesion, 93, 94, 96, 98, 100, 101, 119, 121, 135
Unit identity, 93, 94, 96, 98, 100, 119, 134
U.S. Army: professional culture of, 4, 9, 11, 12–13, 15, 57–58, 135–37; unpreparedness for war, 19, 91; personnel issues of, 20, 77–78, 87, 127–28; European evaluation of, 41, 136; postwar reforms in, 52–53, 87, 127–28; resistance to serving under volunteer officers, 60–61, 62; medical department of, 91; current doctrine, 100, 104, 116; postwar resistance to reform in, 130, 131
U.S. Army War College, 130–31, 132
U.S. Christian Commission, 121, 136
U.S. Colored Troops (USCT), 79–80
U.S. Military Academy: curriculum of, 6, 7, 8; alumni of, 22, 63–64, 71, 76, 82, 85; instructors at, 30, 31, 32; critics of, 36–37, 56–57, 64, 68, 80, 87, 126; budgetary concerns of, 65; Lincoln's selection of alumni, 73; support for, 80–81, 88; postwar reform at, 128
U.S. Navy, 30, 49, 131
U.S. Sanitary Commission, 91, 112, 136
United States Service Magazine, 46, 77, 128–29. *See also* Coppee, Henry
U.S. War Department: unpreparedness for Civil War, 24, 26, 27; and appointment of generals, 61, 77–78; and care

of soldiers, 91, 92; and army organization, 94–95, 97, 100, 126, 128
Upton, Col. Emory, 100, 127, 129, 130

Vermont Brigade, 110
Vermont regiments: 5th Infantry, 113
Vertical bonding or cohesion, 98, 99, 100,
101, 102, 120, 121
Veteranized regiments, 97, 101, 103, 134
Vicksburg, Miss., siege of, 41, 43, 44, 80,
81
Vienna, Va., skirmish at, 60, 61

Wade, Sen. Benjamin, 29, 64, 80
War, definitions of, 19, 21, 25–26
War of 1812, 56, 57, 59
War of the Austrian Succession, 42
War of the Polish Succession, 42
*War of the Rebellion: A Compilation of
the Official Records of the Union and
Confederate Armies*, 5
Ward, Brig. Gen. W. H. H., 98–99
Warren, Maj. Gen. Gouverneur K., 95,
98, 107
Warrior science, 93, 114–15
Washington, George, 10, 56, 65, 76

Watkins, Lt. Col. Guy, 111, 112
Webb, Brig. Gen. Alexander S., 118
Weigley, Russell F., 7
Welles, Gideon, 35, 45
Wellington, General, 76, 125, 126
Western theater, 33, 36, 46, 51–52, 125,
144 (n. 60)
West Point. *See* U.S. Military Academy
Wilderness, Battle of the, 14, 48, 92,
98–99, 105–6, 108, 109–10, 122
Wilkes, George, 68
Wilkes' Spirit of the Times, 68
Willcox, Brig. Gen. Orlando B., 82
Williams, T. Harry, 6, 8
Williamsport, Md., skirmish at, 75
Willoughby, Adj. John, 109
Wilson, Adj. George W., 109
Wilson's Creek, Battle of, 62
Winter Campaigns (de Peyster), 42
Winthrop, Maj. Theodore, 60
Wisconsin regiments: 6th Infantry, 101,
116; 36th Infantry, 119
Wise, Henry A., 22
Wool, Maj. Gen. John, 75
World War I, 123, 132, 136
Wright, Maj. Gen. Horatio G., 98, 100